# UNCLE JOE'S RECORD GUIDE

## By Joe Benson

# HARD ROCK

## VOLUME 1

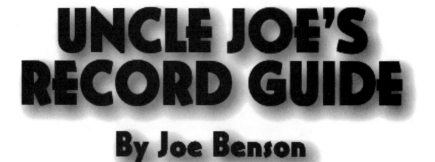

# UNCLE JOE'S RECORD GUIDE

## By Joe Benson

# HARD ROCK

## VOLUME 1

Published independently by

**J. Benson Unlimited**
P.O. Box 12464
Glendale, CA 91224

First printing, June 1988
Second printing, October 1995

Published independently by

**J. Benson Unlimited**
P.O. Box 12464
Glendale, CA 91224

ISBN 0-943031-14-1

Cover design and illustration: Houston & Seattle
Cover photography: Jan Benson

*This book is dedicated to my grandparents who were brave*
*enough to strike out on their own, leaving homes, families*
*and friends to strive for something better.*
*To have a vision is fine, but without courage and stamina*
*you'll never achieve it.*

v

# HARD ROCK, Volume One

# Contents

# Contents

# Contents

# Contents

# Contents

# Contents

# Acknowledgments

Over the years, there have been many, many people who helped and aided this project's development: my entire family, including my wife Jan, my mom Georgia, little sister Janet, brothers Gerard and Jon, and all their families, whose support never failed and without whom this would have been impossible; Michael Anthony, Sammy Hagar, Wendy Laister of Collins Management, Steve Barnett of Hard To Handle Management, Bill Ham of Lone Wolf Management, and SRO/Anthem Management for their time, input and encouragement; Marti Baldassano, Bill Bentley, Phil Carson, Bob Coburn, Mark Felsot, Mary Kaplan, Mike Lancaster, Greg Ladanyi, Patrick Lewis, Jim Nelson, Steven G. Rosen, Kenny Ryback, Bob Small, Rick Snyder, John Valenzuela and Jim Villanueva for their invaluable research assistance; Jim and Barb Houston for their friendship, design expertise and time; Kathrin Breitt, Ann Hitchins and Beverly Rubin for their editing skills and assistance in my continuing education; Sue Evans, Mary Mateljen and Sharon Simpson, the proofing crew; Dean Guiliotis at Ten Arts, the SGR Archives, the Research Garage, Atlantic, Atco, Elektra, Geffen, RCA and Warner Brothers Records for the photo research assistance; Alison Ellner, Lui Garcia, Rich McEwen and Lana Wilson for their feedback, friendship and help; Diana Lindsey, Gary

Lycan, Fred Shuster and Vince Kowalick for their special assistance; B.C., Cindy Davis, Cynthia Fox, Jim Ladd, J.J. Lee, Geno Mitchellini, Beau Rials, Shana and Rita Wilde for their on-air help and stimulation; Bob Moore, Warren Williams, Scott Segelbaum, Ron Escarsega and Ronn Lipkin for their help and encouragement; and the sharpest audience in the world, who never let anything slip past them.

# Preface

Like most Americans, I first linked up with the music that spoke for my generation through radio. I became fascinated with rock & roll's "magical" effect on people (nothing like a good song to get everyone going!). Upon searching for the source of that "magic," I began to see the situation in a different light. I found the business and gossip of rock & roll wasn't nearly as interesting as the music's creation and its effect on the lives of the musicians and their fans. Working in rock & roll radio since the late Sixties has given me a perfect opportunity to watch those effects and track the progression of each generation's music. This book will provide you with that additional insight and place each of your favorite albums in the perspective of the artist's career and contemporary music.

If you use your ears, you don't need self-anointed rock critics to tell you what music is good or bad. If you want to know more about the genesis of the music you grew up with, you'll find **UNCLE JOE'S RECORD GUIDES** invaluable.

**A word of warning**: This book should not be used as a substitute for listening to the albums. Since its beginning, rock & roll has been about the release of energy — physical and/or mental — and while one can spend hours reading and talking about the music and lyrics, there is no substitute for listening to the recordings. Words have never been written that convey the feelings rock & roll music inspires, but **UNCLE JOE'S RECORD GUIDES** can give you an insight into the people that created the music and the processes involved. So listen and read, then listen and enjoy, but don't forget to listen! **ROCK ON!**

# Introduction

Based on the scripts Joe Benson uses on his weekly radio program, UNCLE JOE'S ALBUM ARCHIVES on 97.1 KLSX in Los Angeles, the various volumes of **UNCLE JOE'S RECORD GUIDE** deal with hundreds of the most popular rock albums of all time. Each entry is a self-contained synopsis detailing an album's relationship to the artist's career and contemporary music. A glossary, recommended reading list and song index (arranged by artist) appear at the end of the book. With the emphasis of the **UNCLE JOE'S RECORD GUIDE** series on music and details of the recording process, there is a minimal use of photographs. If you desire greater visual stimulation, the recommended reading list can supply you with the titles of several photographic essays.

In the **UNCLE JOE'S RECORD GUIDE** series, the amount of detail on the creation of each album is proportional to the artistic or commercial success of the work. Likewise, definitive "greatest hits" compilations are detailed to greater length than the more pedestrian efforts.

Throughout the **UNCLE JOE'S RECORD GUIDE** series, individual album entries are formatted as follows:

### Artist's Name

*Album Title* (length of each side)

1st LP (a numeric reference to the release), released 10/95 (the release date). The detailed story of the album's creation and effect on the world of Rock & Roll.

## *Album Sides*

1: "**Song Titles**" and their associated stories.
    B-1: "**Bonus Tracks**," if any, from CD Singles.

Because rock & roll is constantly changing (it would be quite boring if it weren't), **UNCLE JOE'S RECORD GUIDES** are updated on a regular basis. Your inquiries, comments and suggestions are welcome. For update notices or information on new editions of this book, please contact:

**UNCLE JOE'S RECORD GUIDE**
P.O. Box 12464
Glendale, CA 91224

# HARD ROCK
## The First Generation

# The First Generation

The emergence in the late Sixties of Led Zeppelin from the remnants of the Yardbirds officially marked the beginning of the hard rock genre of rock & roll, even though Eric Clapton, Jack Bruce and Ginger Baker — in their super-group Cream — first established the power-trio format of virtuoso musicians that jammed around blues riffs two years earlier. Led Zeppelin's phenomenal commercial and artistic success (without the benefit of a British hit single or MTV exposure) immediately spawned a host of imitators, most of whom picked up on the power trio and jamming aspect, but missed on all other points.

# UNCLE JOE'S RECORD GUIDE

The early Seventies also saw the development of three other major blues-based hard rock bands: Aerosmith, who came into their own about the time Deep Purple's reign began to falter; Bad Company, who were always more blues-oriented than their patrons, Led Zeppelin; and ZZ Top, the Texas blues band that developed into one of the longest-running, most successful, innovative hard rock groups ever. These first generation hard rock bands all effected a lasting impact – not only on the musicians who formed the second and third generation hard rock bands, but also on the millions of fans who participated in the magic of their music.

In addition to spawning many imitators capable of nothing more than the sonic sludge of heavy metal, these first generation bands went through career phases that made them worthy of inclusion in Rob Reiner's satirical hard rock movie, *This Is Spinal Tap*.

This discography emphasizes the music and creative process. For more sordid details – real or imagined – you would be best advised to check out the included **Recommended Reading** list.

The first part of this **RECORD GUIDE** deals with the highly influential first generation hard rock bands. The second part of this book details three of hard rock's best known and most successful offspring.

# Led Zeppelin

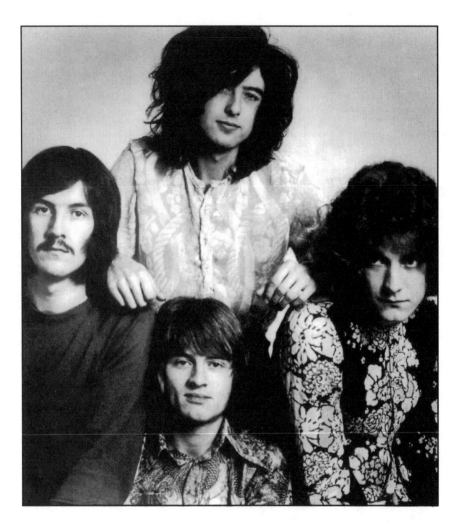

## **Led Zeppelin**
1968

Jimmy Page
John Bonham, Robert Plant
John Paul Jones

# Led Zeppelin

Led Zeppelin became the most successful and influential rock
& roll band of the Seventies — in spite of a continuous drubbing
by music critics. They were so influential that their popularity
continued in the Nineties, years after they disbanded. The
Zeppelin first emerged as a "heavy blues" group assembled
from the remnants of the Yardbirds. Guitar whiz Jimmy Page
adapted the "power-trio-and-a-lead-singer" format of the Who
with the expressed intention of making powerful music that
included both a great dynamic range and an acoustic side.
Page and bassist/keyboardist John Paul Jones were two of
England's most respected session musicians; drummer John
Bonham's talents and power were undeniable. Possessing an
amazing voice and physical presence, Robert Plant quickly
developed his skills as a front man and an unmatched
songwriter. This combination of personalities immediately
jelled — both on stage and in the studio — and the Zeppelin's

songwriting, recordings and live performances are still held as a benchmark by today's musicians. In addition to their manipulation of the media ("Sorry mates, no interviews.") Led Zeppelin's capacity for physical and mental excess, as well as full-time partying on the road, was matched only by the Rolling Stones (although many other bands died trying). Always the premiere concert attraction of the rock & roll world, Led Zeppelin easily surpassed every other band at the ticket office. Even more amazing, the Zeppelin's album sales continue to be as strong as ever, and their popularity with radio audiences has never been greater.

Comprised of four musicians who were virtually unknown in America, Led Zeppelin was initially seen by some as record company hype and a stylistic rip-off of the Jeff Beck Group. In fact, both Beck's and the Zeppelin's debut albums contained covers of the same song, and Beck and Page had both worked in the Yardbirds. But this new "heavy blues" was unlike any pop music of the Sixties. A band without hit singles in 1969 found airplay only on underground FM radio, so live performances became the key to success. Within a year of their formation, Led Zeppelin's incessant touring, phenomenal live show and the intense music produced by the band's interpersonal chemistry propelled them to the top of the rock & roll world. Not only were they a bigger concert draw than the Rolling Stones, but every Led Zeppelin album hit the Top 10. Most of their albums peaked at #1 or #2, and each sold in excess of two million copies — a commercial success surpassed only by the Beatles. In 12 years of complete artistic control over their music and packaging, Led Zeppelin released 10 albums that sold a total of over 60 million copies.

# HARD ROCK - Led Zeppelin

Because of Peter Grant, their strong manager, the Zeppelin was one of the first rock groups to enjoy real business clout and to receive most of the money due them. Their occasional use of outrageous demands for a bigger cut of the action and their sometimes-controversial business practices forever altered the way record companies dealt with rock & roll acts.

In the history of modern rock & roll, Eric Clapton's Cream provided the prototype of a blues-based power trio of virtuoso musicians, the Who established the line-up used by most rock bands since, but Led Zeppelin set the standards against which every hard rock band has since been measured.

## Led Zeppelin Birth Dates

**John Bonham**, May 31, 1948 - September 25, 1980

**John Paul Jones**, January 3, 1946

**Jimmy Page**, January 8, 1944

**Robert Plant**, August 20, 1948

## Led Zeppelin
### *Led Zeppelin* (23-23)

1st LP, released 1/12/69 in the U.S. — 3/28/69 in Britain. At 23, Jimmy Page was the hottest session guitarist in England and a member of the highly innovative Yardbirds (the band whose members previously included guitarists Eric Clapton and Jeff Beck). When the Yardbirds finally folded in August 1968, Page formed a new group with fellow session man John Paul Jones, a multi-instrumentalist who had worked with Beck and the Rolling Stones. A pair of 20-year-olds — vocalist Robert Plant and his old buddy drummer John Bonham — were soon recruited and the quartet began rehearsals. Initially calling themselves the New Yardbirds, the band changed their name to Led Zeppelin just before recording their first album. The name came from a joke made by the Who's rhythm section, Keith Moon and John Entwistle, who observed that another version of the Yardbirds would go over like a lead balloon.

In actuality, Led Zeppelin's four members got along so well musically and personally that after only two-and-a-half weeks practice in early October 1968, this entire album was recorded in just 30 hours and for less than $3,000. The resulting "heavy blues" jams were similar to Jeff Beck's first solo material, but the special interaction of the Zeppelin's members — both on record and live — transcended Beck and the Yardbirds.

One of the most overwhelming debut efforts of the late Sixties , this album was produced by Jimmy Page and engineered by Glyn Johns (who had also worked with the Who and the Rolling Stones) at Olympic Studios in London. The band recorded the songs as they had been rehearsed and performed on stage. Generally, the entire group, including vocalist Plant, recorded these tracks live in the studio. In contrast to later Led Zeppelin albums, Robert received only one writing credit on this album. (His lack of writing credits was due to previous music publishing contractual obligations.)

Even though Led Zeppelin refused to release singles in Britain and were trashed by music critics everywhere, this album reached an astounding #6 in England and #10 in America, while the Beatles *White Album* held at #1. The Zeppelin's debut then remained on the charts for 73 consecutive weeks and eventually sold over four million copies in the U.S. alone. One major reason for the Zeppelin's success was that the group began to tour the United States incessantly even before the release of their first album. In their first 14 months together they played three U.S. and two British tours for a total of 160 dates. (Page and Jones didn't even get paid for that first tour.) That non-stop hard work and sacrifice combined with the incredible strength of their live shows and great music made Led Zeppelin the first superstar band of the Seventies.

** **Special Note**: There was only one completed outtake from the recording sessions for this album. The bluesy "**Baby Come On Home**," one of the first tracks the band finished, was recorded on October 10, 1968, at Olympic Studios in London. It was credited to Bert Berns (who wrote the original version), and both Page and Plant. Unreleased until 1993's *BoxedSet 2*, the song was also included in the remastered versions of *Coda*, released after that date.

## *Led Zeppelin - Side One*

#1:  Evolving from a rehearsal jam, "**Good Times, Bad Times**" was credited to guitarist Jimmy Page, bassist John Paul Jones and drummer John Bonham. Although this marked vocalist Robert Plant's first serious attempt at lyric writing, his previous recording contract kept his name off the credit sheet. Released as a U.S. single, "**Good Times, Bad Times**" nudged the charts at #80 in March 1969.

#2:  One of the few songs on this album that contained overdubs or differed from the early live versions, "**Babe, I'm Gonna Leave You**" was initially credited to Jimmy Page. He had, in fact, played Joan Baez's version of this song for Robert Plant when trying to recruit Robert for the band. The original songwriter, Anne Bredon, later received credit, with Page and Plant. "**Babe, I'm Gonna Leave You**" was one of the first songs on which the band had jammed.

#3:  "**You Shook Me**" was a Willie Dixon blues number that Jeff Beck also covered on his first solo album — released six months before the Zeppelin's. Rock critics went wild, angrily accusing

# HARD ROCK - Led Zeppelin

Jimmy Page of copying his old partner, and compared Plant's vocals with those of Rod Stewart.

**Note**: Music critics typically go wild over popular artists they can not comprehend.

#4: "**Dazed And Confused**" featured Page who played a guitar with a violin bow. Jimmy had worked on this tune while still in the Yardbirds, but the original arrangement came from an uncredited New York folk singer named Jake Holmes. "**Dazed And Confused**," with different lyrics and the working title "I'm Confused," was one of the first that Led Zeppelin worked up. This version was just the second of two takes of "**Dazed And Confused**" the group recorded, with only the violin bow section overdubbed.

## *Led Zeppelin - Side Two*

#1: "**Your Time Is Gonna Come**" was supposedly a group composition but only guitarist Jimmy Page and keyboardist/bassist John Paul Jones received writing credits. The song was recorded live, with the pedal steel guitar overdubbed later. "**Your Time Is Gonna Come**" was never performed on stage.

#2: "**Black Mountain Side**" was credited to Page, but his direct inspiration came from the arrangement of the old English folk song "Black Waterside," as recorded by Bert Jansch and John Renbourn. Viram Jasani played tablas on this version.

#3: "**Communication Breakdown**" was one of the first signature tunes the Zeppelin worked up. The writing credits went to Page, Jones, and drummer John Bonham. This song featured a rare example of Jimmy Page's backing vocals.

"**Communication Breakdown**" was released as the B-side to "**Good Times, Bad Times**" in March 1969.

#4: "**I Can't Quit You Baby**," another classic number by American bluesman Willie Dixon, was one of the first songs Led Zeppelin ever played.

#5: "**How Many More Times**" was built around "How Many More Years" by Howlin' Wolf and "The Hunter," a Booker T. & The MG's blues song recorded by Albert King. (None of these people received songwriting credits or royalties for this recording.) Page lifted the middle guitar solo from the Yardbirds' "Shapes Of Things;" a solo first done by Jeff Beck. The Yardbirds had also recorded a version of "**How Many More Times**." Page, Jones and Bonham received songwriting credits for this tune — one of the first Led Zeppelin performed.

## Led Zeppelin
### *Led Zeppelin II* (21-20)

2nd LP, released 10/22/69 in the U.K. — 10/31/69 in the U.S. —
less than nine months after their first album debuted in the
States. Led Zeppelin recorded their first album within three
weeks of their formation. They then composed and recorded
most of this album during their first two American tours,
between July and September 1969. Some of these songs were
recorded mere hours after being written.

The high energy of the live gigs and partying carried over
into the studio and helped make this Led Zeppelin's most
intense recording. Once again, 25-year-old guitarist Jimmy
Page did an excellent production job for the Zeppelin. This
time the sound was handled by Eddie Kramer (Jimi Hendrix's
engineer), Andy Johns (who had also worked with the Rolling
Stones) and George Chkiantz (who soon became a regular
with the Zep). Vocalist Robert Plant and drummer John
Bonham were both 21 years old, and bassist/keyboardist John
Paul Jones was 23 when this album was released. The intensity
of the basic tracks, recorded live in various studios around
America, is still obvious today.

*Led Zeppelin II* firmly established the band's musical
identity apart from the Yardbirds and Jeff Beck, Jimmy Page's
former partner. On the strength of this, their first #1 charting
multi-million-selling album and their incredible live show, Led
Zeppelin became the first super group of the Seventies — and
eventually one of the biggest bands of all time. Despite
competition from the Beatles' *Abbey Road* and the Rolling

# UNCLE JOE'S RECORD GUIDE

Stones' *Let It Bleed*, as well as a typically thorough trashing from self-anointed rock critics, *Led Zeppelin II* stayed at #1 on the American charts for seven weeks and sold over three million copies within six months of its release! It eventually sold over six million copies in the States.

After New Year's 1970, when the group took their first break from the road, they had played 160 concerts (including three U.S. tours) in the 14 months since they formed!

## *Led Zeppelin II - Side One*

#1:  "**Whole Lotta Love**," credited as a group composition, was initially recorded at Sunset Sound in Los Angeles. The group's performances were so hot that Robert Plant recorded his lead vocals on the first take. Additional instrumental work was done later at Olympic Studios in London and A&R Studios in New York City. Although the band neither approved nor expected this to be a single (edited or otherwise), "**Whole Lotta Love**" charted at #4 in January 1970 in the U.S. and sold over a million copies within five weeks of its release.
**Notes:** Twenty years after this album was released, the group reached an out-of-court settlement over a copyright infringement with bluesman Willie Dixon, whose song "You Need Love" preceded this song by several years.

#2:  "**What Is And What Should Never Be**" was one of Jimmy Page and Robert Plant's first collaborations, and one of the first songs completed for this album. It was recorded before the Zeppelin's second tour at Olympic Studios in London, and finished at both Groove and A&R Studios in New York.

# HARD ROCK - Led Zeppelin

#3: "**The Lemon Song**" was based on two blues numbers the Zeppelin had jammed on since they first practiced together — Howlin' Wolf's "Killing Floor" and Albert Collins's "Crosscut Saw." Neither Collins nor Howlin' Wolf initially received credit or royalties from this song, which was recorded live at New York's Mystic Studios and overdubbed at Mirror Sound in Hollywood.

**Note**: The Zeppelin used the "squeeze my lemon" lyrics from Robert Johnson's "Traveling Riverside Blues" in this, but their own version of "**Traveling Riverside Blues**" wasn't released until 1991.

#4: "**Thank You**," Robert Plant's first full lyrical composition, was dedicated to his wife Maureen. The basic tracks were recorded at A&R Studios in New York and the recording was finished at Morgan Sound in London.

## *Led Zeppelin II - Side Two*

#1: The group composition "**Heartbreaker**," recorded at A&R Studios in New York, became the standard guitar solo cover for anyone who called themselves a player. "**Heartbreaker**" was segued into the next song during the album's final mixing.

#2: Guitarist Jimmy Page and vocalist Robert Plant's "**Livin' Lovin' Maid (She's Just A Woman)**," recorded at Morgan Studios in London, was never performed live. Its lyrical inspiration supposedly came from a West Coast groupie. Released as the B-side to "**Whole Lotta Love**," "**Livin' Lovin' Maid (She's Just A Woman)**" charted at #65.

#3: Even though Robert called "**Ramble On**" his favorite on this album, the Page/Plant composition was never played live. The basic recording took place at Juggy Sound in New York, with some guitar overdubs done at A&R Studios in New York. This song demonstrated a strong J.R.R. Tolkien influence in Plant's writing.

#4: John Bonham's solo on "**Moby Dick**" was mostly done without drumsticks (he used his hands!). The recording of the drum solo and instrumental portions of the Page/Jones/Bonham composition took place in different sessions at Mirror Sound in Los Angeles and May Fair Studios in New York. The song's instrumental open and close had been previously performed live as "The Girl I Love." In later concerts, Bonzo's version of this solo would stretch to an epic 30 minutes.

#5: The Page/Plant tune "**Bring It On Home**" demonstrated the Zep's best use of dynamic range to date. Based on Sonny Boy Williams' "Bring It On Home," this song was recorded at a little Vancouver studio, at Mystic Studios in Los Angeles, and at Atlantic and A&R Studios in New York.

## Led Zeppelin
### *Led Zeppelin III* (22-23)

3rd LP, released 10/5/70 in the U.S. — 10/21/70 in Britain. After two years of heavy nonstop touring, the Zeppelin finally had to take a vacation. While 22-year-old drummer John Bonham and 24-year-old bassist/keyboardist John Paul Jones spent time with their families, 26-year-old guitarist Jimmy Page and 22-year-old vocalist Robert Plant retreated to a small cottage in Wales called Bron-Yr-Aur [pronounced BRON-rahr]. The relaxed atmosphere inspired Page and Plant to co-write several songs and forge a shift in the Zeppelin's musical direction.

The band started to record *Led Zeppelin III* in May 1970. Three months of lively sessions at the old Headley Grange mansion (where some of their fourth album and *Physical Graffiti* would later be done) yielded 17 songs. Using a mansion and the Rolling Stones Mobile Studio permitted Led Zeppelin the luxury of recording, sleeping, eating and/or partying whenever they felt like it — without paying outrageous studio rental fees — and they never had to go home. Some overdubbing and mixing later took place at Island and Olympic Studios in London, and at Ardent Studios in Memphis (where ZZ Top would later work). As usual, Page controlled the production work. Andy Johns handled the sound (he had also worked with the Rolling Stones).

On June 28, 1970, halfway through the recording sessions for this album, the Zeppelin played to more than 200,000 people at England's Bath Festival, and launched another short

U.S. tour. As soon as they finished this recording, they did a short German tour and their sixth American tour, which ended in late September 1970 — one month before *Led Zeppelin III* was released. Instead of doing another tour after this album's release, the band prepared to work on their fourth album.

Rock critics in England and America hated this release. Typically, the critics ignored the progression of the band's music and Page's production; many even claimed Led Zeppelin was trying to imitate Crosby, Stills & Nash. Nonetheless, the overwhelming reaction of the Zeppelin's fans made this album chart at #1 for four weeks straight — proving how out of touch with reality rock critics can be. *Led Zeppelin III* eventually sold over three million copies in the States.

** **Special Notes**: Bron-Yr-Aur translates as "Golden Breast" — perhaps relating to the sunsets on the gentle hills surrounding the cottage.

The outtakes from the *Led Zeppelin III* sessions included: "**Hey, Hey, What Can I Do**," which was used as the only unique Led Zeppelin B-side and not released on a Zeppelin album until the *Boxed Set* in 1992; an acoustic version of "**Bron-Yr-Aur**," which later appeared on *Physical Graffiti*; an acoustic version of "**Down By The Seaside**," which was reworked for *Led Zeppelin IV* and later released on *Physical Graffiti*; "**Poor Tom**," which was later released on *Coda*; and an early version of "**No Quarter**."

# HARD ROCK - Led Zeppelin

## *Led Zeppelin III - Side One*

#1: "**Immigrant Song**" was co-written at the Welsh Bron-Yr-Aur [pronounced BRON-rahr] cottage by guitarist Jimmy Page and vocalist Robert Plant (who was inspired by the Vikings). This track was first recorded at Headley Grange, and finished at Island and Olympic Studios in London. Backed by the outtake "**Hey, Hey, What Can I Do**," "**Immigrant Song**" reached #16 on the American singles charts in January 1971.

#2: "**Friends**" was another Page/Plant composition that came together during their vacation in Wales. For some reason, bassist John Paul Jones did not receive credit for his excellent string arrangement. The segue into the next song was done during the final mixing to cover a tape problem with the beginning of "**Celebration Day**."

#3: "**Celebration Day**," an amazing song in concert, was credited to Page, Plant and Jones. The tune originated at Bron-Yr-Aur.

#4: One of the first songs finished for this album, "**Since I've Been Loving You**" was recorded live at Olympic Studios in London and remains one of the best representations of the Zeppelin's concert sound. Taking inspiration from the Moby Grape song "Never," Page, Plant and Jones shared writing credits for "**Since I've Been Loving You**." The band had recorded one other take, but felt this version was superior. On the compact disc version of this album, you can hear John Bonham's bass drum pedal squeaking throughout the tune.

#5: "**Out On The Tiles**," credited to Page, Plant and Bonham, was inspired by one of the band's drunken trips to New York.

## *Led Zeppelin III - Side Two*

#1:  "**Gallows Pole**," a Leadbelly blues song from the 1920s, underwent serious revisions as the Zeppelin jammed on it. Guitarist Jimmy Page and vocalist Robert Plant took the writing credits. Although Led Zeppelin played this live only once, Page and Plant revived it for their 1994 album and tour.

#2:  Page had written "**Tangerine**" in a different form for the Yardbirds three years earlier. When the Yardbirds attempted to record it, they just couldn't pull it off. In contrast, Page considered this recording to be a perfect expression of his concept of Led Zeppelin's music and it became the last song for which he wrote all the lyrics.

#3:  "**That's The Way**," a Page/Plant composition, was written at the Bron-Yr-Aur [pronounced BRON-rahr] cottage in Wales under the working title "The Boy Next Door." The final lyrics were inspired partially by the social unrest Led Zeppelin saw during their late-Sixties American tours. This acoustic version was recorded at Island Studios in London after a couple of electric renditions didn't capture the feel of the song.

#4:  "**Bron-Y-Aur-Stomp**" started out as a jam between Plant and Page at the cottage in Wales. The earliest version of this song was entitled "Jennings Farm Blues." Robert wrote the lyrics with his dog in mind. Bassist/keyboardist John Paul Jones received a co-writing credit for the final arrangement.

#5:  "**Hats Off To (Roy) Harper**" was a tribute to the English blues-shouter who had hung out with both Pink Floyd and Led Zeppelin. This studio jam, recorded at Olympic Studios in London, was loosely based on Bukka White's "Shake 'Em On Down" and Sonny Terry's "Custard Pie."

## Led Zeppelin
### *Led Zeppelin IV* (23-20)

4th LP, released 11/8/71 in the U.S. — 11/19/71 in Britain. Led Zeppelin's constant touring not only made them lots of money but also helped them become an extremely tight and intuitive musical ensemble.

The writing and recording sessions for this album, on the heels of their sixth American tour in two years, were reportedly very inspired. The recording sessions began at Island Studios in London in early December 1970, then resumed after Christmas at the old Headley Grange mansion, where *Led Zeppelin III* had been recorded. Most of the work was finished by February 1971 — just four months after the release of *Led Zeppelin III*. The Zep's 26-year-old guitarist, Jimmy Page, took complete charge of the production, which concluded at Olympic Studios in London. Once again, the band found working in the Headley Grange mansion allowed them to record, sleep, eat and/or party whenever they felt like it. That environment encouraged song development both in times of quiet reflection, and during spirited rehearsal and recording sessions. Furthermore, the sonic quality of Ronnie Lane's mobile studio matched that of any major studio in Britain.

Musically and personally, things were going so well for the band that the Zeppelin took a break from recording to play some small clubs just for fun. After that crazed small club experience, they decided to downplay their fame by leaving any reference to the name Led Zeppelin off the album cover.

# UNCLE JOE'S RECORD GUIDE

Ultimately, the Viking-like runes they used instead of a title were for artistic effect rather than to make an oblique statement. Each group member chose a rune of his own. John Bonham, the 24-year-old drummer, chose a symbol that supposedly represented the union of a family; 25-year-old keyboardist/bassist John Paul Jones' rune was a sign of confidence and competence; and 23-year-old vocalist Robert Plant's signified peace. Page invented his own, which added to the mystery.

Even though the lengthy album-mastering sessions and hassles with artwork continued throughout Summer 1971, the Zep was back on the road performing much of this music before the album's release. In Spring 1972 after *Led Zeppelin IV* was finally released, they did a big European tour, returned to the States in May and June, then followed another late-Summer U.S. tour with their first swing through Japan. Everywhere Led Zeppelin played, they broke box office records and blew away the crowds.

Interestingly, although *Led Zeppelin IV* charted for over three years, eventually sold over 12 million copies in the U.S. without a hit single (or MTV exposure), and even entered the British charts at #1, it never charted any higher than #2 in the States. *Led Zeppelin IV* was somehow held out of that top position by Santana, Sly & The Family Stone, Carole King and Don McLean!

** **Special Note**: Outtakes from the *Led Zeppelin IV* sessions included: "**Boogie With Stu**," which was recorded immediately after "**Rock & Roll**"; "**Night Flight**"; an electric version of "**Down By The Seaside**"; and early

24

versions of "**No Quarter**" and "**The Rover**." "**No Quarter**" later appeared on *Houses Of The Holy*; all of rest of those songs appeared on *Physical Graffiti*.

## *Led Zeppelin IV - Side One*

#1: "**Black Dog**" was credited to guitarist Jimmy Page, vocalist Robert Plant and bassist John Paul Jones — who came up with the original riff on which this song was based. Named after a stray dog that wandered in and out of the recording sessions, the song featured intricate work with tricky time signatures. Backed with "**Misty Mountain Hop**," "**Black Dog**" reached #15 on the American charts in February 1973, and Plant later identified this as one of his all time favorite Led Zeppelin songs.

**Note**: The band played "**Black Dog**" during their Summer 1971 tours, months before this album was released. Jones said that in concert "this song was always a race to see who would finish first."

#2: "**Rock & Roll**" was a group composition that came together under the working title "Been A Long Time" during a 15-minute Headley Grange jam with pianist Ian Stewart (of the Rolling Stones). John Bonham's opening drum riff was based on Little Richard's "Keep A Knockin'." As a single, "**Rock & Roll**" made it into the American Top 50 in February 1972. As a song, it inspired virtually every rock & roll band in the world.

#3: The melody for "**The Battle Of Evermore**" emerged in the early morning hours at Headley Grange, after the rest of the band had gone to bed, when Jimmy Page picked up John Paul Jones' mandolin and began experimenting with it. Plant's lyrical inspiration came from a book on the Medieval Scottish wars. When Sandy Denny (of Fairport Convention) overdubbed her vocals, she became the only outside musician to ever sing on a Led Zeppelin recording.

#4: "**Stairway To Heaven**" is still considered to be one of the finest rock & roll songs ever written. (It is certainly the most popular.) The lyrics came to Plant one evening during the recording sessions at the Headley Grange mansion, and the vocals were later recorded in just one take. The Zep played "**Stairway To Heaven**" during their Summer 1971 tours, months before this album was released.

**Note**: Although he used a Telecaster to record this, in concert "**Stairway To Heaven**" was the first song on which Page used his legendary double-neck Gibson guitar. That specialized instrument allowed Jimmy to play the 12-string and 6-string parts without changing guitars. Soon, every band with any pretensions used double-necked Gibsons.

In the years after this album was released, fundamentalist preachers consistently used this song to scare their congregations. They claimed "**Stairway To Heaven**" contained Satanic messages hidden by backwards masking (a technique of recording lyrics backwards at a low level in the final mix). That accusation was so blatantly absurd, even some rock critics thought it was true.

# HARD ROCK - Led Zeppelin

## *Led Zeppelin IV - Side Two*

#1:  Bassist/keyboardist John Paul Jones received a co-writing credit with guitarist Jimmy Page and vocalist Robert Plant for "**Misty Mountain Hop**." Recorded at the Headley Grange mansion, "**Misty Mountain Hop**" was the B-side to the "**Black Dog**" single.

#2:  "**Four Sticks**," a Page/Plant collaboration, was so named because John Bonham played his drum part with four drumsticks instead of two. The group spent a lot of time reworking this song in Island Studios in early 1971, but played it live only once.

#3:  The basic inspiration for "**Going To California**" came during the band's recording and partying sessions in Los Angeles. Plant said later that Joni Mitchell's music greatly affected his lyrical approach to this.

#4:  "**When The Levee Breaks**" was a vastly reworked version of the 1929 Memphis Minnie/Kansas Joe McCoy blues classic. The band tried to record this in the studio in early December 1970, but none of those versions clicked. The song finally came together when the Zep returned to Headley Grange. The key element proved to be John Bonham's drums, which were recorded in a large hallway with just a couple of microphones hanging in the adjacent 30-foot-high stairwell. Natural reverberations off the stone walls contributed to what is still considered to be one of the best rock & roll drum sounds ever.

# UNCLE JOE'S RECORD GUIDE

## Led Zeppelin
### *Houses Of The Holy* (22-20)

5th LP, released 3/28/73 — 16 months after *Led Zeppelin IV*. On this album— their first with a title other than their name and their only album with a printed lyric sheet — Led Zeppelin refined and intensified their music with more complex rhythms and interplay, and stretched their creative abilities further than before. In a change of pace, guitarist Jimmy Page and bassist/keyboardist John Paul Jones separately worked up several of these songs in their respective home studios, then presented the arrangements to the rest of the band. The remainder of this music had been developed on stage during the group's incessant touring. While some of this album was recorded in February and March 1972 — before the *Led Zeppelin IV* world tour began — the bulk of these tracks were done in early May and late June 1972 at Stargroves (Mick Jagger's summer mansion, where many bands partied, rehearsed and recorded). The Zeppelin finished *Houses Of The Holy* in October 1972, after their first Asian tour.

At least 16 songs were finished for this album, and those not used on this album later surfaced on *Physical Graffiti*. Eddie Kramer (Jimi Hendrix's engineer), Keith Harwood and Andy Johns (who had also worked with the Stones), and George Chkiantz (a longtime engineer for the Zep) handled the album's sound. As usual, Jimmy Page controlled the production. The huge sound of John Bonham's drums was achieved by setting up his drum kit in the bay window of the large banquet room in the Stargroves mansion, and letting the natural reverberations off the stone walls and high ceiling

# HARD ROCK - Led Zeppelin

come through on the recording. Additional overdubs were done at Olympic Studios in London and Jimi Hendrix's Electric Lady Studios in New York.

When they finished recording this album in October 1972, Led Zeppelin immediately toured Britain, and then took off for the holidays. In March 1973 they again toured Europe, then in May moved back to the States for their eighth American tour. That leg of the U.S. tour marked the first time Led Zeppelin used a large private jet to fly to each gig — and the first time heavy drug use entered into the Zep's legendary partying. When the Asian leg of the *Houses Of The Holy* tour finally ended in Fall 1973, the band took a well-deserved 18-month hiatus from the road.

Originally scheduled for release in August 1972, by the group's heavy touring schedule and nagging problems with production of the album cover artwork delayed *Houses Of The Holy* release for seven months. When it finally hit the stores, the touring Zeppelin was the biggest rock & roll band in the world. *Houses Of The Holy* immediately charted at #1 and eventually sold over six million copies stateside. It is still one of the Zeppelin's most popular collections. Vocalist Robert Plant and the rest of the band averaged 26 years of age when this album was released.

** **Special Notes**: "Houses Of The Holy" was the Zeppelin's nickname for the huge halls and arenas in which they performed.

Outtakes from the *Houses Of The Holy* sessions included two songs that later appeared on *Physical Graffiti*:

29

the title track, "**Houses Of The Holy**," recorded at Olympic Studios; and "**Black Country Woman**," which was recorded at Stargroves. "**Walter's Walk**," also recorded at Stargroves, was eventually included on *Coda*. Another semi-finished track called "Slush" has never been released.

A portion of the *Houses Of The Holy* tour was filmed and released as the movie, *The Song Remains The Same*.

## *Houses Of The Holy - Side One*

#1: Guitarist Jimmy Page worked on "**The Song Remains The Same**" for months before it finally took this form with vocalist Robert Plant's lyrics. Page's original instrumental was called "The Overture." The working title during the first attempts at lyrics was "The Campaign."

#2: Page worked out the arrangement for "**The Rain Song**" at his home studio, then brought the demos to the band's recording sessions at Stargroves.

**Note**: This writing method had been used extensively by Pete Townshend and the Who, but not Led Zeppelin.

#3: "**Over The Hills And Far Away**" was another song that Page worked out at home then presented to the band. Plant worked several days on the lyrics. "**Over The Hills And Far Away**" reached #51 on the U.S. singles charts in May 1973. The B-side was "**Dancing Days**."

#4: "**The Crunge**" was a spontaneous jam at Olympic Studios that included pieces of several old R&B songs, including Otis

# HARD ROCK - Led Zeppelin

Redding's "Mr. Pitiful." Page first worked up the basic riff in the mid-Sixties. The "bridge" in the lyrics refers to the "bridge" (musical transition) in James Brown's song "Sex Machine."

## *Houses Of The Holy - Side Two*

#1: "**Dancing Days**" was co-written by guitarist Jimmy Page and vocalist Robert Plant. The song came together during an extremely spirited session, and the band was reported to have danced about during the playback of the basic tracks. During the final mixing sessions, "**Dancing Days**" replaced "**Houses of the Holy**" in the album's sequencing. ("**Houses of the Holy**" later appeared on Physical Graffiti.)

#2: The title of the group composition "**D'Yer Maker**" came from a Cockney pronunciation of "Did you make her?" — the punch line from a bad joke. ("My wife just went on vacation. Jamaica? No, she went on her own accord.") Neither the title "**D'Yer Maker**" nor the joke appear in the song's lyrics. One of the first tunes completed for this album, "**D'Yer Maker**" hit the American Top 20 in December 1973. "**The Crunge**" was used as the B-side.

#3: Bassist/keyboardist John Paul Jones had first worked up most of "**No Quarter**" in his home studio several years earlier. The band had recorded different versions of "**No Quarter**" at least twice before this was done at Island Studios in London. This song was Jones' first major contribution to be recorded by the band, and his Hammond organ solo became his concert trademark. Plant's lyrics were inspired by the Vikings.

# UNCLE JOE'S RECORD GUIDE

#4: Plant said that as he gazed out over Led Zeppelin's concert audiences he felt as if he were looking at an ocean. "**The Ocean**," inspired by that feeling, was listed as a group composition. The basic tracks were recorded on the fifth take, as indicated by drummer John Bonham's rap at the beginning of the song.

**Note**: During the final mixing, the sound of a telephone ringing was added 1:38 minutes into the song — a clever trick!

## Led Zeppelin
### *Physical Graffiti* (21-18-23-21)

6th LP, released 2/24/75 — two years after *Houses Of The Holy*. Following the exhausting *Houses Of The Holy* world tour, the Zeppelin began rehearsing new material for *Physical Graffiti* in mid-November 1973. Three months later they started recording in earnest with Ronnie Lane's Mobile Studio at the Headley Grange mansion, where most of *Led Zeppelin III* and *IV* had been done. While there was some partying (after all, they *were* Led Zeppelin), the group's mental attitudes were as loose and relaxed as their musical skills were sharp. The music seemed to flow from improvisations, and the ambient sound of the stone rooms and halls of Headley Grange were ingeniously used to great effect. Often, tape machines were simply turned on to record whatever happened — even the sound of conversations and airplanes flying overhead were left in the final mix. Vocalist Robert Plant and drummer John Bonham were both 26 years old, bassist/keyboardist John Paul Jones was 28, and guitarist Jimmy Page was 30 when this magical album was recorded.

With more than enough new material for a single album, the group decided to use older outtakes to transform this into a double album. The sound on the new tracks, as well as the remixing of some of the old ones, was handled by Keith Harwood (who worked on *Houses Of The Holy* and with the Rolling Stones) and Ron Nevison (who had worked with the Who). Once again, Jimmy Page took charge of the production.

# UNCLE JOE'S RECORD GUIDE

When the final mixing and overdubs were finished in July 1974 at Olympic Studios in London, the band knew they had created something special. *Physical Graffiti* was scheduled as the first release for Led Zeppelin's own record label, Swan Song, as the band prepared for their biggest tour ever. However, three months later, as rehearsals began for the Zep's first tour in a year-and-a-half, production of the album's complex cover art became a serious problem. Ultimately, those production problems delayed the release of *Physical Graffiti* until February 1975. By default, Bad Company's successful debut became the first release on the Zeppelin's *Swan Song* label.

Led Zeppelin began their *Physical Graffiti* world tour in Holland in early January 1975. By the time *Physical Graffiti* was finally released , they had finished half of their ninth U.S. tour — a two-month long, 39-concert affair. The album entered the British charts at #1, and spent six weeks at #1 in America as it sold millions and millions of copies (over four million in the States alone). But trouble seemed to haunt the partying band both on the road and during their short summer break. Just before the start of the second leg of the Zeppelin's American tour in late August 1975, Robert Plant and his family were in a terrible auto accident on a Greek island. With the tour suddenly canceled, and Robert and his wife recovering from grievous injuries, Plant encountered tax problems. He was forced to leave England immediately — even before his broken bones had a chance to heal. Page joined his friend upon Robert's arrival in Los Angeles. Soon, they summoned the rest of the band, and the Zeppelin's next recording project was under way.

# HARD ROCK - Led Zeppelin

*Physical Graffiti* is still considered to be one of Led Zeppelin's finest, most diverse recordings — one of the greatest hard rock albums of all time. In the years since its release, both Page and Plant called it their favorite Zep album because of the "feel" and "magic" between the musicians during the recording sessions. Much of that feel is still clearly evident.

## *Physical Graffiti - Side One*

#1:  "**Custard Pie**," a Jimmy Page/Robert Plant composition, evolved from an early 1974 jam at the Headley Grange mansion. Just like their earlier song "**Hats Off To (Roy) Harper**," the lyrical and melodic inspiration for "**Custard Pie**" came from bluesmen Sonny Terry's "Custard Pie" and Bukka White's "Shake 'Em On Down." "**Custard Pie**" was never performed live.

#2:  "**The Rover**" was first recorded in May 1970 during the sessions for *Led Zeppelin IV* at Stargroves (Mick Jagger's summer mansion). This version was recorded the same day as "**D'Yer Maker**" in Spring 1972. "**The Rover**" was never performed in concert.

#3:  "**In My Time Of Dying**" was a group composition based on Blind Willie Johnson's 1927 song, "Jesus, Make Up My Dying Bed." In fact, these lyrics were almost identical to Bob Dylan's early-Sixties version of that song, but neither Bob nor Blind Willie received writing credit for this. One of the first numbers completed for this album in early 1974, "**In My Time Of Dying**" was recorded live at Headley Grange, with Jimmy Page adding only a few overdubs later. The group recorded John Bonham's drums in the large Headley Grange hallway, with only two microphones set up in a 30-foot-high stairwell — the same technique they used on "**When The Levee Breaks**."

**Note**: Robert Plant said this song kept running through his mind as he and his family lay injured in the jeep wreck that resulted in the cancellation of the final leg of the *Physical Graffiti* tour. The final 25 seconds of "**In My Time Of Dying**" — laughter, John Bonham's coughing and conversation — were originally included on the album to add some lightness to the mood. That same 25-second insight into Led Zeppelin's in-studio psyche was left off the first compact disc versions of this album — a smooth move by a record company that wasn't paying attention.

## *Physical Graffiti - Side Two*

#1:  A great rocker, "**Houses of the Holy**" was recorded in June 1972 for the *Houses Of The Holy* album. During the final mixing, it was replaced on that album by "**Dancing Days**." Written by guitarist Jimmy Page and vocalist Robert Plant, "**Houses of the Holy**" was never performed live.

#2:  With a keyboard nod to Robert Johnson's famous car song "Terraplane Blues," and with drummer John Bonham's inspired input, "**Trampled Under Foot**" evolved from an in-studio jam into a love song about an automobile. Credited to Page, Plant and bassist/keyboardist John Paul Jones, it peaked on the U.S. charts at #38 in June 1975. "**Black Country Woman**" was used as the B-side of the "**Trampled Under Foot**" single.

# HARD ROCK - Led Zeppelin

#3:   The classic "**Kashmir**" was credited to guitarist Jimmy Page, vocalist Robert Plant and drummer John Bonham. Developed under the title "Driving To Kashmir," Bonzo first came up with the rhythm, then Jimmy worked up the guitar melody between the November 1973 and February 1974 sessions for this album. When Robert adapted lyrics he had written while driving in the Sahara desert, the song was virtually complete. To this day, "**Kashmir**" remains one of the most requested Zeppelin songs. Page, Plant and Jones have all said it was their personal favorite because it captured everything the band was about — lyrically, as well as in the way it was recorded and performed live.

## *Physical Graffiti - Side Three*

#1: "**In The Light**" was co-written by guitarist Jimmy Page, vocalist Robert Plant and bassist/keyboardist John Paul Jones. The early working version, called "In The Morning," featured completely different lyrics. Jones did a lot of development on this song using an EMS VCS-3 synthesizer, a highly innovative piece of gear in 1974. Although Robert identified this as one of his favorite Zeppelin songs, the band never played "**In The Light**" live.

#2: "**Bron-Yr-Aur**" [pronounced BRON-rahr] was inspired by the pastoral surroundings of the cottage in Wales where Jimmy Page and Robert Plant wrote most of Led Zeppelin's third album. "**Bron-Yr-Aur**" was recorded in 1970 during the Island Studio sessions for *Led Zeppelin III*.

#3: The Page/Plant song "**Down By The Seaside**," written for the third album and recorded in 1972 for the Zeppelin's fourth album, was never performed live.

#4: For several years, Jimmy Page worked sporadically on the instrumental that became "**Ten Years Gone**" when Robert Plant wrote lyrics that tied the arrangement together during the *Physical Graffiti* sessions. Robert later said he was writing about a girlfriend who had insisted he choose between her and music.

# HARD ROCK - Led Zeppelin

## *Physical Graffiti - Side Four*

#1: "**Night Flight**" was recorded in 1971 during the sessions for *Led Zeppelin IV*. It was played live in rehearsals, but never performed in concert. Interestingly, this song marked the first time keyboardist/bassist John Paul Jones was listed before guitarist Jimmy Page and vocalist Robert Plant in the writing credits.

#2: "**The Wanton Song**" was a Page/Plant collaboration recorded in early 1974. Although it was one of Robert's favorite Led Zeppelin songs, the band only played it live a few times early in the *Physical Graffiti* tour.

#3: "**Boogie with Stu**" refers to piano player Ian Stewart (of the Rolling Stones). After "**Rock & Roll**" was recorded during the 1971 Headley Grange sessions for *Led Zeppelin IV*, the Zep continued to party and jam with Stewart. Among the many songs they covered was Ritchie Valens' "OO-My-Head" (Valens — L.A.'s first true rock & roll star — was killed in the 1959 plane crash with Buddy Holly). While the *Physical Graffiti* album's release was held up with artwork problems, Ritchie's mother got wind of the Zeppelin's recording. She immediately threatened to sue, and only then was Ritchie given proper writing credits, royalties and, as a bonus, his mom received a mention in the *Physical Graffiti* liner notes. The original title for "**Boogie with Stu**" was "Sloppy Drunk," which evidently reflected the musicians' condition. "**Boogie with Stu**" was never played live in concert.

#4: "**Black Country Woman**" was worked up for the *Houses Of The Holy* album during the sessions at Stargroves (Mick Jagger's summer mansion). This version of the Page/Plant song was recorded in the Stargroves garden in Spring 1972. An airplane flew overhead as the tape machines began to record and the band decided to leave that sound in the final mix. For some reason, "**Black Country Woman**" was judged inappropriate for *Houses Of The Holy*, but was used as the B-side of "**Trampled Under Foot**." The original title was the "Never Ending Doubting Woman Blues." The title "**Black Country Woman**" reflected the fact that Robert was from the area of England known as the Black Country. This song was performed in concert only once.

#5: "**Sick Again**," another Page/Plant composition, was a rather strange note upon which to end Led Zeppelin's most ambitious album. The lyrics were inspired by the depraved Los Angeles groupie scene that the Zeppelin allegedly nurtured. During the final mix, Page decided to leave Bonham's cough on at the end of the song as another touch of Zeppelin humor.

## Led Zeppelin
### *Presence* (20-25)

7th LP, released 3/31/76 — 13 months after *Physical Graffiti*. Vocalist Robert Plant and his family were in rough shape following their August 1975 car accident — the accident that forced cancellation of the latter part of the *Physical Graffiti* tour. As soon as he was able, Robert left his family and travelled to Malibu, California, to recuperate free of England's 90% taxation. Before long, he was joined by Jimmy Page, the Zeppelin's 31-year-old guitarist. When their songwriting efforts began to flow in mid-September, 29-year-old bassist/keyboardist John Paul Jones and 27-year-old drummer John Bonham were summoned for rehearsals.

The Zeppelin's playing was still tight and intuitive, and their work was as inspired as Plant's pain was acute. In November 1975, when Robert was able to move without too much discomfort, the band went to Musicland Studios in Munich, Germany, to record this album. Even though Plant re-injured himself in the studio, the group finished the job in only 18 working days! Once again, Page handled the production and Keith Harwood (who also worked with the Rolling Stones) engineered the sound.

The entire *Presence* album was written and recorded faster than anything the Zeppelin had done in years. In fact, Page recorded the guitar overdubs for "**Achilles Last Stand**" in one evening, then finished the rest of the album's guitar solos the next day! The speed with which the band worked resulted in a sharp-edged sound; this was their most raw work since *Led Zeppelin II*.

*Presence* immediately hit #1 upon its release and sold over two million copies. Because Plant's condition precluded touring for several months, several of these songs were never performed in concert.

Eight months after this album was released, Plant was ready to go back on the road. Returning from a two year hiatus, Led Zeppelin began their 10th American tour in April 1977. With few rest breaks and much reported travail — including physical violence and increasingly severe drug abuse among a couple of band members and crew — the tour continued through six sold-out dates at Madison Square Garden in July. Then tragedy struck again. On July 27, Robert Plant's 5-year-old son suddenly died in England. With the last 10 dates of the tour canceled, the whole Zeppelin entourage returned to Britain feeling very low, and with a sense of unfinished business.

\*\* **Special Note**: The day after this album was finished, the Rolling Stones began recording their *Black And Blue* album in the same studios.

# HARD ROCK - Led Zeppelin

## *Presence - Side One*

The first two songs on this side were written by guitarist Jimmy Page and vocalist Robert Plant while Plant recuperated in Malibu.

#1:   The lyrics for "**Achilles Last Stand**" were inspired on a trip Page and Plant made through Africa. Page's overdubs were considered the finest guitar orchestration of his career. Plant's vocals were recorded in one take following a two-week stay in a hospital after he re-injured his broken ankle.

#2:   "**For Your Life**" evolved from a rehearsal jam and was never performed in concert. Plant later said the lyrics were a sarcastic dig at an old friend who partied too much.

#3:   "**Royal Orleans**" was the only group composition on this album. Written about some of the band's strange experiences in and around their favorite New Orleans hotel, "**Royal Orleans**" was never performed live.

## *Presence - Side Two*

These songs were all composed while guitarist Jimmy Page and vocalist Robert Plant were in Malibu. The last three were never performed live.

#1: "**Nobody's Fault But Mine**" was based on Blind Willie Johnson's 1928 song of the same name. He did not receive a writing credit.

#2: You can hear Page's speaker cabinet rattling during several passages in "**Candy Store Rock**." Written during a one-hour rehearsal jam, "**Candy Store Rock**" was released as a single in May 1976. "**Royal Orleans**" was the B-side. Neither song charted.

#3: "**Hots On For Nowhere**" evolved from an hour-long jam. The chord changes first evolved in 1974 during early work on "**Custard Pie**."

#4: The lyrics for "**Tea For One**" were inspired by Plant's loneliness when he was away from his wife and family.

# HARD ROCK - Led Zeppelin

## Led Zeppelin
### *The Song Remains The Same* (22-27-24-28)

8th LP, released 9/28/76 — six months after *Presence* and one month before Led Zeppelin's movie *The Song Remains The Same*. Led Zeppelin was always, first and foremost, an outstanding live band. Because several of the multi-track masters were lost, this album was a direct dub from the soundtrack of the Zep's concert movie *The Song Remains The Same*. The concert footage was filmed during the *Houses Of The Holy* tour at Madison Square Garden on July 27, 28, and 29, 1973. Additional filming was planned for the second half of the *Physical Graffiti* tour, but when vocalist Robert Plant's car accident forced the cancellation of that tour leg, the movie project was completed with what little film was available. (Well placed sources observed that most of the close-ups were shot on a sound stage in London.) The fact that the movie took three years and two directors to finish indicated the band's level of interest (or lack thereof) in the project. Their manager, Peter Grant, later referred to the film as "one of the most expensive home movies ever made." Even guitarist Jimmy Page had mixed feelings about the presentation and insisted that the Zeppelin had performed much more effectively in almost every other live show they did. As usual, Page controlled the production. Eddie Kramer (Hendrix's engineer) was brought in to handle the sound. No overdubbing was used to sweeten the occasionally rough performances on this #2 charting, multi-million selling album.

# UNCLE JOE'S RECORD GUIDE

** **Special Note**: Superb versions of "**Since I've Been Loving You**," "**Black Dog**," "**Bron-Yr-Aur**" and "**Heartbreaker**" were included in the final version of the film, but not on this album.

## *The Song Remains The Same - Side One*

#1:  "**Rock & Roll**"

#2:  "**Celebration Day**" did not appear in the film's final cut.

#3:  "**The Song Remains The Same**"

#4:  "**The Rain Song**"

## *The Song Remains The Same - Side Two*

#1:  "**Dazed And Confused**"

# HARD ROCK - Led Zeppelin

## *The Song Remains The Same - Side Three*

#1:  A slightly different version of "**No Quarter**" was used in the final cut of the film.

#2:  Vocalist Robert Plant's introduction to "**Stairway To Heaven**" was edited differently in the film.

## *The Song Remains The Same - Side Four*

#1:  "**Moby Dick**"

#2:  "**Whole Lotta Love**"

## Led Zeppelin
### *In Through The Out Door* (21-22)

9th LP, released 8/15/79 — three-and-a-half years after
*Presence*. After the death of vocalist Robert Plant's 5-year-old
son forced the cancellation of the final leg of the Zeppelin's
1977 world tour, Robert stayed away from the band for
almost 10 months. When he got back in touch with the group,
Robert insisted they explore new musical territory as a
condition of his return. As a result, when the Zep regrouped in
London for six weeks of rehearsals in May and June 1978, they
took a completely different approach to their music.
Keyboardist/bassist John Paul Jones worked on the musical
arrangements as Plant worked on lyrics. Supposedly,
drummer John Bonham's and guitarist Jimmy Page's
substance abuse problems kept them in the compositional
background, although Page received his usual production
credits. Jones' keyboards and melodic textures dominated the
arrangements and he received writing credits for six of the
seven songs on this album — the most ever for the quietest,
most underrated member of Led Zeppelin. Conversely, Page
received no credit for two songs on this album — the only time
in the band's history he didn't have a hand in the songwriting.

   *In Through The Out Door* was recorded under the
working title *Look* in the first three weeks of December 1978.
The recording facility they chose was ABBA's Polar Music
Studios in Stockholm, Sweden, where Genesis had just
finished their *Duke* album. Interestingly, for the first time in
Led Zeppelin's history, there were no wild parties during these
sessions.

# HARD ROCK - Led Zeppelin

Jimmy Page supposedly quipped that the Zep chose the album title *In Through The Out Door* because "that's the hardest way to get back in." They certainly didn't have to worry about being accepted back by their fans. *In Through The Out Door* sold over two million copies in its first 10 days of release. It spent seven weeks at #1 in the States and eventually sold over five million copies. During that time, all eight of the Zeppelin's previous albums also shot back up the charts. To further promote this album's release and highlight the group's newly found vigor, Led Zeppelin played two landmark dates at England's Knebworth Festival in September 1979. A brief European tour was staged during June and July 1980, but alcohol and drug-related problems plagued Page and some of the band's staff. On September 25, 1980, during final rehearsals for the long-anticipated American tour, drummer John Bonham died in his sleep after consuming at least 40 shots of vodka in an afternoon of partying. Less than three months later, on December 4, 1980, the official announcement was made that Led Zeppelin had disbanded.

** **Special Notes**: The group arranged for six different covers to be produced for this album, each wrapped in a plain brown paper cover so the album's purchaser would not know which they would get (a clever marketing trick that sold more records). The supposed inspiration for the cover shot was a bar around the corner from the group's favorite Royal Orleans hotel.

Outtakes from the *In Through The Out Door* sessions included: "**Darlene**," "**Ozone Baby**," "**Wearing And Tearing**," and a working track called "The Hook." All of those outtakes, except "The Hook," later appeared on the *Coda* album.

## *In Through The Out Door - Side One*

#1:    Bassist/keyboardist John Paul Jones had first worked on the **"In The Evening"** melody line at home. This version was a result of his collaboration with guitarist Jimmy Page and vocalist Robert Plant.

#2:    "**South Bound Saurez**," credited to Jones and Plant, was one of only two Led Zeppelin songs for which Jimmy Page did not receive writing credits, "**South Bound Saurez**" was never performed live.

    **Note**: Saurez [pronounced swar-RAY] is Portuguese for party.

#3:    "**Fool In The Rain**" was a Jones/Page/Plant composition. The samba-like percussion section was inspired by the 1978 World Cup Soccer matches in Argentina. Although "**Fool In The Rain**" charted at #21 in January 1980 (Led Zeppelin's sixth American Top 40 hit), it was never performed live.

#4:    "**Hot Dog**," co-written by Page and Plant, evolved from the group's pre-production sessions in London. The quality of Jimmy's guitar work was seen by some as an indication of the degree of his problems. "**Hot Dog**" was used as the B-side to "**Fool In The Rain**."

# HARD ROCK - Led Zeppelin

## *In Through The Out Door - Side Two*

#1: "**Carouselambra**" was another number initially worked up by bassist/keyboardist John Paul Jones. He later collaborated with guitarist Jimmy Page and vocalist Robert Plant for this final version. Supposedly, Plant wrote the lyrics about some of the band's members.

#2: "**All My Love**" was co-written by Jones and Plant one morning before the recording sessions began. Robert's vocals were recorded on the first take; his lyrics were a tribute to the memory of his 5-year-old son Karac, who had died while the Zeppelin toured America in 1977. Robert later identified this as one of his favorite Zeppelin songs of all time.

   **Note**: A 7:02 minute version of this song is supposed to be in Jimmy Page's archives. This is the second of only two Led Zeppelin songs in which Page did not write any music or lyrics.

#3: "**I'm Gonna Crawl**," credited to Page, Plant and Jones, was a tribute to Wilson Pickett and Otis Redding.

# UNCLE JOE'S RECORD GUIDE

## Led Zeppelin
*Coda* (15-19-22)

10th LP, released 11/19/82. In Summer 1981, guitarist Jimmy Page began to assemble this collection of outtakes and soundcheck recordings from the Zeppelin's 11-year career under the working title *Early Days and Later Years*. Bassist/ keyboardist John Paul Jones and vocalist Robert Plant were called in for the final mixing and overdubbing before the compilation was released approximately two years after drummer John Bonham's death. *Coda* charted at #4 in Britain and #6 in the States, and sold over a million copies.

** **Special Note**: Curiously, this compilation did not initially contain one of the most famous Led Zeppelin songs to never appear on a Zeppelin album, "**Hey, Hey, What Can I Do**," which had been recorded during the sessions for their third album and released as the flipside to "**Immigrant Song**." Also missing were any of the unreleased live versions of the R&B medley the band consistently performed during their earliest tours, or any live renditions of "**White Summer**," a Jimmy Page guitar workout carried over from his days with the Yardbirds. In 1993, several additional tracks, including "**White Summer**" and "**Hey, Hey, What Can I Do**," were included on the remastered compact disc version of this compilation.

# HARD ROCK - Led Zeppelin

## *Coda - Side One*

#1: "**We're Gonna Groove**" was recorded during a soundcheck at the Royal Albert Hall on January 9, 1970, near the end of the first British tour for the Zep's second album. "**We're Gonna Groove**," originally a hit for Ben E. King, had been the Zeppelin's show opener when they first performed in public. Guitarist Jimmy Page added a few overdubs to this track in early 1982.

#2: Co-written by Page and vocalist Robert Plant during their stay at the Bron-Yr-Aur [pronounced BRON-rahr] cottage in Wales, "**Poor Tom**" was recorded on June 5, 1970, at Olympic Studios in London during the sessions for *Led Zeppelin III*. "**Poor Tom**" was never performed live.

#3: A cover of the Willie Dixon song "**I Can't Quit You Baby**" had been included on the *Led Zeppelin* album. This version was recorded during a soundcheck at the Royal Albert Hall on January 9, 1970.

#4: "**Walter's Walk**," a Page/Plant song, was recorded during the first sessions for *Houses Of The Holy* on May 15, 1972, at Stargroves (Mick Jagger's summer mansion). "**Walter's Walk**" was never performed live.

## *Coda - Side Two*

None of the songs on this side were ever performed live.

#1:   "**Ozone Baby**," an outtake from the *In Through The Out Door* sessions recorded on November 14,1978, was co-written by guitarist Jimmy Page and vocalist Robert Plant.

#2:   "**Darlene**," another *In Through The Out Door* outtake listed as a group composition, was recorded two days after "**Ozone Baby**."

#3:   "**Bonzo's Montreux**" arose from a drumming experiment that had long fascinated drummer John Bonham. It was recorded by Page and Bonham at Mountain Studios in Switzerland on December 9, 1976, before the *Presence* tour. During that same time frame, Yes was recording their *Going For The One* album in the same studio complex.

#4:   "**Wearing And Tearing**" was another Page/Plant outtake from the *In Through The Out Door* sessions. The riff was first worked up during the *Presence* rehearsals. Supposedly, Plant's final lyrics were about the damage he saw others doing to themselves through drug abuse. Recorded on November 21, 1978, "**Wearing And Tearing**" was never performed in concert while John Bonham was alive.

# HARD ROCK - Led Zeppelin

## *Coda - Side Three*

The songs on this side were released initially on an album in Led Zeppelin's 1990 and 1993 boxed sets. They were included in the remastered CD version of the *Coda* album in late 1993.

#1:   "**Baby Come On Home**" was an outtake from the October 10, 1968 *Led Zeppelin* sessions at Olympic Studios in London. It was credited to Bert Berns (who wrote the original version), guitarist Jimmy Page and vocalist Robert Plant. This track was first released as part of the 1993 *Boxed Set2*.

#2:   "**Traveling Riverside Blues**," credited to Page, Plant and bluesman Robert Johnson, was recorded live for John Peel's Top Gear radio show on the BBC on June 23, 1969. It was first released as part of the 1990 Led Zeppelin *Boxed Set*.

#3:   The Jimmy Page workout "**White Summer/Black Mountain Side**" was recorded and broadcast on the BBC show, Playhouse Theatre Over Radio One, on June 27, 1969. It was first released as part of the 1990 Led Zeppelin *Boxed* Set.

#4:   "**Hey, Hey, What Can I Do**," a group composition, and the most famous Led Zeppelin outtake of all time, was recorded in 1970 at Island Studios in London for *Led Zeppelin III*, and released as the B-side to the "**Immigrant Song**" in November of that year. "**Hey, Hey, What Can I Do**" was never performed live.

## **Led Zeppelin**

1976

Jimmy Page
John Bonham, John Paul Jones
Robert Plant

## Led Zeppelin
***Boxed Set*** (21-28-23) (26-25-24) (23-21-28) (21-28-23)

11th LP, released 10/23/90 in the U.K. — 10/29/90 in the U.S. — roughly in conjunction with the tenth anniversary of the band's dissolution. Led Zeppelin's surviving members had originally been dissatisfied with the quality of the mastering of their compact discs, which had been done without any of the group's input. In early 1990, bassist/keyboardist John Paul Jones took the initiative and approached guitarist Jimmy Page with a list of songs he thought should be included in, and remastered for, a Led Zeppelin compilation. Page decided to handle this project, and scoured the tape vaults for the group's original master tapes. Eventually, he and engineer George Marino digitally remastered these 54 songs, which were mutually chosen by Page, Jones and vocalist Robert Plant. Jimmy arranged the songs in a musical and thematic sequence, rather than the more common chronological order found in most boxed sets. The results proved interesting.

The distinct sonic difference in these remastered songs caused fans to clamor for the remastering and re-release of the original Zeppelin albums. In fact, the reaction of fans to this compilation surprised many in the music business. This Zeppelin retrospective quickly charted at #18 and became the biggest selling box set ever when it sold over three million copies.

** **Special Note**: The *Boxed Set's* artwork was vintage Led Zeppelin, including a tongue-in-cheek reference to UFOs and a classy rendering of the rune-like symbols each Zep member made famous on *Led Zeppelin IV*. Also, four seemingly mysterious digits (54, 69, 79, 00) were included in the artwork. Soon, fans figured out that the numbers referred to the 54 songs and 54 photographs in the set and its detailed booklet; the decade of music covered in the set (1969 to 1979); and 00 was seen as a reference to infinity (∞) and the timelessness of Led Zeppelin's music and appeal.

## *Boxed Set - CD One, Side One*

#1:  "**Whole Lotta Love**," credited as a group composition, was initially recorded at Sunset Sound in Los Angeles for *Led Zeppelin II*. The group's performing was so hot that Robert Plant recorded his lead vocal on the first take. Additional instrumental work was later done at Olympic Studios in London and A&R Studios in New York City. Although the band neither approved nor expected this to be a single (edited or otherwise), "**Whole Lotta Love**" charted at #4 in January 1970 in the U.S. and sold over a million copies within five weeks of its release.

**Note**: Jimmy Page's guitar solo after the sound effects section in "**Whole Lotta Love**" became a standard measure of performance for electric guitarists. Also, 20 years after this album was released, the group reached an out-of-court settlement over a copyright infringement with bluesman Willie Dixon, whose song "You Need Love" preceded this song by several years.

# HARD ROCK - Led Zeppelin

**#2:**  The group composition "**Heartbreaker**" was recorded at A&R Studios in New York for their second album and became a staple of their live set. The guitar solo became standard fare for any guitarist calling himself a player.

**#3:**  Recorded for their first album, "**Communication Breakdown**" was one of the first signature tunes the Zeppelin worked up. The writing credits went to Page, keyboardist/bassist John Paul Jones and drummer John Bonham. This song featured a rare example of Jimmy Page's backing vocals.

**#4:**  One of the few songs on their first album that contained overdubs or differed from the early live versions, "**Babe, I'm Gonna Leave You**" was initially credited to Jimmy Page. (Page had played Joan Baez's version of this song for Robert Plant when he tried to recruit Robert for the band.) The original songwriter, Anne Bredon, later received credit with Page and Plant.

**#5:**  "**What Is And What Should Never Be**" was not only one of the first collaborations between Page and Plant, but also one of the first songs completed for their second album. It was recorded at Olympic Studios in London before the Zeppelin's second tour and finished at both Groove and A&R Studios in New York.

## *Boxed Set - CD One, Side Two*

#1:  "**Thank You**," vocalist Robert Plant's first full lyrical composition, was dedicated to his wife Maureen. The basic tracks were done at A&R Studios in New York and, like much of *Led Zeppelin II*, the recording was finished at Morgan Sound in London.

#2:  "**I Can't Quit You Baby**" was another classic number by American bluesman Willie Dixon that the Zep recorded for their debut album and was, in fact, one of the first songs they ever played.

#3:  "**Dazed And Confused**," featured Page, who played his guitar with a violin bow. Jimmy had worked on this track while he was still in the Yardbirds. The original arrangement came from an uncredited New York folk singer named Jake Holmes. This song, with different lyrics and the working title "I'm Confused," was one of the first Led Zeppelin worked up and just the second of two takes of "**Dazed And Confused**" the group recorded. Only the violin bow section was overdubbed.

#4:  "**Your Time Is Gonna Come**" was supposedly a group composition, but was credited only to Page and bassist/keyboardist John Paul Jones. Recorded live for their first album, only the pedal steel guitar was overdubbed. "**Your Time Is Gonna Come**" was never performed on stage.

#5:  Even though Robert called "**Ramble On**" his favorite song on *Led Zeppelin II*, the Page/Plant composition was never played live. The basic tracks were recorded at Juggy Sound, and guitar overdubs were later done at A&R Studios in New York.

# HARD ROCK - Led Zeppelin

## *Boxed Set - CD One, Side Three*

#1: "**Traveling Riverside Blues**," credited to guitarist Jimmy Page, vocalist Robert Plant and long-dead bluesman Robert Johnson, was recorded live for John Peel's Top Gear radio show on the BBC on June 23, 1969. This track was previously unreleased.

#2: "**Friends**" was a Page/Plant composition that came together during their vacation in Wales before the band recorded *Led Zeppelin III*. For some reason, bassist John Paul Jones did not receive credit for his string arrangement.

#3: "**Celebration Day**," a great song live, was credited to Page, Plant and Jones. The basic tune also came together at Bron-Yr-Aur [pronounced BRON-rahr] and was recorded for the band's third album.

#4: "**Hey, Hey, What Can I Do**," a group composition, was the most famous Led Zeppelin outtake of all time. It was recorded in 1970 at Island Studios in London for *Led Zeppelin III* and released as the B-side to the "**Immigrant Song**" in November of that year. "**Hey, Hey, What Can I Do**" was never performed live.

#5: The Jimmy Page workout "**White Summer/Black Mountain Side**" was recorded and broadcast on the BBC's Playhouse Theatre Over Radio One show on June 27, 1969. This track was previously unreleased.

## *Boxed Set - CD Two, Side One*

#1: "**Black Dog**" was credited to guitarist Jimmy Page, vocalist Robert Plant and bassist John Paul Jones, who came up with the original riff on which the song was based. Named after a stray dog that wandered in and out of the recording sessions for *Led Zeppelin IV*, the song featured tricky time signatures. The band played "**Black Dog**" during their Summer 1971 tours, months before the album was released. Backed with "**Misty Mountain Hop**," "**Black Dog**" reached #15 on the American charts in February 1973. Plant later identified this as one of his favorite Led Zeppelin songs of all time. Jones said that in concert "this song was always a race to see who would finish first."

#2: Page worked up "**Over The Hills And Far Away**" at home, then presented it to the band for the *Houses Of The Holy* album. Plant spent several days working on the lyrics. "**Over The Hills And Far Away**" reached #51 on the U.S. singles charts in May 1973. The B-side was "**Dancing Days**."

#3: "**Immigrant Song**" was co-written at Bron-Yr-Aur [pronounced BRON-rahr] by Page and Plant, who was inspired by the Vikings. This track was first recorded at Headley Grange, and then finished at Island and Olympic Studios in London for *Led Zeppelin III*. Backed by the outtake "**Hey, Hey, What Can I Do**," "**Immigrant Song**" reached #16 on the American singles charts in January 1971.

#4: The melody for "**The Battle Of Evermore**" emerged in the early morning hours at Headley Grange when, after the rest of the band had gone to bed, Jimmy Page picked up John Paul Jones' mandolin and began to experiment with it. Plant's lyrical inspiration came from a book on the Medieval Scottish wars.

# HARD ROCK - Led Zeppelin

When Sandy Denny (of the Fairport Convention) overdubbed her vocals, she became the only outside musician to ever sing on a Led Zeppelin song. "**The Battle Of Evermore**" was originally released on *Led Zeppelin IV*.

#5:  "**Bron-Y-Aur-Stomp**" started out as a jam between Plant and Page at the cottage in Wales where *Led Zeppelin III* was written. The earliest version of this song was entitled "Jennings Farm Blues." Robert wrote the lyrics about his dog . Bassist/keyboardist John Paul Jones received co-writing credit for his contribution to the final arrangement.

#6:  Page wrote "**Tangerine**" in a different form for the Yardbirds three years before Led Zeppelin recorded it for their third album. When the Yardbirds attempted to record it, they just couldn't pull it off. In direct contrast, Page considered this recording to be a perfect expression of his concept of Led Zeppelin's music. It became the last song for which he wrote all the lyrics.

## Boxed Set - CD Two, Side Two

#1:  The inspiration for "**Going To California**" came during the band's partying and recording sessions in Los Angeles. Vocalist Robert Plant said later that he had Joni Mitchell's music in mind when he penned these lyrics. This song was recorded at the Headley Grange mansion during the 1971 sessions for *Led Zeppelin IV*.

#2:  One of the first songs finished for their third album, "**Since I've Been Loving You**," recorded live at Olympic Studios in London, was a good representation of the Zeppelin's concert sound. Taking some inspiration from the Moby Grape song

"Never," guitarist Jimmy Page, Plant and keyboardist/bassist John Paul Jones shared writing credits for "**Since I've Been Loving You**." The band had recorded another version of this song, but felt this one was superior. On the compact disc, you can hear John Bonham's bass drum pedal squeaking throughout the song.

#3:    The title of the group composition "**D'Yer Maker**" came from a Cockney pronunciation of "Did you make her?" — the punch line from a bad joke. ("My wife just went on vacation. Jamaica? No, she went on her own accord.") Neither the title "**D'Yer Maker**" nor the joke appear in the song's lyrics. One of the first tunes completed for the *Houses Of The Holy* album, "**D'Yer Maker**" hit the American Top 20 in December 1973.

#4:    "**Gallows Pole**," a Leadbelly blues song from the 1920s, underwent some serious revisions as the Zeppelin played with it while recording their third album. In the end, the song was credited to guitarist Jimmy Page and vocalist Robert Plant. Although Led Zeppelin only played this song live once, Jimmy Page and Robert Plant reprised it in their 1994 tour.

#5:    "**Custard Pie**" was a Jimmy Page/Robert Plant composition that evolved from an early 1974 jam at the Headley Grange mansion during the *Physical Graffiti* sessions. Just like their earlier "**Hats Off To (Roy) Harper**," the basic lyrical and melodic inspiration for "**Custard Pie**" came from bluesmen Sonny Terry's "Custard Pie" and Bukka White's "Shake 'Em On Down." It was never performed live.

# HARD ROCK - Led Zeppelin

## *Boxed Set - CD Two, Side Three*

#1:  Bassist/keyboardist John Paul Jones got co-writing credit with guitarist Jimmy Page and vocalist Robert Plant for "**Misty Mountain Hop**." Recorded at the Headley Grange mansion for the band's fourth album, "**Misty Mountain Hop**" was used as the B-side to the "**Black Dog**" single.

#2:  Under the working title "Been A Long Time," "**Rock & Roll**" was a group composition from *Led Zeppelin IV*, which came together in about 15 minutes during a warm-up at Headley Grange with pianist Ian Stewart (of the Rolling Stones). John Bonham's opening drum riff came from Little Richard's "Keep A Knockin'." As a single, "**Rock & Roll**" barely broke into the American Top 50 in February 1972. As a song, it inspired virtually every rock & roll band in the world.

#3:  Page worked out the total arrangement for "**The Rain Song**" at his home studio, then brought the demos to the band's *Houses Of The Holy* recording sessions at Stargroves.

#4:  "**Stairway To Heaven**" is still considered to be one of the finest rock & roll songs ever written (it is certainly the most popular). The lyrics came to Plant one evening during the recording sessions at the Headley Grange mansion, and the vocals were later recorded in just one take. The Zep played "**Stairway To Heaven**" during their Summer 1971 tours, months before *Led Zeppelin IV* was released.

**Note**: Although he used a Telecaster to record this, "**Stairway To Heaven**" was the first song on which Page used his legendary double-neck Gibson guitar in concert. That specialized instrument allowed Jimmy to play the 12-string and 6-string parts without changing guitars. Soon, every band with any pretensions used double-necked Gibsons.

# UNCLE JOE'S RECORD GUIDE

Also, in the years after *Led Zeppelin IV* was released, fundamentalist preachers constantly used this song to scare their congregations. They claimed "**Stairway To Heaven**" contained Satanic messages hidden by backwards masking (a technique of recording lyrics backwards at a low level in the final mix). That accusation was so blatantly absurd, even some rock critics thought it was true.

## *Boxed Set - CD Three, Side One*

#1:  Bassist/keyboardist John Paul Jones had first worked on the "**In The Evening**" melody line at home. This version from *In Through The Out Door* was a result of his collaboration with guitarist Jimmy Page and vocalist Robert Plant.

#2:  Page's speaker cabinet can be heard rattling during several passages in "**Candy Store Rock**." Written during a one-hour rehearsal jam for the *Presence* album, "**Candy Store Rock**" was released as a single in May 1976. "**Royal Orleans**" was the B-side. Neither song charted.

#3:  Plant said that he felt as if he were looking at an ocean as he gazed out over Led Zeppelin's concert audiences. "**The Ocean**," inspired by that feeling, was listed as a group composition on the *Houses Of The Holy* album. The basic tracks were recorded on the fifth take, as indicated by drummer John Bonham's rap at the beginning of the song.
**Note**: During the final mixing, the sound of a telephone ringing was added 1:38 minutes into the song — a clever trick!

#4:  A great hard rocker, "**Houses of the Holy**" was replaced on that album by "**Dancing Days**." It later appeared on *Physical*

# HARD ROCK - Led Zeppelin

*Graffiti*. Written by guitarist Jimmy Page and vocalist Robert Plant, and recorded in June 1972 at both Olympic Studios in London and Electric Lady Studios in New York, "**Houses of the Holy**" was never performed live.

## *Boxed Set - CD Three, Side Two*

#1: "**Wearing And Tearing**" was an *In Through The Out Door* outtake co-written by guitarist Jimmy Page and vocalist Robert Plant. The riff was first worked up during the *Presence* sessions. Supposedly, Plant's final lyrics were about the damage he saw others doing to themselves through drug abuse. Recorded on November 21, 1978, "**Wearing And Tearing**" was never performed in concert while John Bonham was alive.

#2: Co-written by Page and vocalist Robert Plant during their stay at the Bron-Yr-Aur [pronounced BRON-rahr] cottage in Wales, "**Poor Tom**" was recorded on June 5, 1970, at Olympic Studios in London during the sessions for *Led Zeppelin III*. "**Poor Tom**" was never performed live.

#3: Recorded for the *Presence* album, "**Nobody's Fault But Mine**" was based on Blind Willie Johnson's 1928 song of the same name. He did not receive writing credit.

#4: "**Fool In The Rain**" was a Jones/Page/Plant composition from *In Through The Out Door*. The samba-like percussion section was inspired by the 1978 World Cup Soccer matches in Argentina. Although "**Fool In The Rain**" charted at #21 in January 1980 (Led Zeppelin's sixth American Top 40 hit), it was never performed live.

# UNCLE JOE'S RECORD GUIDE

## Boxed Set - CD Three, Side Three

#1: "**In The Light**" was co-written by guitarist Jimmy Page, vocalist Robert Plant and bassist/keyboardist John Paul Jones. The early working version, called "Take Me Home," featured completely different lyrics. Jones did a lot of development on this song using an EMS VCS-3 synthesizer, a highly innovative piece of gear in 1974. Although Robert identified this as one of his favorite Zeppelin songs, the band never played "**In The Light**" live.

#2: "**The Wanton Song**" was a Page/Plant collaboration recorded in early 1974. Although it was one of Robert's favorite Led Zeppelin songs, the band only played it live a few times early in the Physical Graffiti tour.

#3: "**Moby Dick**"/"**Bonzo's Montreux**," a combination Jimmy Page worked up, combined segments of "**Bonzo's Montreux**" (from *Coda*) with the drum solo from "**Moby Dick**" (from *Led Zeppelin II*). "**Bonzo's Montreux**" was a drumming experiment that had long fascinated drummer John Bonham. It was recorded by Page and Bonham in Switzerland on December 9, 1976, before the *Presence* tour.

#4: "**I'm Gonna Crawl**" was credited to Page, Plant and Jones. This *In Through The Out Door* song was supposedly a tribute to Wilson Pickett and Otis Redding.

#5: "**All My Love**" was co-written by Jones and Plant one morning before the *In Through The Out Door* sessions began. Robert's lyrics were a tribute to the memory of his 5-year-old son Karac, who had died while the Zeppelin toured America in 1977. Plant's vocals were recorded on the first take. Although he identified this as one of his favorite Zeppelin songs of all time, the band never played "**All My Love**" live.

**Note**: A 7:02 minute version of this song is supposed to be in Jimmy Page's archives. This is one of the only two Led Zeppelin songs in which Page did not write music or lyrics.

## *Boxed Set - CD Four, Side One*

#1:  The classic cut from *Physical Graffiti*, "**Kashmir**," was credited to guitarist Jimmy Page, vocalist Robert Plant and drummer John Bonham. Developed under the title "Driving To Kashmir," Bonzo first came up with the rhythm, then Jimmy worked up the guitar melody between the November 1973 and February 1974 sessions for that album. When Robert adapted lyrics he had written while driving in the Sahara desert, the song was virtually complete. "**Kashmir**" remains one of the most requested Zeppelin songs ever. Page, Plant and Jones have all said it was their personal favorite because it captured everything the band was about — lyrically, as well as in the way it was recorded and performed live.

#2:  With a keyboard nod to Robert Johnson's "Terraplane Blues," and drummer John Bonham's inspired input, "**Trampled Under Foot**" evolved from an in-studio jam into a love song about a car. It was credited to Page, Plant and bassist/keyboardist John Paul Jones, and peaked on the U.S. charts at #38 in June 1975. "**Trampled Under Foot**" first appeared on *Physical Graffiti*.

#3:  "**For Your Life**" evolved from a rehearsal jam for the *Presence* album. It was never performed in concert. Plant later said the lyrics were inspired by a friend who partied too much.

## *Boxed Set - CD Four, Side Two*

#1: Bassist/keyboardist John Paul Jones had worked up most of "**No Quarter**" in his home studio several years before it was recorded for *Houses Of The Holy*. The band had recorded different versions of the song before this one was done at Island Studios in London. "**No Quarter**" was Jones' first major contribution to be recorded by the band, and its Hammond organ solo became his trademark in concert.

#2: "**Dancing Days**" was co-written by guitarist Jimmy Page and vocalist Robert Plant. The song came together during an extremely spirited *Houses Of The Holy* session, and the band was reported to have danced about during the initial playback of the basic tracks.

#3: "**When The Levee Breaks**," from *Led Zeppelin IV*, was a vastly reworked version of the 1929 Memphis Minnie/Kansas Joe McCoy blues classic. The band tried to record this in the studio in early December 1970, but the sound just did not click. Moving back into Headley Grange proved to be the key. John Bonham's drums were recorded in a large hallway, with just a couple of microphones hanging in the adjacent 30-foot-high stairwell. Natural reverberations off the stone walls contributed to what is still considered to be one of the best rock & roll drum sounds ever.

#4: The lyrics for "**Achilles Last Stand**" were inspired on a trip Page and Plant made through Africa. Page's overdubs were considered to be the finest guitar orchestration of his career. Plant's vocal was recorded in one take following a two-week stay in a hospital after he re-injured his broken ankle. This song first appeared on the *Presence* album.

# HARD ROCK - Led Zeppelin

## *Boxed Set - CD Four, Side Three*

#1: Guitarist Jimmy Page had worked for months on "**The Song Remains The Same**" before it finally took this form with vocalist Robert Plant's lyrics. Working titles included "**The Campaign**," "**Slush**" and "**The Overture**." It first appeared on the *Houses Of The Holy* album.

#2: For several years, Jimmy Page worked sporadically on the instrumental that became "**Ten Years Gone**" when Robert Plant wrote lyrics that tied the arrangement together during the *Physical Graffiti* sessions. Robert later said he was writing about a girlfriend who had insisted he choose between her and music.

#3: "**In My Time Of Dying**" was a group composition based on Blind Willie Johnson's 1927 song "Jesus, Make Up My Dying Bed." In fact, these lyrics were almost identical to Bob Dylan's early-Sixties version of that song. One of the first numbers completed for this album in late November 1973, "**In My Time Of Dying**" was recorded live at Headley Grange, with Jimmy Page adding only a few overdubs later on. Just as they had done with "**When The Levee Breaks**," the group recorded John Bonham's drums in a large hallway, using only two microphones set-up in a 30-foot-high stairwell. "**In My Time Of Dying**" was never performed live.

**Note**: Robert Plant said this song kept running through his mind as he and his family lay injured in the jeep wreck that resulted in the cancellation of the final leg of the *Physical Graffiti* tour.

## Led Zeppelin
***Boxed Set2*** (21-25-29) (27-25-24)

12th LP, released 10/2/93. Led Zeppelin's surviving members
had long been dissatisfied with the original quality of the
mastering of the Zep's compact discs, which had been done
without input from the group. In early 1990,
bassist/keyboardist John Paul Jones took the initiative and
approached guitarist Jimmy Page with a list of songs he
thought should be included in and remastered for a Led
Zeppelin compilation. Page took on the project and scoured
the tape vaults for the group's original master tapes.
Eventually he and engineer George Marino digitally
remastered the 54 songs that comprised the Zeppelin's first
*Boxed Set*. These remaining 31 songs were later remastered
so the original albums could be re-released, although *Boxed
Set2* was more of an afterthought. As he did with the first
*Boxed Set*, Page arranged these songs in a musical and
thematic sequence, rather than the more common
chronological order.

The sonic difference was again quite amazing, but sales of
this set (which only charted at #87) were dampened by the
simultaneous release of the remastered versions of the
original Zeppelin albums.

# HARD ROCK - Led Zeppelin

## *Boxed Set2 - CD One, Side One*

#1: Evolved from a rehearsal jam for their first album, "**Good Times, Bad Times**" was credited to guitarist Jimmy Page, bassist John Paul Jones and drummer John Bonham. Even though this marked vocalist Robert Plant's first real attempt at writing lyrics, his previous recording contract kept his name off this credit sheet. Released as a U.S. single, "**Good Times, Bad Times**" nudged the charts at #80 in March 1969.

#2: "**We're Gonna Groove**" was recorded during a soundcheck at Royal Albert Hall on January 9, 1970, near the end of the first British tour for the Zep's second album. "**We're Gonna Groove**" was originally a hit for Ben E. King and had been the Zeppelin's show opener when they first started playing in public. Guitarist Jimmy Page added a few overdubs to this track in early 1982 for its inclusion on the *Coda* album.

#3: "**Night Flight**" was recorded in 1971 during the sessions for *Led Zeppelin IV* and was later included on the *Physical Graffiti* album. Rehearsed on stage, it was never performed in concert. This song marked the first time keyboardist/ bassist John Paul Jones was listed before Jimmy Page and vocalist Robert Plant in the writing credits.

#4: "**That's The Way**," a Page/Plant composition, was originally written at Bron-Yr-Aur [pronounced BRON -rahr] under the working title "The Boy Next Door." The final lyrics were partially inspired by the social unrest Led Zeppelin saw during their late-Sixties American tours. This acoustic version was recorded for *Led Zeppelin III* at Island Studios in London after a couple of electric renditions did not cut it.

# UNCLE JOE'S RECORD GUIDE

#5:  "**Baby Come On Home**" was an outtake from the *Led Zeppelin* sessions on October 10, 1968, at Olympic Studios in London. It was credited to Bert Berns (who wrote the original version), Page and Plant, and was previously unreleased.

## *Boxed Set2 - CD One, Side Two*

#1:  "**The Lemon Song**" was based on Howlin' Wolf's "Killing Floor," a blues song the Zeppelin had been jamming on since their first practice together, and Albert Collins' "Crosscut Saw." Neither Collins nor Howlin' Wolf initially received credit or royalties from this song, which was recorded live at Mystic Studios and Mirror Sound in Hollywood for the Zep's second album.

   **Note**: Vocalist Robert Plant also used the "squeeze my lemon" lyric from Robert Johnson's "Traveling Riverside Blues" in this.

#2:  "**You Shook Me**" was a classic Willie Dixon blues number which Jeff Beck also covered on his first solo album — released six months before Led Zeppelin's first album. Rock critics went wild accusing Jimmy Page of copying his old partner and comparing Plant's vocals with those of Rod Stewart.

   **Note**: Rock critics typically go wild over popular artists they cannot comprehend.

#3:  "**Boogie with Stu**" refers to piano player Ian Stewart (of the Rolling Stones). After "**Rock & Roll**" was recorded during the 1971 Headley Grange sessions for *Led Zeppelin IV*, the Zep continued to party and jam with Stewart. They eventually covered "OO-My-Head" by Ritchie Valens (Valens was L.A.'s first true rock & roll star and was killed in the 1959 plane crash with Buddy Holly). While *Physical Graffiti*'s release was held up with artwork problems, Ritchie's mother got wind of the Zeppelin's recording. She immediately threatened to sue, and only then was given the proper writing credits, royalties and, as a bonus, a mention in the *Physical Graffiti* liner notes. The original title for "**Boogie with Stu**" was "Sloppy Drunk," which evidently reflected the musicians' condition. "**Boogie with Stu**" was never played in concert.

#4:    "**Bron-Yr-Aur**" [pronounced BRON-rahr] was inspired by the pastoral surroundings of the cottage in Wales where guitarist Jimmy Page and Robert Plant wrote most of Led Zeppelin's third album. "**Bron-Yr-Aur**" was recorded in 1970 during the Island Studio sessions for *Led Zeppelin III*, was finally released on *Physical Graffiti* and was never performed live.

#5:    The Page/Plant song "**Down By The Seaside**" was written for the third album and recorded in 1972 for the Zeppelin's fourth album. Included on *Physical Graffiti*, it was never performed live.

## *Boxed Set2 - CD One, Side Three*

#1:    "**Out On The Tiles**," credited to guitarist Jimmy Page, vocalist Robert Plant and drummer John Bonham, was inspired by one of the band's drunken trips to New York. The original tracks were recorded at the old Headley Grange mansion.

#2:    "**Black Mountain Side**" was credited to Page, but his direct inspiration was the arrangement of the old English folk song "Black Waterside" as recorded by Bert Jansch and John Renbourn. Viram Jasani played tablas on this version from the first Zep album.

#3: John Bonham's solo on "**Moby Dick**" was mostly done without drumsticks (he used his hands!). The recording of the drum solo and instrumental portions of the Page/Jones/Bonham composition took place in different sessions at Mirror Sound in Los Angeles and May Fair Studios in New York for *Led Zeppelin II*. The instrumental open and close to the song had been previously performed live as "The Girl I Love." In later concerts Bonzo's version of this solo would stretch to an epic 30 minutes.

#4: "**Sick Again**," another Page/Plant song, was a rather strange note upon which to end *Physical Graffiti*, Led Zeppelin's most ambitious album. The lyrics were supposedly inspired by the depraved Los Angeles groupie scene that the Zeppelin allegedly nurtured. During the final mixing Page decided to leave Bonham's cough on at the end of the song.

#5: "**Hot Dog**" was co-written by Page and Plant, and the quality of Jimmy's guitar work was seen by some as an indication of the degree of his problems during the *In Through The Out Door* sessions. This was used as the B-side to "**Fool In The Rain**."

#6: "**Carouselambra**" was initially worked up by keyboardist/bassist John Paul Jones. He later collaborated with Page and Plant for this final version for In *Through The Out Door*. Plant supposedly wrote the lyrics about some of the band's members.

# HARD ROCK - Led Zeppelin

## *Boxed Set2 - CD Two, Side One*

#1: "**South Bound Saurez**," credited to Jones and Plant, was one of only two Led Zeppelin songs for which Jimmy Page did not receive writing credits. Recorded for *In Through The Out Door*, "**South Bound Saurez**" was never performed live.

**Note**: Saurez [pronounced swar-RAY] is Portuguese for party.

#2: "**Walter's Walk**," a Page/Plant song, was recorded during the first sessions for *Houses Of The Holy* on May 15, 1972, at Stargroves (Mick Jagger's summer mansion). First released on *Coda*, "**Walter's Walk**" was never performed live.

#3: "**Darlene**," listed as a group composition, was another outtake from the *In Through The Out Door* sessions. It was recorded November 16, 1978.

#4: "**Black Country Woman**" was worked up for the *Houses Of The Holy* album during the sessions at Stargroves (Mick Jagger's summer mansion). This version of the Page/Plant song was recorded in the Stargroves garden, where an airplane flew overhead as the tape machines began to record. The song was judged inappropriate for *Houses Of The Holy*, but was used on *Physical Graffiti*. The original title for "**Black Country Woman**" was the "Never Ending Doubting Woman Blues." The name change reflected the fact that Robert was from the area of England known as the Black Country. This song was performed live only once.

#5: "**How Many More Times**" was built around "How Many More Years" by Howlin' Wolf and "The Hunter," a Booker T. & The MG's blues song recorded by Albert King (None of those people received songwriting credits or royalties for this). Page lifted the middle guitar solo from the Yardbirds' "Shapes Of

Things," a solo first done by Jeff Beck. The Yardbirds had also done a version of "**How Many More Times**." Page, Jones and Bonham received the writing credit for this tune from their debut album, one of the first songs Led Zeppelin performed.

## *Boxed Set2 - CD Two, Side Two*

#1: "**The Rover**" was first recorded in May 1970 during the sessions for *Led Zeppelin IV* at Stargroves (Mick Jagger's summer mansion). This version was recorded the same day as "**D'Yer Maker**" in Spring 1972. Released on *Physical Graffiti*, "**The Rover**" was never performed in concert.

#2: "**Four Sticks**" was a Page/Plant collaboration, so named because John Bonham played his drum part with four drumsticks instead of the more usual two. The group spent a lot of time working on this in Island Studios in early 1971 during the *Led Zeppelin IV* sessions, but they performed it live only once.

#3: "**Hats Off To (Roy) Harper**" was a tribute to the English blues-shouter who had been hanging out with both Pink Floyd and Led Zeppelin. This song, recorded at Olympic Studios in London for *Led Zeppelin III*, was loosely based on Bukka White's "Shake 'Em On Down" and Sonny Terry's "Custard Pie."

#4: A cover of the Willie Dixon song "**I Can't Quit You Baby**" had been included on the *Led Zeppelin* album. This version from *Coda* was recorded during a soundcheck at Royal Albert Hall on January 9, 1970.

# HARD ROCK - Led Zeppelin

#5: "**Hots On For Nowhere**" evolved from an hour-long jam during the *Presence* rehearsals.

## Boxed Set2 - CD Two, Side Three

#1: Guitarist Jimmy Page and vocalist Robert Plant's "**Livin' Lovin' Maid (She's Just A Woman)**" was recorded at Morgan Studios in London for *Led Zeppelin II*, but was never performed live. Its lyrical inspiration supposedly came from a West Coast groupie. When "**Livin' Lovin' Maid (She's Just A Woman)**" was released as the B-side to "**Whole Lotta Love**," it charted at #65.

#2: "**Royal Orleans**," the only group composition on *Presence*, was written about some of the band's strange experiences in and around their favorite New Orleans hotel. "**Royal Orleans**" was never performed live.

#3: "**Bonzo's Montreux**" was a drumming experiment that had long fascinated drummer John Bonham. It was recorded by Page and Bonham in Switzerland on December 9, 1976, before the *Presence* tour.

#4: "**The Crunge**" was a spontaneous jam at Olympic Studios that included pieces of several old R&B songs, including Otis Redding's "Mr. Pitiful." Page had first worked up the basic riff in the mid-Sixties. The "bridge" in the lyrics refers to the "bridge" (musical transition) in James Brown's song "Sex Machine." This song was first released on *Houses Of The Holy*.

#5: The Page/Plant tune "**Bring It On Home**" demonstrated the Zep's best use of dynamic range on their second album. Loosely based on Sonny Boy Williams' "Bring It On Home," this song was recorded in Vancouver, at Mystic Studios in Los Angeles, and at Atlantic and A&R Studios in New York.

#6: The lyrics for "**Tea For One**" were inspired by Plant's loneliness away from his wife and family. The song was recorded at Musicland Studios in Munich for the *Presence* album.

# HARD ROCK - Led Zeppelin

## Final Notes:

In early 1982, Robert Plant launched his solo career with the first of several successful albums. By that time, John Paul Jones had become involved with occasional session work and movie soundtrack performances. Not until three years after the end of Led Zeppelin did Page come out of seclusion, making his first on-stage appearance in the 1983 A.R.M.S. Multiple Sclerosis Benefit tour for his old friend Ronnie Lane (of the Faces). Both the British and American legs of that A.R.M.S. tour (which featured several top British musicians) saw Page re-united with Jeff Beck and Eric Clapton, the guitarists who had preceded him in the legendary Yardbirds.

In July 1985, the three surviving Zeppelin members got back together on stage with drummers Phil Collins (of Genesis) and Tony Thompson (of Chic and the Power Station) for a one-time appearance at the giant *Live Aid Benefit Concert* to ease the famine in Africa. In January 1986, the group (without Collins) returned to a rehearsal hall in England to see if anything musical could be worked out. The rehearsals fell apart after three days and Plant went on to record his most significant solo album to date.

On May 14, 1988, the three surviving members teamed with John Bonham's son Jason at an anniversary tribute to Atlantic Records in New York. The "band" was in great form and their performance overshadowed all the other acts featured during the lengthy 13-hour extravaganza. Following that one-time appearance, Plant and Page continued with their solo work, and John Paul Jones returned to his home life and occasional production jobs — until July 1994.

# UNCLE JOE'S RECORD GUIDE

Rumors of an acoustic "Un-Ledded" performance for MTV's *Unplugged* program had circulated for years. When the arrangements were finally announced to the world in July 1994, most fans were perplexed that John Paul Jones would not be joining his old mates. In fact, Jonesy had not even been approached, and his performance with Page and Plant during Led Zeppelin's induction into the Rock & Roll Hall Of Fame later that summer was a last minute deal.

While the result of the Page and Plant collaboration was not a Led Zeppelin album, the material they covered merits inclusion in this book.

# HARD ROCK - Led Zeppelin

## Jimmy Page/Robert Plant
### *No Quarter* (24-26-28)

1st LP, released 11/8/95. Rumors of an acoustic "Un-Ledded" performance for MTV's *Unplugged* program had circulated for years since Led Zeppelin's demise. Vocalist Robert Plant was always the most adamant in denying the reunion, but in early 1994 he finally agreed to discuss the subject with guitarist Jimmy Page. The duo co-wrote a few songs and agreed on a number of major points, including a dedication to taking chances with their songwriting and the re-arrangement of Zeppelin standards, the format of their live performances, specific backing musicians and financial considerations. When the arrangements were finally announced to the world in July, most Led Zeppelin fans were perplexed that John Paul Jones would not be joining his old mates. In fact, Jonesy had not even been approached, and his performance with Page and Plant during Led Zeppelin's induction into the Rock & Roll Hall Of Fame later that summer was a last minute deal.

After their project became official, Page and Plant decided to return to two old Zeppelin haunts to record three new songs for this project. In August they traveled to Marrakech, Morocco, to recapture the middle eastern feel that permeated so much of the Zeppelin's later work. Then they traveled to Snowdonia, Wales, to re-explore the Celtic folksy flavorings of their Bron-Yr-Aur [pronounced BRON-rahr] writing sessions.

Everything came together for the September MTV tapings on a London sound stage. The final cut of the *MTV Unplugged* program also included produced videos from Morocco and

Wales. The *Unplugged* performance showcased Page and Plant, along with a core rock band, an 11-piece Egyptian rhythm and string section, and the 31-piece London Metropolitan Orchestra. The five-piece core band, which began the Page/Plant world tour February 26, 1995, included the rhythm section from Robert's solo band — drummer Michael Lee and bassist Charlie Jones — as well as guitarist Porl Thompson (of the Cure), Nigel Eaton, on hurdy gurdy, orchestral arranger Ed Shearmur on Hammond organ, vocalist Najma Akthar, and an eight-member version of the Egyptian string and percussion ensemble. (A local symphony was used at each date on the tour.) Jim Sutherland played mandolin in the MTV performances.

Initial reaction to the pseudo-Led Zeppelin reunion propelled this album to #4 on the American charts. Both the recorded music and the supporting live performances with a critical success, and throughout the project, Plant and Page continued to enjoy themselves. By the start of the successful world tour in Florida on February 26, 1995, *No Quarter* had sold over a million copies. The first leg of the U.S. tour ended May 26. Following European and Asian dates, the band returned to the States in late summer. The only unanswered question — would they do it again?

# HARD ROCK - Led Zeppelin

## *No Quarter - Side One*

#1: The nature of this excellent reworking of "**Nobody's Fault But Mine**" crystallized the essence of the Page/Plant reunion.

#2: "**Thank You**"

#3: "**No Quarter**" was an interesting Zeppelin song for Page and Plant to cover. The original was a John Paul Jones workout, and both Jimmy and Robert refused to include their old partner in this quasi-Zeppelin reunion.

#4: Another excellent reworking, "**Friends**" featured the eight-piece Egyptian string and percussion ensemble.

#5: One of the three new songs Page and Plant worked up for this project, "**Yallah**" was recorded in the central square of Marrakech with a group of "gnaoui" Moroccan musicians.

## *No Quarter - Side Two*

#1: A polished studio recording, "**City Don't Cry**" was one of the three new songs Page and Plant worked up for this project.

#2: "**Since I've Been Loving You**" was the bluesiest song performed for the MTV Un-Ledded project.

#3: "**The Battle Of Evermore**"

#4: "**Wonderful One**" was another of the new songs composed for this project. The promotional CD single for this song contained two bonus tracks recorded during the MTV taping: "**What Is And What Should Never Be**" and "**When The Levee Breaks**."

# UNCLE JOE'S RECORD GUIDE

## *No Quarter - Side Three*

#1:  "**That's The Way**"

#2:  "**Gallow's Pole**"

#3:  "**Four Sticks**"

#4:  "**Kashmir**"

# Aerosmith

**Aerosmith**
1994

Tom Hamilton,
Brad Whitford,
Steven Tyler,
Joe Perry,
Joey Kramer

# Aerosmith

Formed in Summer 1970, Aerosmith went through a two-and-a-half year gestation period before they were offered their first record contract. Against the odds, their debut album yielded the Boston-based band a hit single; their second release made them cult favorites; and their third turned them into superstars — the biggest American hard rock band ever. The young group achieved so much success early in their recording career that both business and personal problems inevitably followed.

Aerosmith's influence on other musicians ranked them among the most important first generation hard rock bands. Although drug and alcohol abuse and intra-group friction almost destroyed the band in the late Seventies, Aerosmith did not die. Instead, over time the group members cleaned up, regrouped and ultimately scored one of the biggest comebacks of any rock group or artist.

Aerosmith's success tells the story of the remarkable achievements of a great rock & roll band that sold over 64 million records, and reveals the personal triumphs of musicians over the worst demons rock & roll could produce. Neil Peart (of Rush) once observed that "The problem [with rock & roll bands] is rarely a failure of talent, but a failure of character." Ultimately, Aerosmith was dually blessed with the talent and personal character to succeed against the odds!

## Aerosmith Birth Dates

**Jimmy Crespo, Jr.** - July 5, 1955

**Rick Dufay** - February 19,1952

**Tom Hamilton** - December 31, 1951

**Joey Kramer** - June 21, 1950

**Joe Perry** - September 10, 1950

**Ray Tabano** - December 23, 1946

**Steven Tyler** - March 26, 1948

**Brad Whitford** - February 23, 1952

## Aerosmith
### *Aerosmith* (19-17)

1st LP, released 1/5/73. Aerosmith formed in Summer 1970 in the resort town of Sunapee, New Hampshire. Twenty-two-year-old drummer/vocalist Steven Tyler and his band mate, 23-year-old rhythm guitarist Ray Tabano, joined up with two former members of the Jam Band, 19-year-old guitarist Joe Perry and 18-year-old bassist Tom Hamilton. Prior to their first gig in Autumn 1970, the young band recruited 20-year-old drummer Joey Kramer. In late 1970 they moved to Boston; Tabano was replaced by 19-year-old Brad Whitford; and Aerosmith was ready to take on the world.

The band spent the next year-and-a-half playing the resort circuit in the Northeast and the club scene in Boston. By Summer 1972 they had earned themselves a large following and a record contract. During that gestation period, the band lived in the same apartment, played gigs constantly and developed into a very tight musical unit.

Aerosmith entered a recording studio in late 1972 with producer Adrian Barber (who had worked with the Allman Brothers and Cream) and engineer Ray Colcord. Two weeks later, they finished recording material from their live show. But the hard rocking, raw sound failed to make an impact on the American public. Although this album was released in January 1973, it did not appear on the national charts until a full 10 months later, when it peaked at #166. It was not even released in Britain until 22 months later.

The band toured constantly to support this release, and their hard work eventually paid off. The *Aerosmith* album eventually hit #21 in April 1976, three years after its release.

** **Special Note**: On the strength of the single "**Dream On**," — which became a hit three years after this album was released — the *Aerosmith* album eventually sold over two million copies.

## *Aerosmith - Side One*

#1:  "**Make It**" was written by vocalist Steven Tyler.

#2:  Tyler and his old roadie, Steve Emspack, co-wrote "**Somebody**."

#3:  The basic melody for Steven Tyler's "**Dream On**" came to him years earlier, when he was only 17 or 18. "**Dream On**" first charted at #59 in November 1973. In January 1976, after the *Toys In The Attic* album became successful, "**Dream On**" was re-released as a single. Within two months it shot up to #6 and sold over a million copies!

#4:  A great rocker, "**One Way Street**" was credited to Tyler.

# HARD ROCK - Aerosmith

## *Aerosmith - Side Two*

#1: Vocalist Steven Tyler penned "**Mama Kin**" before he joined Aerosmith. David Woodford played saxophone on this track.

#2: Tyler also wrote "**Write Me**."

#3: "**Movin' Out**" was the first Steven Tyler/Joe Perry composition the band ever recorded. "**Movin' Out**" was based on the true story of Aerosmith's eviction from one of the Boston hovels they occupied.

#4: "**Walkin' The Dog**" — a 1963 hit for its author, Rufus Thomas — was one of the first songs that Aerosmith jammed on. Steven later said that their rendition of this and "**Train Kept A Rollin'**" inspired him to join Perry and the others.

# UNCLE JOE'S RECORD GUIDE

## Aerosmith
### *Get Your Wings* (18-20)

2nd LP, released 3/8/74 in the U.S. — 11/74 in Britain.
Aerosmith had been together four years when they recorded
this album in December 1973 and early January 1974. Ray
Colcord (who worked on their first release) shared the
production work with Jack Douglas (who would produce
their next four albums). *Get Your Wings* sold fewer copies
than the group's debut and it charted at only #74, but not until
a full year-and-a-half after its release. But the new music was so
strong that Aerosmith would play at least five of these songs in
concert for years to come.

Twenty-five-year-old vocalist Steven Tyler's songwriting
became stronger and Aerosmith's performance reached a
new level of competence and proficiency during these
sessions. Guitarists Joe Perry and Brad Whitford, bassist Tom
Hamilton and drummer Joey Kramer averaged 22 years of age
by the time *Get Your Wings* was finished. They supported this
release with more non-stop touring, which included opening
for Deep Purple, Black Sabbath, Mott The Hoople and the
Kinks. *Get Your Wings* eventually sold well over two million
copies and its gutsy, raw rock & roll ultimately became
Aerosmith's trademark.

** **Special Note**: The working title for this album, *A Night In
The Ruts*, resurfaced on another album five years later
when the band reached the low point of their career.

94

# HARD ROCK - Aerosmith

## *Get Your Wings - Side One*

#1: "**Same Old Song And Dance**," co-written by vocalist Steven Tyler and guitarist Joe Perry, was recorded in late December 1973. Inspired by one of Joe's old girlfriends, the song was composed when the band was living together in Boston — before they had achieved any success. "**Same Old Song And Dance**" was released as a single in March 1974. Although it garnered a lot of airplay, it did not chart — but it did become Aerosmith's sing-a-long concert tune.

#2: Tyler took credit for "**Lord Of The Thighs**." The last song written and recorded for the album, Steven's inspiration arose from the band's lifestyle and some of the people they met when they recorded this album in New York City.

#3: "**Spaced**" was another Tyler/Perry composition. Co-producer Ray Colcord handled the keyboard parts on this track, which was used as the B-side of the September 1974 single release of "**Train Kept A-Rollin'**."

#4: "**Woman Of The World**" was co-written by Tyler and his old band mate, Don Solomon. The mid-song guitar riff was supposedly lifted from Fleetwood Mac's "Rattlesnake Shake."

## *Get Your Wings - Side Two*

#1: "**S.O.S. (Too Bad)**," written by vocalist Steven Tyler, became an Aerosmith concert standard for years to come.

#2: "**Train Kept A-Rollin'**," co-written in 1951 by Myron "Tiny" Bradshaw, Lois Mann and Howie Kay, had been made famous in 1966 by the Yardbirds with guitarist Jeff Beck. For several years "**Train Kept A-Rollin'**" was Aerosmith's closing number in concert. Joe Perry said one of the highlights of his life occurred on stage in Anaheim, California, when Aerosmith toured with Jeff Beck. As the band launched into this song, Beck came out on stage and joined in. Perry said he thought he "died and went to heaven." Aerosmith released "**Train Kept A-Rollin'**" as a single in September 1974, but it never charted.

#3: Tyler wrote "**Seasons Of Wither**" on a bleak December night when the band was first struggling to achieve fame. Steven, who also played acoustic guitar on this track, later said the song was inspired in part by the barbiturates Tuinal and Seconal.

#4: "**Pandora's Box**," co-written by Tyler and drummer Joey Kramer, was supposedly the first song Joey helped write. "**Pandora's Box**" was used as the flipside to "**Same Old Song And Dance**."

## Aerosmith
### *Toys In The Attic* (18-20)

3rd LP, released 4/1/75. After their first two albums received limited commercial success, Aerosmith finally made their big breakthrough with this great hard rocker. In February 1975 they recorded this album at the Record Plant in New York under the working title *Love At First Bite*. Their second effort with producer Jack Douglas (who later worked with John Lennon and Cheap Trick), this material marked a significant improvement in the Boston-based group's songwriting and performance. For the first time, 26-year-old lead singer Steven Tyler shared most of the compositional chores with various other band members, including 24-year-old bassist Tom Hamilton, and guitarists Joe Perry (24) and Brad Whitford (23). Only 24-year-old drummer, Joey Kramer, received no writing credit.

Released within weeks of Led Zeppelin's *Physical Graffiti* album, Queen's *A Day At The Races* and Bad Company's *Straight Shooter*, Aerosmith's *Toys In The Attic* topped at #11 on the American charts and eventually sold over six million copies. The ensuing tour marked the first time the band performed as a headline act and proved to be their most successful to date. *Toys In The Attic* was undeniably one of the best hard rock albums of the mid-Seventies.

** **Special Note**: On the strength of Aerosmith's reputation earned with fans during the *Toys In The Attic* tour, their first single, "**Dream On**," was re-released in January 1976.

It soon charted at #6 and sold over a million copies. On the heels of that success, "**Walk This Way**" was re-released a year-and-a-half after this album — long after their next album, *Rocks*, had come and gone. Soon, Aerosmith's second belated re-release charted at #10 and sold over a million copies!

## *Toys In The Attic - Side One*

#1:   The title track, "**Toys In The Attic**" was co-written by vocalist Steven Tyler and guitarist Joe Perry. It was also used as the B-side of "**You See Me Crying**."

#2:   "**Uncle Salty**" was co-written by Tyler and bassist Tom Hamilton, who played rhythm guitar on the song.

#3:   Steven wrote "**Adam's Apple**."

#4:   "**Walk This Way**," a Tyler/Perry composition, was recorded in February 1975. The band recorded a jam based on the basic riff when Tyler was out of the studio. Upon his return, Steven immediately wrote the lyrics, with the title and refrain inspired by the movie *Young Frankenstein*. The single bombed the first time it was released, but it reached #10 on the charts when it was re-released in December 1976 — long after Aerosmith's next album *Rocks* had been out. In 1986 Steven and Joe made a cameo appearance on Run DMC's video of their cover of "**Walk This Way**." That appearance sparked Aerosmith's ultra-successful comeback of the mid- Eighties.

#5:   "**Big Ten Inch Record**," credited to Fredrick Weismantel, was originally recorded in 1952 by Bull Moose Jackson.

# HARD ROCK - Aerosmith

## *Toys In The Attic - Side Two*

#1: "**Sweet Emotion**," written by Steven Tyler and bassist Tom Hamilton, became one of Aerosmith's most popular songs. The bass line, one of the most memorable hard rock riffs ever, first came to Hamilton during the *Get Your Wings* sessions. The song finally took form when he was playing with the riff during one of the *Toys In The Attic* sessions. Tyler's final lyrics were supposedly his reflection on guitarist Joe Perry's wife. "**Sweet Emotion**" charted at #36 twice — first in July 1975, and again when it was remixed and re-released in January 1991.

#2: "**No More No More**," another Tyler/Perry composition, featured some great piano work by Scott Cushnie (who accompanied the band on their next tour). Steven supposedly based his lyrics on the band's developing/de-evolving lifestyle.

#3: "**Round And Round**" was co-written by Tyler and guitarist Brad Whitford, who came up with the original riff. This was used as the B-side to "**Walk This Way**."

#4: "**You See Me Crying**" was credited to Tyler, Perry and Tyler's old bandmate Don Solomon. The song came together during the February 1975 sessions for this album, and was released as a single in November 1975. It never charted.

# UNCLE JOE'S RECORD GUIDE

## Aerosmith
*Rocks* (16-19)

4th LP, released 5/1/76. Heady on the breakthrough success of their *Toys In The Attic* album, the surprise Top 10 re-release of "**Dream On**" and life as over-the-top rock stars, Aerosmith was ready to rock! Averaging 24 years of age, bassist Tom Hamilton, drummer Joey Kramer, guitarists Joe Perry and Brad Whitford, and their 28-year-old singer, Steven Tyler, finished much of the preproduction on this material after Christmas 1975. In February 1976 they returned to the Record Plant in New York with producer Jack Douglas (who later worked with Cheap Trick). Work went quickly; they finished this — their first album without any cover songs — in mid-March.

Aerosmith's highest charting release for the next 17 years, *Rocks* hit #3 Stateside and became Aerosmith's second consecutive multi-platinum release. It eventually sold over three million copies. Once again, the Boston-based band had made another of the finest hard rock albums of the mid-Seventies. However, the heavy touring and partying that followed the release of *Rocks* took its toll on all the band members. Both Tyler and Perry developed nasty habits that ultimately came close to destroying both them and the band.

** **Special Note**: This album was dedicated to the memory of Anthony Perry, Joe's father, and Herb Spar, a close friend of the band.

## *Rocks - Side One*

#1: One of the first songs finished for this album, "**Back In The Saddle**" was recorded on February 3, 1976. It was credited to vocalist Steven Tyler and guitarist Joe Perry, who wrote the melody on a six-string bass. After the re-release of "**Walk This Way**" from *Toys In The Attic* became a million-selling Top 10 hit in January 1977, "**Back In The Saddle**" charted at #38 in May 1977.

#2: "**Last Child**" was co-written by Tyler and guitarist Brad Whitford, who created the original riff. Paul Prestopino played the banjo part. "**Last Child**" charted at #21 in Summer 1976.

#3: "**Rats In The Cellar**" was another Tyler/Perry composition. Steven said this song represented the lyrical flipside to "**Toys In The Attic**."

#4: "**Combination**" was the first recorded solo writing effort from guitarist Joe Perry.

## *Rocks - Side Two*

#1: "**Sick As A Dog**" was credited to Steven Tyler and bassist Tom Hamilton. By the time the band finally finished this song, Tom had played guitar and both guitarist Joe Perry and vocalist Tyler added bass parts!

#2: "**Nobody's Fault**" was the second number Tyler and guitarist Brad Whitford wrote for this album.

#3: "**Get The Lead Out**" was credited to Tyler and Perry.

#4: The lyrics of "**Lick And A Promise**," another Tyler/Perry composition, reflected the thrill the band felt when they won an audience over. This was one of the first Aerosmith songs about real emotions they experienced at a particular moment in time.

#5: Tyler wrote "**Home Tonight**," which hit #71 in Fall 1976. A 101-piece orchestra supplied the backing.

## Aerosmith
### *Draw The Line* (18-18)

5th LP, released 12/1/77 – just as Van Halen's debut was unleashed and more than a year-and-a-half after *Rocks*. In Spring 1977 after six years of heavy touring, Aerosmith finally took a vacation to recover from exhaustion, road damage and encroaching substance abuse problems. Several weeks later, they returned to work with producer Jack Douglas. He and guitarist Joe Perry shared half of the songwriting credits on this album with 29-year-old vocalist Steven Tyler. Guitarists Perry and Brad Whitford, bassist Tom Hamilton and drummer Joey Kramer averaged 26 when this album was recorded between June and October 1977. Although this featured the band's most polished songs to date, the writing and recording process proved torturous. The sessions got off to a rocky start in an old monastery. After a couple of unproductive, high-flying months, the group did a few disastrous European concerts. By the time they finished recording in New York, their lives were so out of hand that a couple of songs were co-written by all the band members except Joe Perry — who was half of their main songwriting team!

*Draw The Line* hit #11 on the charts and became the band's third million seller. The following tour, which featured help from keyboardist Mark Radice, was less than memorable.

** **Special Note**: Following the release of *Draw The Line*, Aerosmith headlined the *Cal Jam II* festival in front of 350,000 at the Ontario Motor Speedway near Los Angeles on March 18, 1978. Despite increased intra-band tensions and a couple of serious addictions, they headlined the *Texxas Jam* at the Cotton Bowl in Dallas on July 4th, and appeared in the god-awful *Sgt. Pepper* movie along with the Bee Gees. Aerosmith's version of the Beatles' "**Come Together**," which came from that movie's soundtrack, charted at #23 in September 1978.

## *Draw The Line - Side One*

#1:  "**Draw The Line**," co-written by vocalist Steven Tyler and guitarist Joe Perry, charted at #42 in November 1977, a month before this album was released. The B-side was a collaboration jam by guitarist Brad Whitford, bassist Tom Hamilton and drummer Joey Kramer called "**Subway**." That instrumental was eventually released in the 1994 *Box Of Fire* compilation.

#2:  One of the last songs completed for this album, "**I Wanna Know Why**" was a Tyler/Perry composition that supposedly reflected Steven's reaction to the press.

#3:  "**Critical Mass**" was credited to Tyler, bassist Tom Hamilton and producer Jack Douglas. The group's tour keyboardist, Scott Cushnie, played piano on this track.

#4:  "**Get It Up**" was another Tyler/Perry composition. Karen Lawrence performed backing vocals.

# HARD ROCK - Aerosmith

#5: Joe Perry wrote "**Bright Light Fright**."

## *Draw The Line - Side Two*

This side contained some awesome music!

#1: "**Kings And Queens**" was co-written by producer Jack Douglas and all the group members except guitarist Joe Perry. This charted at #70 in April 1978, with a B-side called "**Circle Jerk**." That instrumental was credited to guitarist Brad Whitford and eventually released in the *Box Of Fire* compilation in 1994. (It was also included as an unmarked bonus track in the 1991 *Pandora's Box* compilation.)

#2: "**The Hand That Feeds**" was the only other song on this album credited to Douglas and all the group members, except Joe Perry.

#3: "**Sight For Sore Eyes**" was credited to vocalist Steven Tyler, Joe Perry, Jack Douglas and David Johansen (of the New York Dolls and Buster Poindexter fame).

#4: "**Milk Cow Blues**" was a group re-arrangement of the 1934 Kokomo Arnold blues number previously covered by Elvis Presley. Aerosmith played this song when they first formed.

## Aerosmith
### *Live! Bootleg* (21-17-19-16)

6th LP, released 10/4/78. Live albums are often used to sum up a band's music, and *Live! Bootleg* marked an end to the first phase of Aerosmith's career. Much of this material was recorded on the 1978 *Draw The Line* tour, which featured help from keyboardist Mark Radice. Even though Aerosmith's longtime producer, Jack Douglas, handled the sound, the album was less than a commercial success.

** **Special Note**: Over the years Aerosmith previously had released five live bootleg EPs. It is highly unusual for a band to endorse a bootleg, much less release one themselves, so the title of this album represented an inside joke Aerosmith shared with their fans.

# HARD ROCK - Aerosmith

## Live! Bootleg - Side One

#1: "**Back In The Saddle**" was recorded in Indianapolis on July 4, 1977.

#2: This version of "**Sweet Emotion**" was recorded in Chicago on March 23, 1978, during the *Draw The Line* tour.

#3: "**Lord Of The Thighs**" was also recorded in Chicago on March 23, 1978.

#4: This raucous rendition of "**Toys In The Attic**" was captured in Boston on March 28, 1978.

## Live! Bootleg - Side Two

#1: "**Last Child**" was recorded at the Paradise Club in Boston on August 8, 1978.

#2: This was a rehearsal of "**Come Together**" recorded in Waltham, Massachusetts, on August 21, 1978.

#3: This version of "**Walk This Way**" was recorded in Detroit on April 2, 1978.

#4: "**Sick As A Dog**" was recorded in Indianapolis on July 4, 1977.

## Live! Bootleg - Side Three

#1: This version of "**Dream On**" was recorded in Louisville , Kentucky, on July 3, 1977.

#2: This version of the Richie Supa song "**Chip Away The Stone**" was recorded at the Santa Monica Civic Auditorium on April 18, 1978. It charted at #77 in January 1979.

#3: "**Sight For Sore Eyes**" was recorded in Columbus, Ohio, on February 24, 1978, near the beginning of the *Draw The Line* tour.

#4: "**Mama Kin**"/"**S.O.S. (Too Bad)**" were recorded at the July 4, 1977 show in Indianapolis.

## Live! Bootleg - Side Four

#1: This medley of the Yardbirds cover of "**I Ain't Got You**" and James Brown's "**Mother Popcorn**" was recorded on April 23, 1973, for a WBCN radio broadcast from Paul's Mall — the first Boston club Aerosmith ever played. David Woodford supplied the saxophone on this.

#2: This cover of the Yardbirds' "**Train Kept A-Rollin'**" was recorded in Detroit on April 2, 1978.

## Aerosmith
### *Night In The Ruts* (18-19)

7th LP, released 11/2/79 — shortly after AC/DC's *Highway To Hell* and just before Rush's *Permanent Waves*. After a few years at the top, Aerosmith's collective substance abuse problems, intra-group tensions and rock star lifestyles were tearing the band apart. The group began preproduction for this album in Spring 1979. A couple of months later they entered a New York studio with English producer Gary Lyons (who had worked with Foreigner). Vocalist Steven Tyler, bassist Tom Hamilton, guitarists Joe Perry and Brad Whitford, and drummer Joey Kramer averaged 28 years of age when *Night In The Ruts* was recorded. In the studio, the recording of instrumental tracks went well, but finishing the lyrics and recording the vocals seemed to take forever. It became obvious that a couple of the members' increasingly severe abuse problems had damaged Aerosmith's creativity and their ability to work as a unit. When the *Night In The Ruts* album was finally finished, founding member Joe Perry quit the band. His replacement, 24-year-old guitarist Jimmy Crespo, was recruited just two weeks before the tour began.

Although it missed the Platinum sales mark (one million copies sold), *Night In The Ruts* made it into the Top 15 — was the last Aerosmith album to do so for the next nine years. Shortly after the tour began, Tyler collapsed on stage and the remaining concert dates had to be canceled. Every band member has since commented that this album and tour marked the lowest point of their careers. With the commercial and artistic failure of this album and the breakthrough success of Van Halen, Rush and AC/DC, most saw 1979-80 as the year the second generation hard rockers surpassed their mentors.

** **Special Note**: *Night In The Ruts* was the original working title for Aerosmith's 1974 album *Get Your Wings*.

## *Night In The Ruts - Side One*

#1: "**No Surprize**" was co-written by vocalist Steven Tyler and guitarist Joe Perry.

#2: "**Chiquita**" was another Tyler/Perry song.

#3: "**Remember (Walking In The Sand)**" was a Top 5 hit for Shangri-Las in 1964. Aerosmith's cover version hit #67 in February 1980.

#4: The Tyler song "**Cheese Cake**" was supposedly recorded on the first take.

# HARD ROCK - Aerosmith

## *Night In The Ruts - Side Two*

#1: "**Three Mile Smile**" was co-written by vocalist Steven Tyler and guitarist Joe Perry. Although guitarist Jimmy Crespo did not receive credit for the solo he played in this song, he was later recruited to replace Perry.

#2: "**Reefer Headed Woman**" had no credits listed — a rather strange happenstance considering Lester Melrose, Joe Bennett and Willie Gillum wrote the song in 1945.

#3: "**Bone To Bone (Coney Island White Fish Boy)**" was another Tyler/Perry song. The title and lyrics referred to used condoms floating down the Hudson River. This track was used as the B-side to "**Remember (Walking In The Sand).**"

#4: "**Think About It**," a 1968 Yardbirds song, was co-written by Keith Relf, Jim McCarty and Jimmy Page.

#5: "**Mia**" was inspired by Steven Tyler's new baby daughter.

## Aerosmith
### *Aerosmith's Greatest Hits* (18-20)

8th LP, released 10/4/80. This compilation, released while the band went through personnel changes and personal problems, featured edited versions of a couple songs — a fact not mentioned anywhere on the cover or in the liner notes. Also included was the studio version of Aerosmith's cover of the Beatles' "**Come Together**." Although it only charted at #53, *Aerosmith's Greatest Hits* eventually sold over seven million copies!

### *Greatest Hits - Side One*

#1:  "**Dream On**," from the *Aerosmith* album, charted at #6 and sold over a million copies upon its re-release in January 1976.

#2:  This was the shorter, edited single version of "**Same Old Song And Dance**," originally included on the *Get Your Wings* album.

#3:  This shorter edit of "**Sweet Emotion**," originally included on *Toys In The Attic*, charted at #36 in July 1975.

#4:  "**Walk This Way**" first appeared on *Toys In The Attic*. It peaked at #10 in January 1977.

#5:  "**Last Child**," from *Rocks*, charted at #21 in Summer 1976.

# HARD ROCK - Aerosmith

## *Greatest Hits - Side Two*

#1:  "**Back In The Saddle**," from *Rocks*, hit #38 in May 1977.

#2:  "**Draw The Line**," the title track of that album, charted at #42 in November 1977.

#3:  "**Kings And Queens**," from *Draw The Line*, peaked at #70 in Spring 1978.

#4:  This cover of the Beatles' "**Come Together**," from the *Sgt. Pepper* movie soundtrack, hit #23 in September 1978.

#5:  "**Remember (Walking In The Sand)**," from *Night In The Ruts*, charted at #67 in February 1980.

## Aerosmith
### *Rock In A Hard Place* (21-20)

9th LP, released 8/4/82 – almost three years after *Night In The Ruts*. Aerosmith spent most of 1980 rehearsing new material without vocalist Steven Tyler, who was recovering from a motorcycle accident and slipping deeper into addiction. When nothing had been recorded by Summer 1981, 29-year-old guitarist Brad Whitford left the band in disgust. Months later, in mid-December, 29-year-old guitarist Rick Dufay was recruited, but he and 26-year-old guitarist Jimmy Crespo did not quite click with the rest of the band. The creative spark was missing for the 34-year-old Tyler, drummer Joey Kramer and bassist Tom Hamilton, both of whom were 30 years old.

After recording most of this music in early 1982 with engineer Tony Bongiovi (who also worked with the Talking Heads), Aerosmith convinced their longtime producer Jack Douglas to make an attempt to save the album. The sessions continued sporadically through Spring and early Summer 1982. Intra-group friction was reportedly at an all-time high as some members' substance abuse problems overwhelmed their lives.

Even though the group toured extensively in support of this album, *Rock In A Hard Place* became the first Aerosmith release in eight years that failed to crack the Top 30 (it peaked #32). Near the end of the *Rock In A Hard Place* tour, original guitarists Joe Perry and Brad Whitford attended the 1984 Valentine's Day show in Boston. Two months later, they agreed to rejoin the band if Steven would clean up his chemical problems.

## *Rock In A Hard Place - Side One*

#1: "**Jailbait**" was credited to vocalist Steven Tyler and guitarist Jimmy Crespo, even though Crespo was supposedly the sole creative force behind its development.

#2: One of the first numbers recorded for this album, the Rich Supa song "**Lightning Strikes**" featured original guitarist Brad Whitford's only appearance on this album.

#3: "**Bitch's Brew**" was another Tyler/Crespo composition that survived the chaotic early sessions.

#4: Tyler and Crespo also wrote "**Bolivian Ragamuffin**," one of the first songs the band worked up for this album.

#5: The Arthur Hamilton standard "**Cry Me A River**" had previously been covered by Joe Cocker.

# UNCLE JOE'S RECORD GUIDE

## *Rock In A Hard Place - Side Two*

#1: "**Prelude To Joanie**" was credited to vocalist Steven Tyler.

#2: Guitarist Jimmy Crespo co-wrote "**Joanie's Butterfly**" with producer Jack Douglas. Steven Tyler's name also appeared in the credits.

#3: "**Rock In A Hard Place (Cheshire Cat)**" was credited to Tyler, Crespo and Douglas.

#4: "**Jig Is Up**" was co-written by Tyler and Crespo.

#5: "**Push Comes To Shove**" was Tyler's song.

## Aerosmith
### *Done With Mirrors* (16-16)

10th LP, released 11/23/85 – almost three years after *Rock In A Hard Place*. During the early and mid-Eighties, bands such as Van Halen, Rush, Motley Crue and Ratt performed sold-out concert tours and sold millions of albums. But Aerosmith — the primary inspiration to those second and third generation hard rock groups — was missing in action.

Once Aerosmith's original members vowed to clean up their various substance abuse problems, the five members officially regrouped in April 1984. They played a short series of gigs called the *Back In The Saddle* tour. Once they proved they still had audience appeal, Aerosmith secured a new record contract and spent a month working up new material.

During this time, producer Ted Templeman (who had worked with Van Halen and the Doobie Brothers) mentioned at the 1985 Grammy Awards telecast that Aerosmith was the only other major band he would like to work with. Three months later, in July 1985, his wish became reality. With Templeman at the helm, the original Aerosmith recorded together for the first time in six years. At Fantasy Studios in Berkeley (where Journey recorded), Ted actually taped Aerosmith's first run-throughs on the sly. That technique worked so well at capturing the band's edgy performance that several of those first takes made the final version of the album. *Done With Mirrors* was finished in New York in August 1985, but the band member's substance abuse was apparently still out of control. Those personal problems, combined with terrible marketing, doomed this project. *Done With Mirrors* peaked at #36 and was only certified Gold (500,000 sold). The *Done With Mirrors* tour began in January 1986, but was canceled in early May when the group's problems went completely out of control and they could no longer perform.

In late 1986, after the *Done With Mirrors* album failed commercially and the band had finally became involved in a serious detox effort, the rap group Run DMC covered "**Walk This Way**." Suddenly, positive public recognition thrust Aerosmith back into the limelight. To everyone's surprise, one of America's greatest hard rock groups had another chance at a comeback. They were not about to blow it again!

** **Special Note**: The single "**Darkness**" was included on the compact disc and cassette, but not on the vinyl album — strange marketing!

# HARD ROCK - Aerosmith

## *Done With Mirrors - Side One*

#1: "**Let The Music Do The Talking**" was a remake of the title track from guitarist Joe Perry's first solo album. This was the closest thing to a memorable song on *Done With Mirrors*.

#2: "**My Fist Your Face**" lyrically recalled vocalist Steven Tyler's days in a Massachusetts detox center.

#3: "**Shame On You**"

#4: Even Tyler later admitted that "**The Reason A Dog**" was only half finished.

## *Done With Mirrors - Side Two*

#1: "**Sheila**"

#2: "**Gypsy Boots**"

#3: "**She's On Fire**"

#4: "**The Hop**"

#5 (on the CD and cassette): "**Darkness**" was released as a single backed with live versions of "**My Fist Your Face**" and "**The Hop**." It never charted.

# UNCLE JOE'S RECORD GUIDE

## Aerosmith
### *Classics Live!* (19-20)

11th LP, released 4/1/86. Aerosmith's original record company put together this collection with virtually no input from the band. The live songs had been recorded between 1977 and 1980. One previously unreleased 1983 studio track was included as a bonus. All but the last song had been recorded by the original Aerosmith line-up, although some overdubs were done by Jimmy Crespo in early 1986. When this release charted at #84 and sold more copies than Aerosmith's *Done With Mirrors* album, the band's original record company and management decided to release a follow-up live compilation.

# HARD ROCK - Aerosmith

## *Live Classics - Side One*

#1:  "**Train Kept A-Rollin'**"

#2:  "**Kings And Queens**"

#3:  "**Sweet Emotion**"

#4:  "**Dream On**"

## *Live Classics - Side Two*

#1:  "**Mama Kin**"

#2:  "**Three Mile Smile/Reefer Headed Woman**"

#3:  "**Lord Of The Thighs**"

#4:  This previously unreleased studio version of "**Major Barbara**" was recorded in 1983 with guitarists Jimmy Crespo and Rick Dufay, who had replaced Joe Perry and Brad Whitford.

## Aerosmith
### *Classics Live II* (20-20)

12th LP, released 6/3/87. After the first *Live Classics* album sold well, Aerosmith's old management and record company put together this compilation consisting of live tracks performed by the band's original line-up. This time, however, the band's involvement was solicited for the song selection and for use of their personal tapes. While *Classics Live II* sold very few copies, at least some documentation on the performances was provided in the liner notes.

# HARD ROCK - Aerosmith

## *Live Classics II - Side One*

All but the last song on this side were recorded live on December 31, 1984, at Boston's Orpheum Theatre.

#1: "**Back In The Saddle**"

#2: "**Walk This Way**"

#3: "**Movin' Out**"

#4: "**Draw The Line**" was recorded on March 18, 1978, at the *Cal Jam II* concert in Ontario, California.

## *Live Classics II - Side Two*

All but the third song on this side were recorded on December 31, 1984, at the Orpheum Theatre in Boston.

#1: "**Same Old Song And Dance**"

#2: "**Last Child**"

#3: "**Let The Music Do The Talking**" was recorded on March 12, 1986, at the Worcester Centrum in Worcester, Massachusetts.

#4: "**Toys In The Attic**"

# UNCLE JOE'S RECORD GUIDE

## Aerosmith
### *Permanent Vacation* (26-27)

13th LP, released 9/12/87. When Aerosmith's *Done With Mirrors* album proved a commercial bomb, most people wrote-off the band as burned-out heroes of yesteryear. It appeared that one of America's greatest hard rock groups had fallen completely out of step with the second and third generation bands that ruled the charts in the mid-Eighties — the very groups they had inspired. But the late 1986 success of Run DMC's cover of "**Walk This Way**" thrust Aerosmith back into the limelight. Given another chance, the Boston-based boys emerged with this music and proved the doubters wrong in a big way.

By the time the three months of recording sessions began in March 1987, all of Aerosmith's original members (especially 39-year-old lead singer Steven Tyler and 36-year-old guitarist Joe Perry) had finally cleaned up their substance abuse problems. That lifestyle change contributed to a much better relationship between Aerosmith's chief songwriters, and proved to be a creative catalyst for the rest of the band. *Permanent Vacation* marked the first time Aerosmith recorded drug-free; the first time they collaborated with producer Bruce Fairbairn (who worked with Bon Jovi and Loverboy); the first time they recorded out of the U.S. (Fairbairn's studio was in Vancouver, British Columbia); and the first time they used outside writers (such as Bryan Adams' partner, Jim Vallance).

# HARD ROCK - Aerosmith

Fairbairn proved the perfect creative inspiration for Tyler, Perry, guitarist Brad Whitford, bassist Tom Hamilton and drummer Joey Kramer. Until then, Tyler had never demonstrated such remarkable vocal control and range, nor had Aerosmith covered such diverse material. Not since *Toys In The Attic* had the band rocked with such an intense edge. Instead of the loose, rowdy music that had been characteristic at the end of the first phase of their career, Aerosmith's new sound reflected a return to a tight performance by a very intuitive ensemble.

*Permanent Vacation* sold over three million copies, peaked at #11 in the U.S., and became Aerosmith's first hit album across the Atlantic, where it reached #37 on the British charts. The *Permanent Vacation* world tour began October 16, 1987, and eventually ran 11 months with 150 shows. The combined artistic and commercial success of that tour and this exceptional record, as well as Aerosmith's transformed personal energy, contributed to make their return from the brink truly one of the biggest comebacks in rock & roll history.

## *Permanent Vacation - Side One*

#1: "**Heart's Done Time**" was co-written by guitarist Joe Perry and Desmond Child. The background in this song included the sound of killer whales.

#2: "**Magic Touch**" was co-written by Joe Perry, vocalist Steven Tyler and Jim Vallance (Bryan Adams' writing partner).

#3: "**Rag Doll**" was a collaboration by Perry, Tyler, Jim Vallance and Holly Knight (who had worked with Heart and Pat Benatar). Vallance played organ during the session. "**Rag Doll**" charted at #17 in August 1988 — almost a year after this album was released.

#4: "**Simoriah**," another Tyler/Perry/Vallance song, was used as the B-side to "**Dude (Looks Like A Lady)**."

#5: "**Dude (Looks Like A Lady)**" was penned by Steven Tyler, Joe Perry and Desmond Child. "**Dude (Looks Like A Lady)**" became Aerosmith's first legitimate hit in years. It charted at #14 in December 1987

#6: "**St. John**" was Tyler's song, based on a riff from Aerosmith's earliest days together.

# HARD ROCK - Aerosmith

## *Permanent Vacation - Side Two*

#1: "**Hangman Jury**" was co-written by vocalist Steven Tyler, guitarist Joe Perry and Jim Vallance (Bryan Adams' writing partner). Producer Bruce Fairbairn recorded the sound of his rocking chair for the opening of this great song.

#2: Tyler and Perry co-wrote "**Girl Keeps Coming Apart**." This song was used as the B-side to "**Angel**."

#3: "**Angel**," co-written by Steven Tyler and Desmond Child, marked the first time the band experimented with an outside writer. They were quite worried about including the track on this album. Their fears were unfounded. "**Angel**" became Aerosmith's biggest hit to date when it charted at #3 in March 1988. Drew Arnott supplied the mellotron performance on the recording.

#4: Guitarist Brad Whitford penned "**Permanent Vacation**" with Steven Tyler.

#5: "**I'm Down**" was a cover of the Beatles song Aerosmith had used for years as a warm-up.

**Note**: Before Aerosmith formed in 1970, Steven Tyler needed an audition tape and used Joe Perry's band for backing. The song they performed was "**I'm Down**."

#6: The instrumental "**The Movie**" was listed as a group composition. It began as an in-studio jam between bassist Tom Hamilton and drummer Joey Kramer.

## Aerosmith
### *Gems* (26-29)

14th LP, released 11/2/88. Following the comeback success of *Permanent Vacation*, this compilation was assembled by Aerosmith's original record company with minimal input from the band. Rather than a collection of hits, these were the band's signature songs, with one outtake thrown in as a bonus. *Gems* charted at #133.

### *Gems - Side One*

#1:  Co-written by vocalist Tyler and guitarist Perry, "**Rats In The Cellar**" was from the *Rocks* album.

#2:  "**Lick And A Promise**" was a Tyler/Perry composition from *Draw The Line*.

#3:  This previously unreleased studio version of Richie Supa's "**Chip Away The Stone**" was an outtake from the *Draw The Line* sessions. (Richie played piano on this version.) Aerosmith's original release of this song appeared on the *Live! Bootleg* album.

#4:  "**No Surprize**" was a Steven Tyler/Joe Perry song from the *Night In The Ruts* album.

#5:  Steven Tyler's "**Mama Kin**" was originally included on the band's first album.

#6: "**Adam's Apple**," another Tyler song, had first appeared on *Toys In The Attic*.

## *Gems - Side Two*

#1: Co-written by vocalist Steven Tyler and guitarist Brad Whitford, "**Nobody's Fault**" had originally appeared on *Rocks*.

#2: "**Round And Round**," another Tyler/Whitford song, was taken from *Toys In The Attic*.

#3: "**Critical Mass**," co-written by Tyler, bassist Tom Hamilton and producer Jack Douglas, was from *Draw The Line*.

#4: Tyler's song "**Lord Of The Thighs**" first appeared on *Get Your Wings*.

#5: "**Jailbait**" was co-written by Tyler and guitarist Jimmy Crespo for the *Rock In A Hard Place* album.

#6: This cover of the Yardbirds' classic "**Train Kept A Rollin'**" was taken from *Get Your Wings*.

## Aerosmith
*Pump* (24-24)

15th LP, released 9/23/89 — two years after *Permanent Vacation*. Their second album with co-producer Bruce Fairbairn (who also worked with AC/DC and later with Van Halen) and their second effort utilizing outside writers, *Pump* became the biggest album of Aerosmith's career. After four months of preproduction that began in late 1988, in April 1989 Aerosmith started recording *Pump* at Fairbairn's Little Mountain Studios in Vancouver, British Columbia. The group described the three months of rewriting, rearranging and recording as some of their most intense work ever. Fairbairn's discipline drove the band to try harder than they imagined possible. The result was the best songwriting and most consistent performances of Aerosmith's career. Keyboardist John Webster joined vocalist Steven Tyler (41), guitarists Joe Perry (39) and Brad Whitford (36), bassist Tom Hamilton (38) and drummer Joey Kramer (39) in the studio. Thom Gimbel helped with the keyboard and saxophone parts on the tour, which began October 18, 1989, in Germany, and concluded 18 months and 163 concerts later.

A truly great rock & roll album, *Pump* charted at #5 in the States, #3 in Britain, and sold over nine million copies.

# HARD ROCK - Aerosmith

## *Pump - Side One*

#1:  "**Young Lust**" was co-written by vocalist Steven Tyler, guitarist Joe Perry and lyricist Jim Vallance (who worked with Bryan Adams and .38 Special). This song was used as the flipside to "**Love In An Elevator**."

#2:  Tyler and Perry co-wrote "**F.I.N.E.**" (Fucked-Up, Insecure, Neurotic, Emotional) with their old writing partner Desmond Child. Tyler has hinted that his life inspired the lyrics.

#3:  Catherine Epps supplied the voice for " **Goin' Down**," the opening segment to Tyler and Perry's " **Love In An Elevator**." "**Love In An Elevator**" was released as a single before the album came out, and charted at #5 in November 1989. The song was supposedly inspired by one or more true incidents.

#4:  The lyrics to the Tyler/Perry composition "**Monkey On My Back**" were inspired by Tyler's drug addiction. "**Monkey On My Back**" was used as the B-side to "**Janie's Got A Gun**."

#5:  The instrumental piece called "**Water Song**" was specifically written as the introduction to "**Janie's Got A Gun**." In addition to the group, Randy Raine-Reusch was involved in the composition and performance of "**Water Song**." One of Aerosmith's most affecting songs, "**Janie's Got A Gun**" was inspired by a true story of child abuse. Co-written by Tyler — who composed the basic melody in his basement months before he completed the lyrics — and bassist Tom Hamilton, "**Janie's Got A Gun**" charted at # 4 in February 1990 and later won a Grammy Award for the *Best Rock Performance By A Duo Or Group*.

## *Pump - Side Two*

#1: "**Dulcimer Stomp**" was an in-studio jam that was segued into "**The Other Side**" during the final mixing. Randy Raine-Reusch was involved in the creation of "**Dulcimer Stomp**." Vocalist Steven Tyler co-wrote "**The Other Side**" with Jim Vallance (Bryan Adams' longtime collaborator). The fourth single released from this album, "**The Other Side**" charted at #22 in September 1990.

#2: "**My Girl**" was credited to Tyler and guitarist Joe Perry. It was used as the B-side to "**The Other Side**."

#3: "**Don't Get Mad, Get Even**" was another Tyler/Perry composition.

#4: "**HooDoo**" was the instrumental opening segment of "**VooDoo Medicine Man**." Randy Raine-Reusch was involved in the composition and performance of "**HooDoo**." Co-written by Tyler and guitarist Brad Whitford, "**VooDoo Medicine Man**" was used as the B-side to "**What It Takes**."

#5: "**What It Takes**" was co-written by Tyler, Perry and their old buddy Desmond Child. The third single released from this album, "**What It Takes**" hit #9 in Spring 1990.

#6: Added onto the album as an unmarked bonus track, "**Toe Jam**" was a group jam with Randy Raine-Reusch.

## Aerosmith
### *Pandora's Box* (38-36) (38-36) (36-39)

16th LP, released 11/19/91. In the wake of the tremendous comeback success of *Pump*, this compilation was assembled by Aerosmith's original record company as a retrospective of their nine albums released between 1972 and 1982. The 52 songs included 24 unreleased live and studio outtakes, and the collection was compiled, digitally re-mastered and produced by Don Devito. *Pandora's Box* charted at #45 and was certified Gold when it sold over 500,000 copies.

** **Special Note**: In Greek mythology, *Pandora's Box* was the source of incomparable chaos in the world.

## *Pandora's Box - CD One, Side One*

#1: "**When I Needed You**" was vocalist Steven Tyler's first recorded composition, recorded by his group Chain Reaction on October 6, 1966, when Steven was 18 years old. He later observed that the band never got paid for it.

#2: "**Make It**" was a Tyler song from Aerosmith's first album.

#3: This was a previously unreleased version of "**Movin' Out**" from the first Aerosmith album. This first song Tyler and guitarist Joe Perry ever wrote together was composed while they sat on a waterbed.

#4: "**One Way Street**" was a Tyler-penned song from the *Aerosmith* album.

#5: This previously unreleased version of "**On The Road Again**" was recorded May 8, 1972, while the band rehearsed their first album. This was one of the first songs they ever performed.

#6: Tyler wrote "**Mama Kin**" before he joined Aerosmith. David Woodford played the saxophone on this recording, which was recorded for the band's debut album.

#7: The Tyler/Perry tune "**Same Old Song And Dance**" was recorded in late December 1973 for the *Get Your Wings* album. Inspired by one of Joe's ex-girlfriends, they composed the song when the band still lived together in a small Boston apartment long before they achieved any success.

#8: This cover of the Yardbirds' classic "**Train Kept A Rollin'**" was originally included on the *Get Your Wings* album.

#9: Joe Perry called "**Seasons Of Wither**" one of his favorite Steven Tyler ballads. Recorded in late December 1973 (or early January 1974) for the *Get Your Wings* album, Tyler said he was inspired in part by the barbiturates Tuinal and Seconal.

## *Pandora's Box - CD One, Side Two*

#1: This previously unreleased version of vocalist Steven Tyler's song "**Write Me A Letter**" was recorded live at the Boston Gardens in November 1976.

**#2:** The basic melody for "**Dream On**" first came to Tyler when he was 17 or 18. This was recorded for the band's debut album in 1972, and eventually became their first hit when it reached #6 four years later.

**#3:** "**Pandora's Box**," co-written by Tyler and drummer Joey Kramer, was taken from the *Get Your Wings* album. This was supposedly the first song Joey ever had a hand in writing.

**#4:** This version of the classic Griffith/Gilmore song "**Rattlesnake Shake**" was taken from a live 1971 Cincinnati radio broadcast.

**#5:** The Rufus Thomas composition "**Walkin' The Dog**," one of the first songs on which Aerosmith jammed, was recorded from the same 1971 Cincinnati radio broadcast as "**Rattlesnake Shake**."

**#6:** This version of "**Lord Of The Thighs**" was recorded at the *Texxas Jam* at the Cotton Bowl in Dallas, Texas, on July 4, 1978.

## *Pandora's Box - CD Two, Side One*

**#1:** "**Toys In The Attic**," co-written by vocalist Steven Tyler and guitarist Joe Perry, was recorded in February 1975 at the Record Plant in New York.

**#2:** "**Round And Round**" was co-written by Tyler and guitarist Brad Whitford, who came up with the original riff during the February 1975 *Toys In The Attic* sessions.

**#3:** "**Krawitham**," a previously unreleased instrumental outtake from the *Draw The Line* sessions, was recorded in New York on May 2, 1977. Writing credit went to drummer Joey Kramer, guitarist Brad Whitford and bassist Tom Hamilton.

#4: "**You See Me Crying**" was credited to Tyler, Perry and Don Solomon (an old band mate of Tyler's). The song came together during the February 1975 *Toys In The Attic* sessions.

#5: "**Sweet Emotion**," written by Steven Tyler and bassist Tom Hamilton, has proven to be the band's most popular song. The bass line, one of the most memorable hard rock riffs ever, first came to Hamilton during the *Get Your Wings* sessions. This song finally took form when he was playing with the riff while waiting for the rest of the band during one of the *Toys In The Attic* sessions. Tyler's final lyrics were supposedly a reflection on guitarist Joe Perry's ex-wife. "**Sweet Emotion**" charted at #36 both in Summer 1975 and a special remix charted at #36 again in January 1991.

#6: "**No More No More**," another Tyler/Perry composition, featured some fine piano work by Scott Cushnie. Steven supposedly based his lyrics on the true story of the band. "**No More No More**" had first appeared on *Toys In The Attic*.

#7: "**Walk This Way**," a Tyler/Perry composition, reached #10 on the singles charts in early 1977. Tyler was not in the studio when the band jammed and recorded the basic riff. Upon his return, Steven immediately wrote the lyrics, with the title and refrain inspired by the movie *Young Frankenstein*. In 1986, Tyler and Perry made a cameo appearance on Run DMC's cover of this song. That appearance sparked Aerosmith's successful comeback of the mid-Eighties.

#8: "**I Wanna Know Why**" was a Tyler/Perry composition originally included on *Draw The Line*. The lyrics reflected Steven's reaction to the press.

**#9:** "**Big Ten Inch Record**" was credited to Fredrick Weismantel and originally recorded in 1952. Aerosmith first recorded it for *Toys In The Attic*. This previously unreleased live version was done at the *Texxas Jam* in Dallas on July 4, 1978.

## *Pandora's Box - CD Two, Side Two*

**#1:** "**Rats In The Cellar**" was co-written by vocalist Steven Tyler and guitarist Joe Perry for the *Rocks* album. Steven said this song represented the flipside of "**Toys In The Attic**."

**#2:** "**Last Child**" was co-written by vocalist Steven Tyler and guitarist Brad Whitford, who created the basic riff and brought it to the band during the *Rocks* recording sessions. Paul Prestopino supplied the banjo work.

**#3:** "**All Your Love**," another Tyler/Whitford song, was taken from *Toys In The Attic*.

**#4:** "**Soul Saver**," co-written by Tyler, bassist Tom Hamilton and producer Jack Douglas, was from the *Draw The Line* album.

**#5:** "**Nobody's Fault**" was a Tyler/Whitford song from *Rocks*.

**#6:** "**Lick And A Promise**" was a Tyler/Perry composition from *Rocks*. The lyrics reflected how the band felt when they won an audience over. It was a rare early Aerosmith song about a real emotion at a particular moment in time.

**#7:** This previously unreleased live version of the Tyler song "**Adam's Apple**" was recorded in Indianapolis on July 4, 1977. The song originally appeared on *Toys In The Attic*.

#8:   This was a previously unreleased remix of "**Draw The Line**," co-written by Tyler and Perry and recorded sometime between June and December 1977.

#9:   "**Critical Mass**" was taken from *Draw The Line*. The writing credit went to Tyler, bassist Tom Hamilton and producer Jack Douglas. Scott Cushnie supplied the piano work.

## *Pandora's Box - CD Three, Side One*

#1:   This previously unreleased version of "**Kings And Queens**" was recorded live in Boston on March 28, 1978. Producer Jack Douglas and every band member except guitarist Joe Perry received a writing credit for this song.

#2:   A cover of the Kokomo Arnold song, "**Milk Cow Blues**" was recorded for *Draw The Line* when the band almost ran out of material. This was another one of the first songs they had ever played.

#3:   "**I Live In Connecticut**" was an outtake from the *Night In The Ruts* rehearsals in March 1979. The writing credit went to vocalist Steven Tyler and guitarist Joe Perry.

#4:   "**Three Mile Smile**" was a Tyler/Perry composition taken from the *Night In The Ruts* album.

#5:   "**Let It Slide**" was another outtake from the rehearsals for *Night In The Ruts*. This Tyler/Perry song was recorded in March 1979.

#6:   "**Cheese Cake**," a Tyler song from *Night In The Ruts*, was recorded live on the first take.

#7:   "**Bone To Bone (Coney Island White Fish Boy)**" was a Tyler/Perry song from *Night In The Ruts*. The title and lyrics referred to used condoms floating down the Hudson River.

#8:   The Tyler/Perry song "**No Surprize**" from *Night In The Ruts* was based on a true story.

#9:   This cover of the Beatles' "**Come Together**" was recorded August 21, 1978. Both Jack Douglas (Aerosmith's regular producer) and George Martin (the Beatles' producer) supervised the recording sessions. This track was used in the lame *Sgt. Pepper* movie and first appeared on *Aerosmith's Greatest Hits*.

#10:  "**Downtown Charlie**" was an unreleased group jam recorded August 8, 1978, for *Draw The Line*.

## *Pandora's Box - CD Three, Side Two*

#1:   "**Sharpshooter**" was co-written by guitarist Brad Whitford and vocalist/guitarist Derek St. Holmes (who worked extensively with Ted Nugent) before Brad left Aerosmith. After his departure, he recorded it with St. Holmes, bassist Dave Hewitt, drummer Steve Pace and producer Tom Allom in late 1980 and early 1981 for the *Whitford/St. Holmes* album.

#2:   Written by guitarist Joe Perry, "**Shithouse Shuffle**" was recorded on May 30, 1979. Aerosmith's internal hassles (and the song's fine title) kept it unreleased until this compilation was unleashed.

#3:   The Perry song "**South Station Blues**" was recorded for his Joe Perry Project album *I've Got The Rock N' Rolls Again*. It was

139

produced by Bruce Botnick (who worked with the Doors and Rolling Stones) and featured drummer Ronnie Stewart, bassist David Hull and guitarist Charlie Farren.

#4:  "**Riff & Roll**" was a previously unreleased *Rock In A Hard Place* jam recorded on September 16, 1981. Vocalist Steven Tyler shared the writing credits with guitarist Jimmy Crespo.

#5:  "**Jailbait**" was co-written by Tyler and Crespo for the 1982 *Rock In A Hard Place* album.

#6:  This alternate take of Steven Tyler's "**Major Barbara**" was recorded during the *Rock In A Hard Place* sessions.

#7:  This was an unreleased version of Richie Supa's "**Chip Away The Stone**," recorded in an early *Draw The Line* session on June 4, 1978.

#8:  This previously unreleased cover of the Beatles' "**Helter Skelter**" was recorded in 1975. No one from the band could remember much about the recording session!

#9:  "**Back In The Saddle**" was co-written by Tyler and Joe Perry — who wrote the melody on a six-string bass. One of the first songs finished for *Rocks*, this was recorded February 3, 1976.

#10: "**Circle Jerk**" was an unlisted bonus track on the boxed set. That instrumental was credited to guitarist Brad Whitford and first used as the B-side to "**Kings And Queens**" from *Draw The Line*. It was "officially" released in the *Box Of Fire* compilation in 1994.

## Aerosmith
### *Get A Grip* (26-29)

17th LP, released 4/20/93 — three years after *Pump*. Following their year-and-a-half long *Pump* world tour, Aerosmith spent eight months relaxing with their families. Refreshed and recharged, they began preproduction for this album in Fall 1991. As they had with *Permanent Vacation* and *Pump*, vocalist Steven Tyler and guitarist Joe Perry wrote several songs in collaboration with Jim Vallance and Desmond Child, who provided a different perspective on their music. In January 1992, the Boston-based group rejoined co-producer Bruce Fairbairn (who had just finished work on AC/DC's *Live* album) at A&M Studios in Los Angeles. Just eight weeks later, they had recorded an entire album. But the band wasn't satisfied. They still felt a need to stretch their limits. In late Spring 1992, Tyler and Perry began to record additional demos at Perry's home studio in Boston. Guitarist Brad Whitford, bassist Tom Hamilton and drummer Joey Kramer joined them a couple of weeks later. Soon, the group had worked up the basics for 10 more new songs.

In September 1992, Aerosmith regrouped at Fairbairn's Little Mountain Studio in Vancouver — where *Permanent Vacation* and *Pump* both had been recorded. By late November, all of the new material was recorded — with most of the basic tracks recorded live in the studio. When Brendan O'Brien (who also produced Pearl Jam) finished the final mixing at Can-Am Studios in Tarzana, California, Aerosmith had kept only five of the songs from their original version of *Get A Grip*. (They later used the outtakes as B-sides.) The final

141

version of this album emerged with a stronger guitar orientation than *Pump*, and Whitford and Perry took great pride in how different their guitar work sounded on each of the songs.

Five weeks after this album debuted at #1, Aerosmith launched another massive world tour, which included their first jaunts into South America and a number of Eastern European countries. With their old friend Thom Gimbel rejoining them on keyboards, backing vocals and saxophone, the band's live set continually changed and evolved. Eventually stretching into a 20-month-long marathon before ending at the band's Boston club Mama Kin in December 1994, the tour showcased some of Aerosmith's strongest live performances ever.

*Get A Grip* sold over 12 million copies and yielded five hit singles — Aerosmith's most successful album ever. Once again in their long career, Aerosmith had fought their way to the top of the rock & roll world!

### *Get A Grip - Side One*

#1: The album's "**Intro**" was vocalist Steven Tyler's clever invention. This and the next song were used to open every date on the *Get A Grip* tour.

#2: One of the first songs completed for this album, "**Eat The Rich**" was co-written by Tyler, guitarist Joe Perry and lyricist Jim Vallance (who has worked for years with Bryan Adams). Steven arranged the rhythmic Polynesian log drum parts.

#3: "**Get A Grip**" was another Tyler/Perry/Vallance composition recorded in Los Angeles for the first rendition of this album. The original riff had been written during a jam at the Long View Farm studio in Massachusetts months before they considered any lyrics for it.

#4: The Tyler and Perry song "**Fever**" was recorded during the first *Get A Grip* sessions in early 1992. Guitarist Brad Whitford played all of the lead parts in this song. Joe Perry said he felt it contained the strongest rhythm work he had ever done. Bassist Tom Hamilton later identified this as one of his favorite songs on the album.

#5: Credited to Tyler, Perry and Mark Hudson, "**Livin' On The Edge**" was written and demoed at Perry's home studio after the first version of this album was recorded. The whole band hadn't even worked on this song before they started to record it in Vancouver. "**Livin' On The Edge**," combined with several bonus tracks, became the first CD single from *Get A Grip*, and charted at #18 in May 1993. Joe Perry later said this was his favorite song on the album.

    B-1: This acoustic rendition of "**Livin' On The Edge**" was later developed into the final album version.

    B-2: This original demo of "**Livin' On The Edge**," as it was recorded at Joe Perry's home studio, was amazingly close to the final version of the song.

    B-3: "**Don't Stop**" was an outtake from the first sessions for *Get A Grip*.

    B-4: "**Can't Stop Messin'**" was one of the last songs completed for the album, written and recorded at the same time as "**Shut Up And Dance**." Guitarist Brad Whitford later said this was his favorite song from the *Get A Grip* sessions. "**Can't Stop Messin'**" was included as a bonus track on the British version of this album.

#6: "**Flesh**," co-written by Tyler, Perry and Desmond Child, was one of the last songs completed for the album.

#7: Guitarist Joe Perry wrote and sang "**Walk On Down**."

## *Get A Grip - Side Two*

#1: Co-written by vocalist Steven Tyler and guitarist Joe Perry, and their old friends Jack Blades and Tommy Shaw (of Damn Yankees) "**Shut Up And Dance**" was one of the last songs completed for the album, and the last single to be released. Although it was rarely played live, each performance was an exercise in wild abandon — Aerosmith at their best!

   B-1: Steven Tyler co-wrote "**Deuces Are Wild**" with Jim Vallance (Bryan Adams' longtime collaborator). The song was an outtake from the May 1989 *Pump* sessions, and had been first released on 1994's MTV *Beavis & Butt-head* album.

   B-2: The same acoustic version of "**Crazy**" previously used as a B-side to the "**Crazy**" single.

   B-3: This was the previously unreleased "Butcher Brothers" dance remix of "**Line Up**."

#2: Tyler, Perry and Taylor Rhodes co-wrote "**Cryin'**" near the end of the sessions. The entire band had not even played the tune until two days before they recorded it. Tyler's favorite *Get A Grip* song, this was the second single released from the album. It charted at #12 and sold over a million copies in Fall 1993.

   B-1: An acoustic version of "**Cryin'**."

B-2: The original demo of "**Cryin'**" as it was recorded at Joe Perry's home studio.

#3: "**Gotta Love It**," co-written by Tyler, Perry and Mark Hudson, was one of the last songs finished for this album. Brad Whitford later said this contained his favorite guitar solo on *Get A Grip* and bassist Tom Hamilton identified this as one of his favorite songs on the album.

#4: "**Crazy**" was co-written by Tyler, Perry and Desmond Child. Desmond also played keyboards on this track.
> B-1: A differently mixed orchestral version of "**Crazy**."
> B-2: A radically different acoustic version of "**Crazy**."
> B-3: The orchestral version of "**Amazing**."
> B-4: The album version of "**Gotta Love It**."

#5: One of the first songs finished for the album, but one of the last chosen for the final mix, "**Line Up**" was co-written by Tyler, Perry and Lenny Kravitz.

#6: Keyboardist Richie Supa and Steven Tyler co-wrote the classic "**Amazing**." Recorded during the earliest sessions for this album, Richie played keyboards and Don Henley (of the Eagles) added some backing vocals to the song. In December 1993, "**Amazing**" charted at #24. The band did not perform this highly personal song live until the latter portion of the *Get A Grip* tour.

#7: "**Boogie Man**" was an instrumental jam left over from the first rendition of this album.

## Aerosmith
### *Big Ones* (35-38)

18th LP, released 11/1/94. Released in part to fulfill a contractual obligation, this greatest hits compilation covered the most recent, most artistically and most commercially successful phase of Aerosmith's career. Containing two songs specially recorded for this release, *Big Ones* charted at #6 and sold over five million copies.

## *Big Ones - Side One*

#1: "**Walk On Water**" was recorded specifically for this compilation in April and June 1994 in New York and Italy. Michael Beinhorn handled the production. Vocalist Steven Tyler and guitarist Joe Perry had co-written this number with Tommy Shaw and Jack Blades (of Damn Yankees).

#2: Released as a single before the *Pump* album came out, "**Love In An Elevator**" charted at #5 in September 1989. The song, co-written by Steven Tyler and Joe Perry, was supposedly inspired by one or more true incidents.

#3: "**Rag Doll**" was a collaboration by Perry, Tyler, Jim Vallance and Holly Knight (who had worked with Heart and Pat Benatar). "**Rag Doll**" charted at #17 in August 1988 — almost a year after *Permanent Vacation* was released.

**#4:** "**What It Takes**" was co-written by Tyler, Perry and their old buddy Desmond Child. The third single released from *Pump*, "**What It Takes**" hit #9 in Spring 1990.

**#5:** "**Dude (Looks Like A Lady)**" was another Tyler/Perry/Child composition from the *Permanent Vacation* album. "**Dude (Looks Like A Lady)**" became Aerosmith's first legitimate hit in years when it charted at #14 in December 1987.

**#6:** One of Aerosmith's most affecting songs, "**Janie's Got A Gun**" was inspired by a true story of child abuse. Co-written by Tyler and bassist Tom Hamilton for the *Pump* album, "**Janie's Got A Gun**" charted at # 4 in February 1990.

**#7:** "**Cryin'** " was co-written by Tyler, Perry and Taylor Rhodes. Tyler's favorite *Get A Grip* song, "**Cryin'** " was the second single released from the album. It charted at #12 and sold over a million copies in September 1993.

## *Big Ones - Side Two*

**#1:** Keyboardist Richie Supa and vocalist Steven Tyler co-wrote the classic "**Amazing**." Recorded during the earliest sessions for *Get A Grip*, the song featured Richie on keyboards and Don Henley (of the Eagles) on backing vocals. In December 1993, "**Amazing**" charted at #24.

**#2:** "**Blind Man**" was co-written by Tyler, Perry and Taylor Rhodes, the same trio responsible for "**Cryin'**." "**Blind Man**" was recorded in April and June 1994 in New York and Italy just for this compilation. Michael Beinhorn handled the production.

**#3:** Steven Tyler co-wrote "**Deuces Are Wild**" with Jim Vallance (Bryan Adams' longtime collaborator). This rocker was an outtake from the May 1989 *Pump* sessions, and had been first released on 1994's MTV *Beavis & Butt-head* album.

#4:  Tyler and Vallance also co-wrote "**The Other Side**." The fourth single released from *Pump*, "**The Other Side**" charted at #22 in September 1990.

#5:  "**Crazy**" was co-written by Tyler, guitarist Joe Perry and Desmond Child for *Get A Grip*. Desmond also played keyboards on this track.

#6:  Tyler, Perry and Vallance shared writing credits for "**Eat The Rich**," one of the first songs completed for *Get A Grip*.

#7:  Steven Tyler and Desmond Child co-wrote "**Angel**." This song marked the first time the band experimented with an outside writer, and they were quite worried about including it on *Permanent Vacation*. Their fears were unfounded. "**Angel**" became their biggest hit ever when it charted at #3 in February 1988.

#8:  Credited to Tyler, Perry and Mark Hudson (of the Hudson Brothers), "**Livin' On The Edge**" was written and demoed at Perry's home studio after the first version of *Get A Grip* was recorded. "**Livin' On The Edge**" became the first single from the final version of the album, and charted at #18 in May 1993. Joe Perry later said this was his favorite song on *Get A Grip*.

## Aerosmith
### *Box Of Fire*

Released 11/8/94. This special boxed set of Aerosmith's first dozen albums represented their entire output with their first record company, Columbia Records. All the original master tapes were digitally reprocessed and the CDs were re-mastered with 20-bit Super Bit Mapping that was absolute state of the art in 1994. The result was an amazing improvement in sonic quality. Also included was a five-song bonus CD of rare B-sides and special recordings.

### *Box Of Fire Bonus CD*

#1:  "**Sweet Emotion (1991)**" was a special re-mix of the Aerosmith classic released in conjunction with the *Pandora's Box* compilation in November 1991. The song, written by Steven Tyler and bassist Tom Hamilton, has proven to be the band's most popular number. The bass line, one of the most memorable hard rock riffs ever, first came to Hamilton during the *Get Your Wings* sessions. This song finally took form when he was playing with the riff while waiting for the rest of the band during one of the *Toys In The Attic* sessions. Tyler's final lyrics were supposedly a reflection on guitarist Joe Perry's ex-wife. "**Sweet Emotion**" charted at #36 both in Summer 1975, and this special re-mix charted at #36 again in January 1991.

#2:   Recorded for the *Less Than Zero* soundtrack in 1987, this was Aerosmith's loose rendition of the Huey "Piano" Smith song "**Rocking Pneumonia And The Boogie Woogie Flu**."

#3:   A collaboration jam by guitarist Brad Whitford, bassist Tom Hamilton and drummer Joey Kramer, "**Subway**" was recorded during the chaotic *Draw The Line* sessions. Its only previous release was as a B-side for the "**Draw The Line**" single in November 1977.

#4:   "**Circle Jerk**" was a Whitford jam recorded during the chaotic *Draw The Line* sessions, and later used as a B-side of "**Kings And Queens**" in Spring 1978.

#5:   This symphonic version of "**Dream On (MTV Anniversary)**" was recorded especially for the *MTV Anniversary* show and later used in the *Last Action Hero* film and its soundtrack.

# ZZ Top

**ZZ Top**

1994

Billy Gibbons, Frank Beard, Dusty Hill

# ZZ Top

Formed as a boogie & blues power trio in late 1969, ZZ Top's gestation took place over several years. The band performed six out of seven days in bars and clubs around Texas before their 1973 hit, "**La Grange**," exposed them to a national audience. The first phase of their career concluded three years later after the Top had played to millions of fans, sold millions of albums, and taken their hard-rocking three-piece boogie & blues format as far as it could possibly go. The end of that phase could have been a perfect time for the group to take a break, enjoy their riches, lose their creative spark and make a failed comeback attempt. Indeed, ZZ Top did take a three-year break, but the musical evolution they made upon their return was nothing short of incredible. They stayed firmly based in the blues as their songwriting style, and individual performances improved; their unique arrangements tightened, and their execution grew more sophisticated. The trio's experimentation with electronics and digital sampling proved them second to no other hard rock band. The combination of new developments and techniques generated enormous album sales and sold-out concert tours. The second phase of ZZ Top's career became even more successful than their first.

Even with so much commercial success while in pursuit of their unique musical vision, a more fitting tribute to the trio's talent was the superb quality of their performances during 1994's *Antenna Tour*. After 25 years together, ZZ Top not only enjoyed each other's company more than ever, their musical abilities were at an all-time high!

### ZZ Top Birth Dates

**Frank Beard** - June 11, 1949
**Billy Gibbons** - December 16, 1949
**Dusty Hill** - May 19, 1949

## ZZ Top
### *First Album* (18-18)

1st LP, released 1/71. The Houston-based ZZ Top formed as a boogie & blues band in early 1969. Early on, 19-year-old guitarist Billy Gibbons (a veteran of the Moving Sidewalks) and manager Bill Ham guided the band through a couple personnel changes before recruiting 19-year-old drummer Frank Beard in late 1969. Beard led them to his old partner from the Dallas band American Blues, 19-year-old bassist Dusty Hill . Within a couple of months, ZZ Top recorded this very raw, electric-blues album. Ham produced the sessions in a small, no frills concrete block studio, laying down some of the best blues recorded in the early Seventies. Then Bill secured the band a contract on London Records, and — even before this debut was released — he began booking the Top in clubs all around Texas.

ZZ Top's *First Album* is still a superb listening album!

** **Special Note**: Frank Beard was identified as "Rube" on the album credits, which was notable because no one ever called him by that name.

## First Album - Side One

#1: "**(Somebody Else Been) Shaking Your Tree**" was written by guitarist Billy Gibbons. Released as a single with "**Neighbor, Neighbor**" as the B-side, this never charted.

#2: "**Brown Sugar**" was another "Reverend" Billy Gibbons song.

#3: "**Squank**" was credited to Gibbons, bassist Dusty Hill and manager/producer Bill Ham.

#4: "**Goin' Down To Mexico**" was another Gibbons, Hill and Ham composition. Dusty handled the lead vocal on this one.

#5: "**Old Man**" was the only group composition on this album.

## First Album - Side Two

#1: "**Neighbor, Neighbor**" was credited to guitarist Billy Gibbons.

#2: Gibbons, drummer Frank Beard and manager/producer Bill Ham co-wrote "**Certified Blues**."

#3: Gibbons penned "**Bedroom Thang**."

#4: "**Just Got Back From Baby's**" was co-written by Gibbons and Ham. The band reprised this song on their 1994 *Antenna Tour*.

#5: "**Backdoor Love Affair**," which became one of the classic ZZ Top songs, was another Gibbons/Ham composition.

## ZZ Top
### *Rio Grande Mud* (21-21)

2nd LP, released 4/72. Another minimally produced boogie & blues album recorded in a small concrete block studio, the ultra-raw sound of *Rio Grande Mud* did nothing to raise the Houston-based band beyond regional cult status. However, ZZ Top's emerging group personality began to appear on this album, but with less emphasis on guitarist Billy Gibbons and more on the entire band's performance. Bassist Dusty Hill handled two of the lead vocals (he and Billy often traded leads in their live shows), and drummer Frank Beard received three co-writing credits for his contributions to the arrangements. Bill Ham (their manager and producer) booked the band into 300 gigs in the year following the release of their debut album. Although the 22-year-olds became a tight musical unit, it would be another year before the rest of America first recognized ZZ Top. *Rio Grande Mud* peaked at #104 a month after it was released.

** **Special Note**: The band played to 100,000 people at ZZ Top's *First Annual Texas Size Rompin' Stompin' Barn Dance And Bar-B-Q* in Austin, Texas, in July 1972 — just three months after this album was released. Even though they were not selling a lot of records, the Top were certainly developing a monster reputation.

# UNCLE JOE'S RECORD GUIDE

## *Rio Grande Mud - Side One*

#1: "**Francine**" had been co-written several years earlier by guitarist Billy Gibbons and two other friends. Bassist Dusty Hill handled the lead vocals on this version. "**Francine**" eventually charted at #69 in June 1972. The B-side featured a Spanish version of the song that has never been released on an album.

#2: "**Just Got Paid**" was credited to Gibbons and manager/ producer Bill Ham. The band reprised this great rocker in 1973 as the B-side to "**La Grange**," and again in their 1991 and 1994 world tours.

#3: "**Mushmouth Shoutin'**" was another Gibbons/Ham tune.

#4: "**Ko Ko Blue**" was the only group composition on this album. At least part of the inspiration came from blues singer Kokomo Arnold.

#5: "**Chevrolet**" was another Gibbons song that Dusty sang.

## *Rio Grande Mud - Side Two*

#1:  "**Apologies To Pearly**" was co-written by the group with manager/producer Bill Ham. Pearly Gates was the name of Billy Gibbons' prized Les Paul guitar, but he used a Stratocaster on this song (hence the title).

#2:  "**Bar-B-Q**" was credited to Ham and Gibbons.

#3:  "**Sure Got Cold After The Rain Fell**" was an extended Gibbons jam. Bassist Dusty Hill sang lead vocals.

#4:  "**Whiskey 'N Mama**" was co-written by the band and manager Bill Ham. The earliest version of this song was called "G 4/4" — blues in the key of G in 4/4 time.

#5:  "**Down Brownie**" was another Gibbons number.

## ZZ Top
### *Tres Hombres* (17-17)

3rd LP, released 7/73. After playing 300 gigs per year for three years, the 23-year-olds Billy Gibbons, Dusty Hill and Frank Beard's writing, singing and playing styles had become much tighter and better focused. But ZZ Top was still identified as a Southwestern phenomenon, just as Styx and REO Speedwagon were considered Midwest bands, and J. Geils was associated with the East Coast. In early 1973, ZZ Top recorded some basic tracks in the tiny concrete block studio they had used for their first two albums, then moved to Ardent Studios in Memphis. Once there, they set up their equipment, turned on the tape recorders, and captured everything as it was played live. Their changes in recording technique and buffed-up writing style worked so well that the sound of this album took the band to a new level.

Propelled by the hit single "**La Grange**," *Tres Hombres* became ZZ Top's first Top 10 charting, million-selling album. Bill Ham produced the Texas-style boogie & blues album as Terry Manning engineered the sound. Guitarist Gibbons and bassist Hill split the lead vocals, and all three band members contributed to songwriting. *Tres Hombres* is considered to be one of the classic American rock & roll albums of the mid-Seventies.

** **Special Note**: *Tres Hombres* is Spanish for "Three Men."

## *Tres Hombres - Side One*

#1:  "**Waiting For The Bus**," co-written by guitarist Billy Gibbons and bassist Dusty Hill, always segued into "**Jesus Just Left Chicago**." That combination featured some fine jamming and became a ZZ Top concert standard for the rest of their career.

#2:  "**Jesus Just Left Chicago**" was listed as a group composition.

#3:  "**Beer Drinkers & Hell Raisers**" was another group composition. Dusty and Billy shared the lead vocals.

#4:  "**Master Of Sparks**" was credited to Billy Gibbons.

#5:  "**Hot, Blue And Righteous**" was another Gibbons song on which he traded vocals with Dusty.

## *Tres Hombres - Side Two*

#1:  "**Move Me On Down The Line**" was co-written by guitarist Billy Gibbons and bassist Dusty Hill.

#2:  "**Precious And Grace**" was a group composition. (The band loved to claim that this song was based on a true story.)

#3:  "**La Grange**" was the group composition that put ZZ Top on the map. Supposedly composed during a ride to the recording studio, it was also the only hit single of 1973 that was written about a brothel. With "**Just Got Paid**" (from *Rio Grande Mud*) as the B-side, "**La Grange**" charted at #41 in May 1974 — almost a full year after this album was released!

#4:  Billy and Dusty co-wrote "**Sheik**."

#5:  "**Have You Heard**" was another Gibbons/Hill composition on which they both sang lead.

## ZZ Top
### *Fandango!* (16-18)

4th LP, released 5/75 – almost two years after *Tres Hombres*. Recorded live in New Orleans, the first side of this album captured the essence of early ZZ Top — intense Texas boogie & blues. Guitarist Billy Gibbons traded lead vocals with bassist Dusty Hill, and drummer Frank Beard propelled the performance. The second side of this album was composed of studio tracks recorded during the *Tres Hombres* tour, and included the huge hit single "**Tush**."

Bill Ham (the group's manager) produced the album, and Terry Manning (who worked on the next five ZZ Top albums) engineered the recording. Bob Ludwig was responsible for the final mastering. The band, whose members averaged 25 years of age, continued their constant touring and partying as this became their second Top 10 charting album. Initially, *Fandango* was seen by many as a filler album: an album released to buy time while the band continued their lucrative touring. In the years since, *Fandango* has provided an insight into the reason the band's music and performance made them so successful.

** **Special Note**: By this time the Top was firmly established as "That little ol' band from Texas," and their song "**Beer Drinkers & Hell Raisers**" best described their ever-burgeoning audiences.

## *Fandango! - Side One*

This side was recorded live at the Warehouse in New Orleans. Because no overdubs were used, you hear exactly what that audience heard!

#1: "**Thunderbird**" was a group composition that took its lyrical inspiration from true life experiences. The song began its life as an instrumental called "C-shuffle," inspired by a band called the Nightcaps, and had been the ZZ Top's show opener for years.

#2: "**Jailhouse Rock**" was the Leiber/Stoller song Elvis Presley first made famous. Bassist Dusty Hill, who sang this song, is a big fan of "The King."

#3: "**Backdoor Medley**"
    I. Guitarist Billy Gibbons and manager/producer Bill Ham co-wrote "**Backdoor Love Affair**."
    II. "**Mellow Down Easy**" was written by blues legend Willie Dixon.
    III. "**Backdoor Love Affair, No. 2**" was a Gibbons composition.
    IV. "**Long Distance Boogie**" evolved from a group jam.

## *Fandango! - Side Two*

All the songs on this side were group compositions recorded between concerts on the *Tres Hombres* tour.

#1: "**Nasty Dogs And Funky Kings**" was absolutely kick-ass.

#2: "**Blue Jean Blues**" was used as the B-side of "**Tush**," and became a concert favorite for the next several years. Guitarist Billy Gibbons shared the lead vocals with bassist Dusty Hill.

#3: "**Balinese**" [pronounced Bahl-eh-NEEZ] was named after one of the band's favorite nightclubs, which was located on a Galveston pier. The club had been a real "swinging" hot spot in the Fifties.

#4: "**Mexican Blackbird**" was supposedly inspired by a real woman.

#5: "**Heard It On The X**" was inspired by the same million-watt Mexican radio station that the Doors had written about in "The WASP (Texas Radio And The Big Beat)." Dusty and Billy traded vocals on this track.

#6: "**Tush**" was sung by bassist Dusty Hill. ZZ Top's second hit single, this #20 charting song first came together during a soundcheck jam session. One of Dusty's "typical" observations inspired the lyrics.

## ZZ Top
*Tejas* (19-17)

5th LP, released 12/76. After two Top 10 albums and two hit singles, ZZ Top found themselves in a struggle with their hell-raising boogie band image, as well as the exhaustion caused by constant roadwork and partying. The band barely took a break before they went into the studio to record these group compositions with producer/manager Bill Ham and engineer Terry Manning. These tunes generally lacked the trademark ZZ Top edge, but the band was not short on showmanship. They followed this release with their infamous *Worldwide Texas Tour*, which included a wolf, rattlesnakes, a steer and a buffalo live on stage — a stunt that earned them an enormous amount of publicity and cost a fortune. The whole tour was reported to have either lost a ton of money or been one of the highest grossing events in history — depending on who told the story. Whatever the true story, the *Worldwide Texas Tour* and years of live gigs burned out the 27-year-old band members enough to induce them to take a three year vacation while their manager, Bill Ham, renegotiated record contracts.

Although *Tejas* eventually sold over a million copies, this album barely broke into the Top 20 on the charts — even with all the publicity from the huge tour. The Top was ready for a break; a break that would either signal the end of the band's career or give them a chance to make a comeback.

** **Special Note**: *Tejas* is Spanish for "Texas."

## *Tejas - Side One*

#1: "**It's Only Love**" charted at #44 in Fall 1976 with "**Asleep In The Desert**" as the B-side. The great bass drum sound came about when the microphone accidentally fell against the drum head during the session.

#2: "**Arrested For Driving While Blind**" charted at #91 in Spring 1977. "**It's Only Love**" was used as the B-side.

#3: "**El Diablo**" was the third single released from this album. It did not chart.

#4: "**Snappy Kakkie**" featured a great groove.

#5: "**Enjoy And Get It On**" was used as the B-side of "**El Diablo**."

## *Tejas - Side Two*

#1:  "**Ten Dollar Man**"

#2:  "**Pan Am Highway Blues**"

#3:  "**Avalon Hideaway**" was named after a Houston drugstore and grill.

#4:  Guitarist Billy Gibbons played (what passed for) a violin part on "**She's A Heartbreaker**." He had never before, nor would he ever again, play the violin. He and bassist Dusty Hill traded lead vocals on this.

#5:  "**Asleep In The Desert**" was the only song on this album that was not listed as a group composition — Billy took credit for it. It was also the only piece that was fully arranged when the band first went into the studio. The middle section originally came from a piece Billy called "Pearly's Prayer," another musical reference to his favorite guitar.

## ZZ Top
### *The Best Of ZZ Top* (17-18)

6th LP, released 11/77. This collection of songs, compiled by the band's record company, was released to recap the first phase of their career and finish up ZZ Top's first recording contract. It eventually charted at #94 and sold over a million copies.

** **Special Note**: No songs from ZZ Top's most recent album, *Tejas*, were included in this compilation.

### *The Best Of ZZ Top - Side One*

#1:   "**Tush**," the group's first Top 20 hit, originally appeared on 1975's *Fandango*.

#2:   "**Waiting For The Bus**" first appeared on *Tres Hombres*.

#3:   "**Jesus Just Left Chicago**" also came from *Tres Hombres*.

#4:   "**Francine**" first appeared on *Rio Grande Mud*.

#5:   "**Just Got Paid**" also came from *Rio Grande Mud*.

## *The Best Of ZZ Top - Side Two*

#1: ZZ Top's first hit single, "**La Grange**" was from 1973's *Tres Hombres* album.

#2: A concert favorite, "**Blue Jean Blues**" first appeared on *Fandango*.

#3: "**Backdoor Love Affair**" was originally released on ZZ Top's *First Album*.

#4: "**Beer Drinkers & Hell Raisers**" was taken from *Tres Hombres*.

#5: "**Heard It On The X**" originally appeared on *Fandango*.

## ZZ Top
### *Deguello* (18-17)

7th LP, released 11/79 – almost three years after their last studio effort. Following six years of constant roadwork, ZZ Top completed one of the world's biggest rock & roll tours in 1976 and decided to take a short vacation. When drummer Frank Beard, bassist Dusty Hill and guitarist Billy Gibbons finally realized how much unwinding they needed, the vacation stretched to two-and-a-half years. That break gave the Top's manager, Bill Ham, a chance to negotiate a lucrative, new recording contract with the label that would be their home for the next 14 years. The second phase of ZZ Top's career was about to begin.

The trio — all sporting long beards for the first time — finally returned to the studio in early 1979, to update their blues-based boogie with jazz-like tonal-textures and astounding instrumental technique. All three even learned to play saxophone for this recording. After the basic tracks for the group compositions were finished, Gibbons spent a few more weeks overdubbing guitars and vocals. As usual, the sound was handled by their longtime producer, Bill Ham, and engineers Terry Manning and Bob Ludwig (who was responsible for the final mastering).

This outstanding comeback album proved to be very successful — musically, sonically and commercially. *Deguello* charted at #24, soon sold over a million copies and yielded another trademark song, "**Cheap Sunglasses**." The quality of the new music, combined with the rejuvenated Top's live show, foretold of great things to come.

** **Special Notes**: The title *Deguello* [pronounced Deh-GWAY-yo] translated from Spanish to English as "Cut off their heads" or "Give no quarter"— General Santa Ana's instructions to his troops at the Alamo.

When Frank Beard decided his attempts at a beard were less than successful, he shaved before the tour began, and left it to Billy and Dusty to further develop the trademark ZZ Top whiskers.

## *Deguello - Side One*

#1: "**I Thank You**" was a cover of an old Isaac Hayes tune the Top used as a warm-up piece before serious work began in the studio. Guitarist Billy Gibbons changed the "me's" in the lyrics to "it," which completely altered the gist of the song. "**A Fool For Your Stockings**" appeared as the B-side of "**I Thank You**," which charted at #34 in April 1980.

#2: "**She Loves My Automobile**," the first new song finished for this album, was supposedly recorded on the first take. The band said this initial recording "went so smooth and felt so good" that it set the tone for the rest of the album. They did spend a considerable amount of time learning to play the saxophone parts they overdubbed later.

#3: "**I'm Bad, I'm Nationwide**" became a concert favorite.

#4: "**A Fool For Your Stockings**" was a great blues workout.

#5: "**Manic Mechanic**"

## *Deguello - Side Two*

#1: This version of the Elmore James blues classic "**Dust My Broom**" was recorded as the band warmed up in the studio. Bassist Dusty Hill handled the lead vocals.

#2: "**Lowdown In The Street**" was inspired by the Austin, Texas music scene of the Seventies.

#3: "**Hi Fi Mama**" featured bassist Dusty Hill's vocals — a rare occasion on ZZ Top's later records, although he still shared those duties with Billy Gibbons during the band's live shows. The group played their own saxophones on this track.

#4: "**Cheap Sunglasses**" became ZZ Top's comeback single and provided them with another trademark — "cheap, black shades." While it received lots of airplay, "**Cheap Sunglasses**" only charted at #89 in Summer 1980.

#5: "**Esther Be The One**" was used as the B-side to "**Cheap Sunglasses**."

## ZZ Top
### *El Loco* (20-17)

8th LP, released 7/81 – more than a year-and-a-half after *Deguello*. After three years out of the business, the comeback success of ZZ Top's 1979 *Deguello* album and tour came as a big surprise. On a creative roll, the Top decided to intensify their musical experimentation in the studio. In addition to that development, the group compositions featured more humorous lyrics than ever before. As usual, guitarist Billy Gibbons, bassist Dusty Hill and drummer Frank Beard worked with their producer/manager Bill Ham and ace engineers Terry Manning and Bob Ludwig.

Even though *El Loco* charted at #17 and sold over a million copies, the Top prepared to make more stylistic and image changes.

** **Special Note**: The title *El Loco* was Texan slang for "The crazy person." The funky photograph on the album cover showed the band caught red-handed with "Loco Weed."

## *El Loco - Side One*

#1:  "**Tube Snake Boogie**" featured one of ZZ Top's most infectious grooves ever. As the second single released from this album, the song did not chart.

#2:  "**I Wanna Drive You Home**"

#3:  "**Ten Foot Pole**"

#4:  "**Liela**" charted at #77 in Fall 1981.

#5:  "**Don't Tease Me**" was used as the B-side to "**Liela**."

## *El Loco - Side Two*

#1:   "**It's So Hard**"

#2:   "**Pearl Necklace**" was a Texan slang term for the result of one of the band's favorite pastimes. Guitarist Billy Gibbons said that the rhythm guitar track was inspired by Keith Richards (of the Rolling Stones).

#3:   The band loved to say that "**Groovy Little Hippy Pad**" was inspired by drummer Frank Beard's place. The song was composed during preproduction at Frank's home studio. First they recorded the synthesizer parts, and then added the rest of the instrumentation. That was the first time the Top ever used this technique to record songs.

#4:   Guitarist Billy Gibbons had written part of "**Heaven, Hell Or Houston**" during a soundcheck about 10 years before the band recorded this version. This song was used as the B-side to "**Tube Snake Boogie**."

#5:   "**Party On The Patio**" was later used as the B-side to the November 1985 hit "**Sleeping Bag**."

## ZZ Top
### *Eliminator* (22-24)

9th LP, released 3/83 – almost two years after *El Loco*. Following the extended studio stretch that resulted in the *El Loco* album, ZZ Top was ready for a change in their writing style and recording techniques. With the basics for several songs written during the previous two Top tours, guitarist Billy Gibbons first experimented with a lot of preproduction work at drummer Frank Beard's home studio. Then Billy, Frank and bassist Dusty Hill then went back to the Memphis studio they used for their classic *Tres Hombres* album. They set up their equipment in the exact same way and in the exact same room as they had 10 years earlier for the *Tres Hombres* sessions. Next, they recorded the basic tracks for these group compositions live in the studio. Even with the extensive overdubs and synthesizer work added later, the Top's new music retained a special raw edge and *really* rocked. In the seven weeks of *Eliminator* sessions, ZZ Top reinvented its music with the help of manager/producer Bill Ham. As usual, Terry Manning engineered the sound and Bob Ludwig handled the mastering. Released when the "little ol' band from Texas" averaged 33 years of age, *Eliminator* is still an outstanding rock & roll album!

It was with this album that ZZ Top first ventured into music videos. Their debut of the now famous *Eliminator* video trilogy — "**Gimme All Your Lovin'**," "**Sharp Dressed Man**," and "**Legs**" — not only established the band as a video pioneer on the newly-launched MTV, but introduced some of the Top's most enduring trademark symbols — the ZZ Top keychain, the red *Eliminator* '33 Ford Coupe, the ZZ Girls and the ZZ Top hand jive gestures. This great music, combined with those videos and icons, helped make *Eliminator* the Top's most successful album ever, and one of the biggest releases of 1983 <u>and</u> 1984. *Eliminator* charted for 141 weeks straight, and sold over eight million copies. Although it charted no higher than #9 in the States, *Eliminator* hit #3 in Britain. This album proved so popular that ZZ Top had long finished their American tour and were about to wrap up their world tour when their record company finally released "**Legs**" as a single. "**Legs**" went on to become the biggest hit of the Top's career and one of the most enduring songs of 1984.

** **Special Notes**: Billy Gibbons attributed his guitar sound on this album to Tom Scholz (who had been a scientist before he formed the band Boston). Scholz invented a small personal amplifier called the Rockman, and during the preproduction sessions for this album, Billy had fun experimenting with the different sounds the device produced.

   The album title *Eliminator* was derived from Billy's 1933 Ford Coupe hot rod —another ZZ Top trademark.

   As a further measure of the trio's popularity, ZZ Top drew twice as many votes as George Bush and Michael Dukakis combined in the 1984 presidential poll of the television show *Saturday Night Live*!

# HARD ROCK - ZZ Top

## *Eliminator - Side One*

#1: "**Gimme All Your Lovin'**" charted at #37 in May 1983. "**If I Could Only Flag Her Down**" was used as the flipside.

#2: "**Got Me Under Pressure**" became a concert standard.

#3: The second single released from this album, "**Sharp Dressed Man**" only charted at #56 in August 1983. The song was partially inspired by the fashion-conscious English fans the Top had seen on their 1982 British tour.

#4: "**I Need You Tonight**"

#5: "**I Got The Six**" was the B-side of "**Sharp Dressed Man**."

## *Eliminator - Side Two*

#1: "**Legs**" became the biggest hit of ZZ Top's career a full year after this album was released. It was inspired by a woman guitarist Billy Gibbons and bassist Dusty Hill saw walking in the rain near their Memphis studio. This million-selling, #8 charting song was later adapted for a pantyhose commercial.

#2: "**Thug**"

#3: "**TV Dinners**" originally entitled "Problems," was supposedly inspired by a jumpsuit!

#4: "**Dirty Dog**" was first entitled "Scurvy Dog."

#5: "**If I Could Only Flag Her Down**" was the B-side to "**Gimme All Your Lovin'**."

#6: "**Bad Girl**" was used as the B-side to "**Legs**."

## ZZ Top
### *Afterburner* (20-18)

10th LP, released 10/85 – a year-and-a-half after *Eliminator*.
In February 1985, on the heels of the tremendous success
generated by their *Eliminator* album and tour, guitarist Billy
Gibbons, bassist Dusty Hill and drummer Frank Beard
returned to their favorite Memphis studio with their
producer/manager Bill Ham. This time the band and Ham
opted to work with sound engineer Joe Hardy (who had done
R&B sessions for Stax during the Sixties) and mastering
engineer Bob Ludwig.

Throughout their three months of recording sessions the
band experimented extensively with several kinds of sounds,
digital sampling and synthesizers. In fact, as he recorded the
final guitar tracks Billy Gibbons played through a stack of
more than twenty different types of amplifiers – switching
them on and off for various effects. Although the resulting
music reflected a more electronic direction for ZZ Top,
*Afterburner* also marked a continuation of the style the band
established with *Eliminator*.

Released when the group averaged 36 years of age,
*Afterburner* charted at #4 in America and #2 in Britain, the
Top's highest-ever chart position on either side of the Atlantic.
The album also sold three million copies faster than any other
1985 release. Some felt the musicianship on *Afterburner*
lacked ZZ Top's trademark spark, but the following 212-date,
15-month world tour was their most successful to date.

## *Afterburner - Side One*

#1: The synthesized drums on "**Sleeping Bag**" included the digitally sampled and processed sounds of doors being slammed on a junked Buick. This million-selling single, with "**Party On The Patio**" from the *El Loco* album as the B-side, reached #8 in November 1985.

#2: "**Stages**" charted at #21 in February 1986.

#3: "**Woke Up With Wood**" was the B-side of "**Velcro Fly**."

#4: The band made an outstanding video for "**Rough Boy**," and the song became a concert highlight. As the third single released from this album, "**Rough Boy**" charted at #22 in May 1986. "**Delirious**" was the B-side.

#5: "**Can't Stop Rockin'**," sung by bassist Dusty Hill, had first been worked up for the *Eliminator* album. It was also used as the B-side to "**Stages**."

## *Afterburner - Side Two*

#1:  Five years after the release of this album, "**Planet Of Women**" was used as the B-side to "**Doubleback**," which was recorded and released in conjunction with the movie *Back To The Future III*.

#2:  "**I Got The Message**"

#3:  "**Velcro Fly**" was written and recorded while the boys messed around in a three-hour jam session. The final drum sound was recorded in the middle of a racquetball court! The fourth and last single released from this album, "**Velcro Fly**" charted at #35 in Summer 1986. "**Woke Up With Wood**" was the B-side.

#4:  "**Dipping Low In The Lap Of Luxury**"

#5:  "**Delirious**" had originally been worked up for the 1980 *Deguello* album.

## ZZ Top
### *The ZZ Top Sixpack*

Released 10/87. This specially packaged collection of six compact discs was released at the request of the Top's record label, who felt they should have new product available when *Billboard* magazine ran a special 56-page feature on "That little ol' band from Texas." Because only four ZZ Top albums had been released on compact disc by early 1987, the band and manager/producer Bill Ham decided the time was right to release the entire catalog on the new digital format. Guitarist Billy Gibbons, bassist Dusty Hill, drummer Frank Beard and Bill Ham spent six months in the studio in Memphis, assisted by engineer Joe Hardy, digitally remixing the original analog master tapes of the group's first five albums, and the more-recent *El Loco*. Bob Ludwig was recruited to master the entire set. While the special *Sixpack* packaging was only available for a limited time, the remastered music still sounds great! For details on this compilation's discography, please refer to the appropriate ZZ Top albums in this *UNCLE JOE'S RECORD GUIDE*.

# UNCLE JOE'S RECORD GUIDE

## ZZ Top
### *Recycler* (21-20)

11th LP, released 10/90 – five years and an extensive world tour after the release of *Afterburner*. When the trio regrouped in mid-1989 for preproduction sessions, they had been personally inspired and recharged by their involvement with the Delta Blues Museum in Clarksdale, Mississippi. In retrospect, it was only logical that they considered "recycling" their blues roots into their more recent musical direction.

In early 1990, guitarist Billy Gibbons, bassist Dusty Hill and drummer Frank Beard once again returned to the Memphis Sound studios with their producer/manager Bill Ham and engineer Terry Manning (who had worked extensively with the band earlier in their career). Although most of this material had been worked up before the Top's trip to Memphis, the songs underwent serious revisions when the group's equipment did not arrive in time. The trio jammed on blues favorites for a couple of days, then began to re-arrange their new songs before the errant equipment truck finally arrived. At that point, the Top made the decision to return to their blues roots, although they still used many of the technological tricks they had developed when they recorded their previous couple of albums. Another byproduct of the bluesy jamming was a loose funkiness that returned to the Top's tempo. All of the *Recycler* songs were listed as group compositions. At 41 years of age, each member was performing at their peak.

# HARD ROCK - ZZ Top

*Recycler* reached #6 in the States and sold over four million copies worldwide. The *Recycler* tour featured the band's most complex staging and inspired jamming to date. After so many years together, ZZ Top rediscovered how much they loved the blues and how much fun they could have when they played.

** **Special Note**: In conjunction with this release, ZZ Top commissioned another exotic hot rod, this time a highly-altered, eggplant purple 1948 Cadillac called *CadZZilla*. The group saw *CadZZilla* as a metaphor for themselves — a classic recycled to highlight its pleasurable strong points.

## *Recycler - Side One*

#1: "**Concrete And Steel**," the first song released from this album. It was later used as the B-side of "**Give It Up**."

#2: "**Love Thing**"

#3: "**Penthouse Eyes**"

#4: "**Tell It**"

#5: One of the first songs recorded in Memphis for this album, "**My Head's In Mississippi**" featured a killer riff.

## *Recycler - Side Two*

#1:  "**Decision Or Collision**"

#2:  "**Give It Up**" charted at #79 in February 1991.

#3:  "**2000 Blues**" was one of the first *Recycler* songs the band recorded in Memphis.

#4:  "**Burger Man**"

#5:  Recorded before the rest of this album, "**Doubleback**" charted at #50 in June 1990 — four months before the album was released. The song was written in conjunction with the movie *Back To The Future III*, in which the boys made a cameo appearance. They later observed that most of their albums were soundtracks, but the movies had not yet been made!

## ZZ Top
### *Greatest Hits* (36–36)

12th LP, released 5/92. This compilation was released, partially, to finish up the band's second recording contract. Unlike their first *Best Of ZZ Top* package, guitarist Billy Gibbons, bassist Dusty Hill and drummer Frank Beard all helped select this music. This *Greatest Hits* collection also contained two new tracks, one previously unreleased alternate take, and four songs that were digitally remixed and remastered for *The ZZ Top Sixpack*. By the time this collection charted at #9 and sold over a million copies, ZZ Top had signed a new contract potentially worth over $40 million.

### *Greatest Hits - Side One*

#1: "**Gimme All Your Lovin'**" came from the *Eliminator* album.

#2: "**Sharp Dressed Man**" was also from *Eliminator*.

#3: "**Rough Boy**" first appeared on the *Afterburner* album.

#4: This version of "**Tush**," originally released on *Fandango*, was digitally remixed and remastered for *The ZZ Top Sixpack*.

#5: "**My Head's In Mississippi**" was taken from *Recycler*.

#6: This version of "**Pearl Necklace**," originally released on *El Loco*, was digitally remixed and remastered for *The ZZ Top Sixpack*.

# UNCLE JOE'S RECORD GUIDE

#7: "**I'm Bad, I'm Nationwide**" was from the *Deguello* album.

#8: This version of the Doc Pomus tune, "**Viva Las Vegas**," was recorded specifically for this compilation. Bassist Dusty Hill, who was a life-long Elvis Presley fan, sang the lead vocals on this song that Elvis originally made famous.

#9: "**Doubleback**" was from the *Recycler* album.

## Greatest Hits - Side Two

#1: Inspired by Jimmy Reed's "Real Gone Lover," "**Gun Love**" was recorded just for this compilation.

#2: "**Got Me Under Pressure**" first appeared on *Eliminator*.

#3: "**Give It Up**" was from *Recycler*.

#4: "**Cheap Sunglasses**" was from the *Deguello* album.

#5: "**Sleeping Bag**" first appeared on the *Afterburner* album.

#6: "**Planet Of Women**" was taken from the *Afterburner* album.

#7: This version of ZZ Top's first hit single "**La Grange**," which originally appeared on *Tres Hombres*, was digitally remixed and remastered for *The ZZ Top Sixpack*.

#8: "**Tube Snake Boogie**," originally released on *El Loco*, was digitally remixed and remastered for *The ZZ Top Sixpack*.

#9: This alternate version of "**Legs**" was previously unreleased.

## ZZ Top
### *Antenna* (25-29)

13th LP, released 1/94 – about four years after their last studio
album. After signing a new record contract potentially worth
millions, guitarist Billy Gibbons, bassist Dusty Hill and
drummer Frank Beard started rehearsing new material in
Summer 1992. Averaging 43 years of age, the group kept their
jams firmly grounded in their unique eclectic blues. This was
ZZ Top's first album to have a theme or concept before the
group began recording. They drew inspiration from the music
they grew up listening to on the powerful Mexico-based rock
& roll radio stations of the late Fifties and early Sixties – the
same stations that inspired ZZ Top's "**Heard It On The X**"
and the Doors' "The WASP (Texas Radio And The Big Beat)."
This time the Top explored a number of darker, more serious
subjects in their lyrics, as well as their usual tongue-in-cheek
double entendres. Four Billy Gibbons numbers, as well as
several group compositions, had been worked up when the
trio entered Ardent Studios in Memphis in July 1993. Engineer
Joe Hardy (who had worked on *Afterburner* and done R&B
sessions for Stax during the Sixties) joined them. Six months
later, the album was finished. This release marked the first
time since 1973's *Tres Hombres* album that Billy took an
individual writing credit, and the first time he ever shared
production credits with the band's manager/producer, Bill
Ham.

The renewed sense of camaraderie between the band
members was one of the biggest achievements of the
*Antenna* sessions. With their 25th anniversary in mind, the

trio began their world tour in Europe in April 1994, then hit the U.S. in mid-May. As the tour progressed, ZZ Top turned in some of the best musical performances of their career. *Antenna* reached #14 in the States and sold over a million copies, proving ZZ Top was still on top of the game!

## *Antenna - Side One*

#1:  "**Pincushion**" was the first song released from this album.

#2:  "**Breakaway**" was credited to guitarist Billy F. Gibbons.

#3:  The last song finished for the album, "**World Of Swirl**" was developed from another of Billy's demos. The lyrics and working title "Everything," were inspired by the Stax record slogan, "Everything and more."

#4:  The boys described "**Fuzzbox Voodoo**" as being halfway between "**Tush**" and "**Legs**." The original riff was inspired by a rare, early fuzz-tone distortion device (a Marshall Supa-Fuzz) Billy received as a gift.

#5:  The first song recorded for this album, "**Girl In A T-Shirt**" was credited to Billy Gibbons.

## *Antenna - Side Two*

#1:  "**Antenna Head**" featured bassist Dusty Hill on lead vocals.

#2:  "**PCH**" was inspired by a motorcycle ride along the Pacific Coast Highway in Southern California.

#3:  Guitarist Billy F. Gibbons took the sole writing credit for "**Cherry Red**."

#4:  "**Cover Your Rig**" was written as a cautionary tale about the use of condoms.

#5:  "**Lizard Life**"

#6:  Dusty also did lead vocals on **"Deal Goin' Down**."

## ZZ Top
### *One Foot In The Blues* (32-36)

14th LP, released 11/22/94. ZZ Top was always, first and foremost, a blues-based band. This compilation of previously released material aptly demonstrated the scope of the Texas trio practicing their craft. Assembled while the Top was overseas on their *Antenna Tour*, the band took a very active — albeit long distance — part in selecting their favorites for this package. Although it was released — without promotion or in-store support — in the 1994 pre-Christmas rush of album releases, *One Foot In The Blues* sold steadily and appeared at #11 on the debut Billboard Blues chart 10 months after the album's release.

** **Special Note**: The photo on the album cover came from one of the Top's first publicity photo sessions in early 1970.

### *One Foot In The Blues - Side One*

#1:   "**Brown Sugar**" was a "Reverend" Billy Gibbons song from the Top's debut album.

#2:   "**Just Got Back From Baby's**," originally released on ZZ Top's *First Album*, was co-written by guitarist Billy Gibbons and Bill Ham, the band's manager. The group reprised this song to great effect on their 1994 *Antenna* world tour.

**#3:** "**A Fool For Your Stockings**" was recorded for 1980's *Deguello* album.

**#4:** "**I Need You Tonight**" was from the landmark 1983 release, *Eliminator*.

**#5:** "**She Loves My Automobile**," the first song finished for *Deguello*, was supposedly recorded on the first take. The band said this initial recording "went so smooth and felt so good" that it set the tone for the rest of the album. They did spend a considerable amount of time learning to play the saxophone parts they overdubbed later.

**#6:** "**Hi Fi Mama**" featured bassist Dusty Hill's vocals — a rare occasion on ZZ Top's later records, although he still shared those duties with Billy Gibbons during the band's live shows. The group also played their own saxophones on this *Deguello* track.

**#7:** "**Hot, Blue And Righteous**" was a *Tres Hombres* Gibbons-penned song on which he traded vocals with Dusty.

**#8:** One of the first songs recorded in Memphis for the *Recycler* album, "**My Head's In Mississippi**" featured a killer riff.

## *One Foot In The Blues - Side Two*

**#1:** "**Lowdown In The Street**," from the *Deguello* album, was inspired by the Austin, Texas music scene of the Seventies..

**#2:** "**If I Could Only Flag Her Down**," from the *Eliminator* album, was the B-side to "**Gimme All Your Lovin'**."

# UNCLE JOE'S RECORD GUIDE

#3: "**Apologies To Pearly**," from the Top's second album, *Rio Grande Mud*. It was co-written by the group and their manager/producer, Bill Ham. Pearly Gates was the name of Billy Gibbon's prized Les Paul guitar, but he used a Stratocaster on this song (hence the title).

#4: "**Sure Got Cold After The Rain Fell**" was an extended Gibbons jam from *Rio Grande Mud*. Bassist Dusty Hill sang lead vocals.

#5: "Another *Rio Grande Mud* cut, "**Bar-B-Q**" was credited to Ham and Gibbons.

#6: "**Old Man**" was the only group composition on the Top's *First Album*.

#7: Another song from their debut album, "**Certified Blues**" was co-written by Gibbons, drummer Frank Beard and manager/producer Bill Ham.

#8: "**2000 Blues**" was one of the first *Recycler* songs the band recorded in Memphis.

#9: Guitarist Billy Gibbons had written part of "**Heaven, Hell Or Houston**" during a soundcheck about 10 years before the band recorded this version for *El Loco*.

# HARD ROCK
## The Second Generation

# The Second Generation

The first generation of hard rock bands listened to the blues in their teens, and then used the blues as the basis for their own compositions. The second generation hard rock bands grew up listening to first generation bands, such as Led Zeppelin and Aerosmith, and used them as their inspiration. When AC/DC, Rush and Van Halen first performed in front of audiences, they played covers of songs by the first generation bands — not of Willie Dixon and Muddy Waters like the first generation. By the early Eighties, each of these three major second generation bands had become the most popular rockers in the world. A new generation of musicians, the third, began to use AC/DC, Rush and Van Halen songs as their inspiration.

# UNCLE JOE'S RECORD GUIDE

Three major second generation bands detailed here adopted a different format and developed their own style of hard rock, but the roots of their music were the same as the first generation. In turn, their influence on the playing styles, song arrangements, stage performance and record production techniques of the third generation hard rock bands was equally monumental. While many of the first generation bands now exist only on recordings, all three of the major second generation hard rockers are fully functioning and still producing some of their finest material.

## AC/DC

1993

Cliff Williams, Malcolm Young, Angus Young, Chris Slade, Brian Johnson

# AC/DC

AC/DC began in early 1973 as a grungy Australian bar band. By the time they hired one of their roadies (Bon Scott) as their lead vocalist in mid-1974, the band's distinctive brand of hard-edged rock had been honed razor sharp by hundreds of gigs on Australia's killer circuit of small rock & roll clubs. Espousing a party-till-you-puke attitude in their lyrics, AC/DC became masters at taking the energy levels of their performance to the edge. Their first foray in 1976 across the ocean failed because America, even more than England, proved unready for so much raw power. After a couple more false starts, 1979's *Highway To Hell* came closest to breaking the band out of its cult status. Following Bon Scott's untimely death in 1980, they quickly recorded a follow-up. That new album, *Back In Black*, became one of the biggest hard rock albums of all time. If the story of AC/DC were to end there, the influence of their sound and fury on every third generation hard rock band would still qualify them as legends. But soon, AC/DC descended into a five-year slump worthy of Rob Riener's satirical movie *This Is Spinal Tap*. In 1986 the band finally found their musical direction again. In early 1988 AC/DC released an album equal in quality and fury to their early days. With their next release, their comeback compared to Aerosmith's.

With worldwide albums sales in excess of 80 million, AC/DC has achieved hard rock commercial success second only to Led Zeppelin — all without one recorded acoustic guitar or a soft ballad!

AC/DC has always utilized the same format as the Rolling Stones — two guitarists, a vocalist, drummer and bassist. But more than most other bands, AC/DC's sound and success depended upon the elusive magical spark of creativity, and a talented producer. But they so perfectly defined the very essence of rock & roll that Keith Richards (of the Rolling Stones) identified AC/DC as his favorite band — an endorsement not to be taken lightly!

# HARD ROCK - AC/DC

## AC/DC Birth Dates

**Mark Evans** - March 2, 1956

**Brian Johnson** - October 5, 1947

**Phil Rudd** - May 19, 1954

**Bon Scott** - July 9, 1946-September 19, 1980

**Chris Slade** - October 30, 1946

**Cliff Williams** - December 14, 1949

**Simon Wright** - June 19, 1963

**Angus Young** - March 31, 1959

**Malcolm Young** - January 6, 1953

# UNCLE JOE'S RECORD GUIDE

## AC/DC
### *High Voltage* (21-21)

1st Australian LP, released 2/75. Formed in 1973 by 20-year-old Malcolm Young, AC/DC started to tear things up when 15-year-old guitarist Angus Young joined his brother in 1974. When they recorded this album later that year, the group's line-up included 28-year-old vocalist Bon Scott, Angus and Malcolm Young on guitars, 18-year-old bassist Mark Evans, and 20-year-old drummer Phil Rudd. Scott and the Young brothers co-wrote all but two of the songs on this raw debut album. Two former members of the Easy Beats, Harry Vanda and George Young (Angus and Malcolm's older brother), produced the record at their home studio.

While this album didn't provide the young band with a major commercial breakthrough, it did provide additional income as the group developed their unique brand of hard-edged rock playing gigs on Australia's killer circuit of small rock & roll clubs.

# HARD ROCK - AC/DC

## *High Voltage - Australian Side One*

#1: It is doubtful that bluesmen Joe Williams and Big Bill Broonzy, who co-wrote "**Baby Please Don't Go**," ever envisioned it with this much energy. This was a great performance!

#2: "**She's Got Balls**"

#3: "**Little Lover**"

#4: "**Stick Around**"

## *High Voltage - Australian Side Two*

#1: "**Soul Stripper**," credited to Angus and Malcolm Young, was one of the few songs AC/DC recorded during vocalist Bon Scott's life that he didn't co-write.

#2: "**You Ain't Got A Hold On Me**"

#3: "**Love Song**"

#4: "**Show Business**"

## AC/DC
***T.N.T.*** (23-21)

2nd Australian LP, released 12/75. AC/DC spent 1975
cranking out hundreds of gigs on Australia's circuit of small
rock & roll clubs. On their way to becoming Australia's top
band, the group honed the edge of their hard rocking
performances. Espousing a party-till-you-puke attitude in their
lyrics, AC/DC took their performance to the edge. This music
was recorded in Fall 1975 by the guitar-playing Young
brothers, 22-year-old Malcolm and 16-year-old Angus,
29-year-old vocalist Bon Scott, 19-year-old bassist Mark Evans,
and 21-year-old drummer Phil Rudd. Scott and the Young
brothers co-wrote all but two of these songs. Harry Vanda and
George Young (Angus and Malcolm's older brother)
co-produced this at their home studio. While the recording
lacked polish, the young band's performance on this
collection of tunes was several steps above their debut. Most
of this album would soon be released in the U.S. under the title
*High Voltage*.

# HARD ROCK - AC/DC

## *T.N.T. - Side One*

#1: "**It's A Long Way To The Top (If You Want To Rock 'N' Roll)**" featured a bagpipe in the chorus!

#2: "**Rock 'N' Roll Suicide**"

#3: "**The Jack**" was inspired by a situation one of the young band members found himself in. The original lyrics were far more racy than this version.

#4: "**Live Wire**"

## *T.N.T. - Side Two*

#1: "**T.N.T.**"

#2: "**Rocker**"

#3: "**Can I Sit Next To You**," credited to Angus and Malcolm Young, was one of the few songs AC/DC recorded during vocalist Bon Scott's life that he didn't co-write.

#4: "**High Voltage**" was actually written around the chords A, C, D, and C.

#5: This cover of Chuck Berry's "**School Days**" rocked!

# UNCLE JOE'S RECORD GUIDE

## AC/DC
### *High Voltage* (U.S.) (22-22)

1st U.S. LP, released 5/76 — re-released 7/81. This album was a compilation of the band's first two Australian releases — *High Voltage* (released in February 1975) and *T.N.T.* (released in December 1975). Formed in 1973 by 20-year-old Malcolm Young, AC/DC began to really click a year later when Malcolm's 15-year-old brother, Angus, joined the lead guitarist. The line-up that recorded this music in mid-1975 included 29-year-old vocalist Bon Scott, Angus and Malcolm Young on guitars, 19-year-old bassist Mark Evans, and 20-year-old drummer Phil Rudd. Scott and the Young brothers co-wrote all but one of the songs included on this album. Two former members of the Easy Beats, Harry Vanda and George Young (Angus and Malcolm's older brother), produced both the *High Voltage* and *T.N.T.* albums from which this was compiled. Both of those albums were recorded at the Young's home studio. Although AC/DC was hailed as Australia's top band in 1976, this album was released to a completely apathetic American audience — although it did contain some hard, hard, raw rock & roll.

** **Special Note**: In the wake of the great success generated by the *Back In Black* album in late 1980, and the even more successful re-release of *Dirty Deeds Done Dirt Cheap* in early 1981, AC/DC's record company re-released this American version of *High Voltage* in July 1981. The second time around, it peaked at #146 and eventually sold over

208

two million copies — a vast improvement over its initial performance! To date, total worldwide sales of both versions of *High Voltage* exceed five million.

## *High Voltage - U.S. Side One*

The song line-up on this side was identical to the first side of AC/DC's second Australian album, *T.N.T.* which had been released six months before this album.

#1: **"It's A Long Way To The Top (If You Want To Rock 'N' Roll)"** featured a bagpipe in the chorus!

#2: **"Rock 'N' Roll Suicide"**

#3: **"The Jack"** was inspired by a situation one of the young band members found himself in.

#4: **"Live Wire"**

## *High Voltage - U.S. Side Two*

#1:  "**T.N.T.**"

#2:  "**Can I Sit Next To You**," credited to Angus and Malcolm Young, was one of the few songs AC/DC recorded during vocalist Bon Scott's life that he didn't co-write.

#3:  "**Little Lover**" had appeared on the original Australian version of this album.

#4:  "**She's Got Balls**" was also taken from the original High Voltage album.

#5:  "**High Voltage**," taken from the *T.N.T.* album, was written around the chords A, C, D, and C.

## AC/DC
### *Dirty Deeds Done Dirt Cheap*
(21-23, Australian)(18-22, U.S.)

3rd Australian LP, released 12/76 — 7th U.S. LP, released 4/81.
This batch of songs was recorded just before the young
Australian group first toured England. Their line-up featured
29-year-old Bon Scott on vocals, 17-year-old Angus and
23-year-old Malcolm Young on guitars, 20-year-old Mark
Evans on bass and 21-year-old Phil Rudd on drums. As usual,
Malcolm and Angus co-wrote all of the songs with Bon (who
had started with the band as their roadie). The Young
brothers older sibling, George, shared production credits
with Harry Vanda. The quick sessions were done in April 1976
at the band's home studio (Albert Studios) in Sydney.

*Dirty Deeds Done Dirt Cheap* was a great success in
Australia. However, with typical lack of foresight, AC/DC's
American record company decided this music wasn't
commercially viable — so they passed on releasing it.

After the immense breakthrough success of *Back In Black*
in late 1980, AC/DC's American record company realized
they still owned the rights to this album but had never released
it. Sensing a quick dollar could be made, they re-sequenced
these songs and released *Dirty Deeds Done Dirt Cheap*— over
the band's strong objections — in early 1981, barely a year
after Bon Scott's death. *Dirty Deeds Done Dirt Cheap* peaked
at #3 on the charts and sold over three million copies —
charting a full notch higher but selling seven million copies less
than *Back In Black*. To date, total worldwide sales of both

211

# UNCLE JOE'S RECORD GUIDE

versions of *Dirty Deeds Done Dirt Cheap* exceed seven million.

## *Dirty Deeds... - Australian Side One*

#1: "**Dirty Deeds Done Dirt Cheap**"

#2: "**Ain't No Fun (Waiting Around To Be A Millionaire)**"

#3: "**There's Gonna Be Some Rockin'**"

#4: "**Problem Child**" was a great rocker!

## *Dirty Deeds... - Australian Side Two*

#1: "**Squealer**"

#2: "**Big Balls**"

#3: "**R.I.P. (Rock In Peace)**" has never been released in America.

#4: "**Ride On**" was the most bluesy recording AC/DC ever made.

#5: "**Jailbreak**" featured one of the band's most intense performances ever. Eventually released in 1984 in the U.S., this song was a highlight of *The Razor's Edge* tour which ran from 1990 through 1991.

## *Dirty Deeds... - U.S. Side One*

#1:  "**Dirty Deeds Done Dirt Cheap**" became a staple on American rock radio.

#2:  "**Love At First Feel**" was previously unreleased on an AC/DC album.

#3:  "**Big Balls**"

#4:  "**Rocker**," previously unreleased in the U.S., was taken from the band's second Australian album, *T.N.T.*

#5:  A great rocker from the original *Dirty Deeds Done Dirt Cheap* album, "**Problem Child**" was previously released on the American version of *Let There Be Rock*.

## *Dirty Deeds... - U.S. Side Two*

#1:  "**There's Gonna Be Some Rockin'**"

#2:  "**Ain't No Fun (Waiting Around To Be A Millionaire)**"

#3:  "**Ride On**" was the most bluesy recording AC/DC ever made.

#4:  "**Squealer**"

## AC/DC
### *Let There Be Rock* (20-22)

4th Australian LP, 2nd U.S. LP, released 7/77 — just as the young band began their second U.S. tour. Except for one track, this album was recorded in Australia in January and February 1977 — right after AC/DC's return from their first trip to London, England. Extremely inspired by that experience, the boys' enthusiasm carried over into the studio.

Considered to be the best example of AC/DC's early sound, *Let There Be Rock* featured an intense performance by 30-year-old vocalist Bon Scott, and the music he co-wrote with 17-year-old Angus and 24-year-old Malcolm Young featured a very sharp edge. *Let There Be Rock* demonstrated an excellent use of dynamics. This style later served as a major inspiration to many of the third generation hard rock bands in the Eighties. The production was handled by two former members of the Easybeats, Harry Vanda and George Young (the eldest brother of the guitar playing duo Angus and Malcolm). The songwriting trio of the Young brothers and Scott were backed by 22-year-old Phil Rudd on drums and 20-year-old bassist Mark Evans (who quit after the tour).

*Let There Be Rock* was an artistic success, but a commercial stiff in the States. None-the-less, its charting rank of #154 still surpassed AC/DC's first two U.S. albums. *Let There Be Rock* did reach #17 in Britain, and eventually sold over four million copies worldwide.

# HARD ROCK - AC/DC

## *Let There Be Rock - Side One*

#1:  "**Go Down**"

#2:  "**Dog Eat Dog**"

#3:  "**Let There Be Rock**"

#4:  "**Bad Boy Boogie**"

## *Let There Be Rock - Australian Side Two*

#1:  "**Overdose**"

#2:  "**Crabsody In Blue**" was a very bluesy song that was never released in America.

#3:  "**Hell Ain't A Bad Place To Be**"

#4:  "**Whole Lotta Rosie**" was one of the best hard rock songs of 1977.

# UNCLE JOE'S RECORD GUIDE

## *Let There Be Rock - U.S. Side Two*

#1: The only song on this album recorded before AC/DC's first British tour, "**Problem Child**" was actually released eight months before this on the Australian *Dirty Deeds Done Dirt Cheap*.

#2: "**Overdose**"

#3: "**Hell Ain't A Bad Place To Be**"

#4: "**Whole Lotta Rosie**" was one of the best hard rock songs of 1977.

## AC/DC
### *Powerage* (18-21)

5th Australian LP, 3rd U.S. LP, released 6/78. As they prepared to enter their Sydney recording studio in January 1978, all of the members in the young Australian group grew dissatisfied with their failure at a commercial breakthrough. The guitar-playing brothers, 25-year-old Malcolm and 18-year-old Angus Young, along with their songwriting partner/vocalist 31-year-old Bon Scott and 23-year-old drummer Phil Rudd, had played together for over five years when this album was recorded. They had produced some great rock & roll records and become the most popular band in Australia, but still had not quite achieved a big breakthrough across the Pacific ocean. By the end of the *Powerage* tour, AC/DC knew they had to sink or swim.

*Powerage*, the last album AC/DC recorded in their own Albert Studios, was AC/DC's last studio effort for several years with their original producers, Harry Vanda and George Young. A young engineer named Mark Opitz handled the sound (he next produced another young Australian band called INXS). *Powerage* also marked the first recorded appearance of 28-year-old bassist Cliff Williams (who replaced Mark Evans after the *Let There Be Rock* tour). *Powerage* charted at #133 in the States and #26 in England, after the band toured there extensively. Within a few years, *Powerage* sold over a million copies in the U.S., and four million worldwide.

# UNCLE JOE'S RECORD GUIDE

## *Powerage - Side One*

#1:  "**Rock 'N' Roll Damnation**"

#2:  "**Down Payment Blues**"

#3:  "**Gimme A Bullet**"

#4:  "**Riff Raff**"

## *Powerage - Side Two*

#1:  "**Sin City**"

#2:  "**What's Next To The Moon**"

#3:  "**Gone Shootin'** "

#4:  "**Up To My Neck In You**"

#5:  "**Kicked In The Teeth**"

## AC/DC
### *If You Want Blood (You've Got It)* (27-25)

6th Australian LP, 4th U.S. LP, released 11/78. Recorded live in Australia and in the U.S. during the young Australian band's 1978 *Powerage* tour, this album effectively summed up the first phase of AC/DC's career. The line-up — Malcolm and Angus Young, Bon Scott, Phil Rudd and Cliff Williams — played rock solid. Their pent-up frustration from a lack of a major breakthrough added even more energy to their performance. This was the last recording for several years on which AC/DC worked with their original producers, Harry Vanda and George Young.

Although it only charted at #113 in the States, this album did hit #26 in Britain and eventually sold over a million copies in the States and four million worldwide. Many still consider *If You Want Blood (You've Got It)* to be one of the best live hard rock albums of all time.

# UNCLE JOE'S RECORD GUIDE

## *If You Want Blood (You've Got It) - Side One*

#1: **"Riff Raff"**

#2: **"Hell Ain't A Bad Place To Be"**

#3: **"Bad Boy Boogie"**

#4: **"The Jack"**

#5: **"Problem Child"**

## *If You Want Blood (You've Got It) - Side Two*

#1: This wild version of **"Whole Lotta Rosie"** opened with the crowd chanting "Angus! Angus!"

#2: **"Rock 'N' Roll Damnation"**

#3: **"High Voltage"**

#4: **"Let There Be Rock"**

#5: **"Rocker"**

## AC/DC
### *Highway To Hell* (21-21)

7th Australian LP, 5th U.S. LP, released 8/79. 1979 became a year of change for AC/DC. Frustrated by the lack of commercial breakthrough, they changed management, and signed with the people who handled Aerosmith and the Scorpions. AC/DC also dropped their old producers, and recorded for the first time with Robert John "Mutt" Lange (who had worked wonders for the Cars and Def Leppard). Under Lange's guidance, guitarists Malcolm and Angus Young (aged 26 and 20, respectively), 32-year-old vocalist Bon Scott, 29-year-old bassist Cliff Williams and 24-year-old drummer Phil Rudd began recording at London's Roundhouse Studios in January 1979. As usual, Malcolm and Angus co-wrote all of the songs with Bon. But working with their new producer proved different from than anything the band had done before, and it took an unusually long six months to record this album. Malcolm and Angus co-wrote all of the songs with Bon. The results were definitely their best to date; this was their first American Top 20 album and first Top 10 in Britain, where it peaked at #8. *Highway To Hell* came very close to giving the boys their big breakthrough when it hit #17 during their successful U.S. tour. This excellent album eventually sold over four million copies in America, and another five million worldwide.

Unfortunately, on February 19, 1980, seven months and a successful world tour after this release, Bon Scott was dead at the age of 33 — a victim of his hard partying lifestyle.

## *Highway To Hell - Side One*

#1:  Their strong performance on "**Highway To Hell**" demonstrated AC/DC's newly found self-confidence. "**Highway To Hell**" charted at #47 in the States in November 1979 and has been a staple of rock radio ever since.

#2:  "**Girls Got Rhythm**" was one of the best hard rock songs of the late Seventies.

#3:  "**Walk All Over You**"

#4:  "**Touch Too Much**"

#5:  "**Beating Around The Bush**"

## *Highway To Hell - Side Two*

#1:  The boys did a superb job of focusing their energy and songwriting talents on "**Shot Down In Flames**."

#2:  "**Get It Hot**"

#3:  This was a re-arranged version of "**If You Want Blood (You've Got It)**," a song that had been part of AC/DC's live set for quite some time.

#4:  "**Love Hungry Man**"

#5:  "**Night Prowler**," a very dark song, concluded with vocalist Bon Scott's interpretation of comedian Robin Williams' most famous Mork & Mindy line — "Nanoo, Nanoo."

## AC/DC
### *Back In Black* (22-20)

8th Australian LP, 6th U.S. LP, released 8/80. On February 19, 1980, just before the recording sessions for this album were to begin, AC/DC's vocalist Bon Scott died at the age of 33 — a victim of his hard partying lifestyle. Two months later, after some quick rehearsals and writing sessions with 32-year-old vocalist Brian Johnson, the band began to record in the Bahamas. The interaction between the Australian band and their new vocalist was perfect. Starting in April at Compass Point Studios, Johnson, guitarists 27-year-old Malcolm and 21-year-old Angus Young, 30-year-old bassist Cliff Williams and 26-year-old drummer Phil Rudd worked quickly, and the project was finished by late May. Once again, the production was handled by Robert John "Mutt" Lange (who next worked wonders for Def Leppard and Foreigner).

*Back In Black* was AC/DC's first album to chart in the American Top 5 (it hit #4), and a long, immensely successful world tour followed its release. On August 22, 1981, part way through the extended *Back In Black* world tour, AC/DC headlined the *Monsters Of Rock Festival* at Castle Donington in England. The Australian band was at the top of the rock & roll world!

Their finest recorded effort to date, *Back In Black* was dedicated to the memory of Bon Scott. It sold over 10 million copies in the U.S., another seven million worldwide, and is still considered to be one of the best hard rock albums of all time!

# UNCLE JOE'S RECORD GUIDE

## *Back In Black - Side One*

#1: "**Hells Bells**"

#2: "**Shoot To Thrill**"

#3: "**What Do You Do For Money, Honey**"

#4: "**Giving The Dog A Bone**"

#5: "**Let Me Put My Love Into You**"

## *Back In Black - Side Two*

#1: "**Back In Black**" charted at #37 in February 1981.

#2: AC/DC's first American Top 40 hit, "**You Shook Me All Night Long**" reached #35 in November 1980.

#3: "**Have A Drink On Me**"

#4: "**Shake A Leg**"

#5: "**Rock And Roll Ain't Noise Pollution**"

## AC/DC

### *For Those About To Rock We Salute You* (21-20)

9th Australian LP, 8th U.S. LP, released 12/81 — about a year and a half after *Back In Black*. While AC/DC toured long and hard to follow-up their breakthrough success with the *Back In Black* album, their American record company re-released *High Voltage*, and, over the band's objection, finally released *Dirty Deeds Done Dirt Cheap*. Hitting #3, *Dirty Deeds Done Dirt Cheap* became the best charting AC/DC album to date. However, releasing a four-and-a-half year-old album recorded with Bon Scott, AC/DC's recently deceased vocalist, did not sit well with the group. In Fall 1981, contractual obligations forced the road-weary band to end their tour and return to the recording studio.

As usual for the second phase of their career, 28-year-old Malcolm and 22-year-old Angus Young co-wrote everything on this album with 34-year-old vocalist Brian Johnson. Bassist Cliff Williams (who was 31) and drummer Phil Rudd (who was 27) supplied the backing. The recording sessions at two different studios in Paris supposedly became quite strained with producer Robert John "Mutt" Lange (a perfectionist who also worked with the Cars and Def Leppard). This became Lange's last project with AC/DC.

The creative spark that inspired the finer moments on *Back In Black* did not appear in the songwriting or performances on this album. Only the chart position and tour grosses of *For Those About To Rock We Salute You* were bigger and better than before. This album lodged at #1 in the U.S. for three weeks and reached #3 in Britain. It sold just under three million copies Stateside, and another three million worldwide. Even though AC/DC had followed-up *Back In Black* — one of the biggest hard rock albums of all time — with their only U.S. #1 charting effort, *For Those About To Rock We Salute You* was viewed by many as an artistic disappointment.

** **Special Note**: The Australian version of this album featured a different song sequence — presumably closer to the group's artistic vision.

## *For Those About To Rock... - U.S. Side One*

#1:  The grandiose "**For Those About To Rock (We Salute You)**" was the highlight of this album and the following tour. In concert, cannon fire accompanied the song.

#2:  "**Put The Finger On You**"

#3:  "**Let's Get It Up**" charted at #44 in the U.S. in February 1982.

#4:  "**Inject The Venom**"

#5:  "**Snowballed**"

# HARD ROCK - AC/DC

## *For Those About To Rock... - U.S. Side Two*

#1: "**Evil Walks**"

#2: "**C.O.D.**"

#3: "**Breaking The Rules**"

#4: "**Night Of Long Knives**"

#5: "**Spellbound**"

## *For Those About To Rock... - Australian Side One*

#1: "**For Those About To Rock (We Salute You)**"

#2: "**Evil Walks**"

#3: "**C.O.D.**"

#4: "**Spellbound**"

#5: "**Put The Finger On You**"

# UNCLE JOE'S RECORD GUIDE

## *For Those About To Rock... - Australian Side Two*

#1:  "**Let's Get It Up**"

#2:  "**Inject The Venom**"

#3:  "**Breaking The Rules**"

#4:  "**Snowballed**"

#5:  "**Night Of Long Knives**"

## AC/DC
### *Flick Of The Switch* (19-18)

10th Australian LP, 9th U.S. LP, released 9/83. Following their less-than-satisfying experiences when recording *For Those About To Rock We Salute You*, AC/DC decided to return to the simplified, raw sound they had achieved on their earliest releases. This album marked their first attempt at self-production after a decade of playing together. The lack of an outside producer to handle problems in the studio, caused various problems. Ultimately, intra-band tensions and a lack of desire to go back out on the road prompted original drummer Phil Rudd to leave the group when they finished this album. His replacement, 20-year-old Simon Wright, was hired just in time for the following tour, which didn't set any sales records. When *Flick Of The Switch* charted at only #15 and sold less than a million copies Stateside (barely two million worldwide), it became obvious that AC/DC had commercial and artistic problems on their hands. After the *Flick Of The Switch* tour ended on August 18, 1984, with another headlining gig at the *Monsters Of Rock Festival* at Castle Donington, they wisely took a long vacation.

# UNCLE JOE'S RECORD GUIDE

## *Flick Of The Switch - Side One*

#1:  "**Rising Power**"

#2:  "**This House Is Burning On Fire**"

#3:  "**Flick Of The Switch**"

#4:  "**Nervous Shakedown**"

#5:  "**Landslide**" — definitely not the Stevie Nicks number!

## *Flick Of The Switch - Side Two*

#1:  "**Guns For Hire**" barely reached #84 on the American singles charts in November 1983.

#2:  "**Deep In The Hole**"

#3:  "**Bedlam In Belgium**"

#4:  "**Badlands**"

#5:  "**Brain Shake**"

## AC/DC
### *'74 Jailbreak* (13-12)

10th U.S. LP, released 11/84. While AC/DC was on hiatus following their disappointing *Flick Of The Switch* effort, this compilation was released to keep their name in the public's eye. More an EP than an LP, *'74 Jailbreak* was composed of songs by the band's original line-up. The band recorded most of the material in late 1974 with Vanda and Young (the group's original production team). The line-up included 28-year-old vocalist Bon Scott, 16-year-old Angus and 21-year-old Malcolm Young on guitars, 18-year-old Mark Evans on bass and 20-year-old Phil Rudd on drums.

All of these songs, except the title track, had been previously released on AC/DC's first Australian album, but omitted from the group's first American release, *High Voltage*. The intensity of these vintage performances put AC/DC's previous two studio efforts to shame. Still, *'74 Jailbreak* only charted at #76 and sold under a million copies.

## *'74 Jailbreak - Side One*

All of these songs, with the exception of the first track, had originally appeared on AC/DC's 1974 Australian debut, *High Voltage*.

#1: "**Jailbreak**" had been first released in Australia in 1976 on the original version of *Dirty Deeds Done Dirt Cheap*. This featured one of the band's most intense performances ever, and was a highlight of *The Razor's Edge* tour, which ran from 1990 through 1991.

#2: "**You Ain't Got A Hold On Me**"

#3: "**Show Business**"

## *'74 Jailbreak - Side Two*

#1: "**Soul Stripper**," credited to Angus and Malcolm Young, was one of the few songs AC/DC recorded during vocalist Bon Scott's life that he didn't co-write.

#2: This cover of the Joe Williams and Big Bill Broonzy blues song "**Baby Please Don't Go**," was a great performance!

## AC/DC
### *Fly On The Wall* (20-20)

11th LP, released 6/85 — almost two years after their last studio album. Following the disappointing results of their *Flick Of The Switch* effort, AC/DC took a long break. In late 1984, 34-year-old bassist Cliff Williams, 21-year-old drummer Simon Wright, 37-year-old vocalist Brian Johnson and guitarists 25-year-old Angus and 31-year-old Malcolm Young regrouped at the Mountain Studio in Montreux, Switzerland. Johnson and the Young brothers co-wrote all of this material, and Angus and Malcolm co-produced it. The results were better than their last effort, but the boys still had not regained their sharp edge.

*Fly On The Wall* was the first AC/DC album that featured songs that obviously dealt with real-life situations instead of the bad boy bravado the band had always embraced. In another change of pace, AC/DC cut back on their marathon touring. The results were immediate — the quality of both their shows and lifestyles improved. *Fly On The Wall* charted at #32 in the States, #7 in the U.K., and sold just under a million copies here and about two million worldwide.

** **Special Note**: In January 1985, part way through the recording sessions for this album, AC/DC headlined in front of 342,000 at the *Rock In Rio* festival in Brazil.

# UNCLE JOE'S RECORD GUIDE

## *Fly On The Wall - Side One*

#1:  "**Fly On The Wall**"

#2:  "**Shake Your Foundations**"

#3:  "**First Blood**"

#4:  "**Danger**"

#5:  "**Sink The Pink**" became a concert highlight.

## *Fly On The Wall - Side Two*

#1:  "**Playing With The Girls**"

#2:  "**Stand Up**"

#3:  "**Hell Or High Water**"

#4:  "**Back In The Business**"

#5:  "**Send For The Man**"

## AC/DC
### *Who Made Who* (20-19)

12th LP, released 9/86. This compilation was the official soundtrack of the Stephen King movie *Maximum Overdrive*. Three of these songs were brand new, one was a previously unreleased number recorded with Bon Scott in 1976, and the rest were greatest hits material. While the movie did not achieve much commercial success, AC/DC's new music (especially the album's title cut) was the best the band released in a long time. This was one kick-ass collection of rock & roll!

Although the band never toured to support *Who Made Who* — which only charted at #33 Stateside and #11 in Britain — this album still sold over three million copies Stateside and another three million worldwide — the biggest AC/DC commercial success in five years!

# UNCLE JOE'S RECORD GUIDE

## *Who Made Who - Side One*

#1: "**Who Made Who**" was an excellent, brand new song — the best the band had done in years.

#2: "**You Shook Me All Night Long**" was previously released on *Back In Black*.

#3: "**D.T.**," another new song, was written and produced by Angus and Malcolm Young.

#4: "**Sink The Pink**" was taken from *Fly On The Wall*.

#5: "**Ride On**" was a number from the band's earliest days, recorded with original singer Bon Scott in 1976.

## *Who Made Who - Side Two*

#1: "**Hells Bells**" came from *Back In Black*.

#2: "**Shake Your Foundations**" first appeared on the *Fly On The Wall* album.

#3: "**Chase The Ace**," the third new number on this album, was written and produced by Angus and Malcolm Young.

#4: "**For Those About To Rock (We Salute You)**" was the title cut of that album.

## AC/DC
### *Blow Up Your Video* (21-23)

13th LP, released 2/88 — more than two-and-a-half years after their last studio effort. This important album marked the first time in almost a decade that AC/DC worked with their original producers — Harry Vanda and George Young (brother of Angus and Malcolm). It was also the first time in several years that AC/DC found themselves with an American Top 10, million-selling album.

Under relaxed circumstances, they recorded a total of 19 songs in the South of France in August and September 1987. As usual, the guitar-playing brothers, 28-year-old Angus and 34-year-old Malcolm Young, shared the songwriting credits with 39-year-old vocalist Brian Johnson. The rhythm section consisted of 37-year-old bassist Cliff Williams and 24-year-old drummer Simon Wright.

*Blow Up Your Video* not only contained AC/DC's most menacing music in years, but also marked the return of the hard edge and dynamic range to their music. This great hard rock album — the band's highest charting release in seven years — reached #12 in American and #2 in Britain, and sold over a million copies. Unfortunately, the following world tour proved arduous. Part way through the European swing, Malcolm Young was replaced on stage by his cousin Steve Young. Then, at the tour's end, drummer Simon Wright left the band permanently.

# UNCLE JOE'S RECORD GUIDE

## *Blow Up Your Video - Side One*

#1:  "**Heatseeker**"

#2:  "**That's The Way I Wanna Rock 'N' Roll**"

#3:  "**Mean Streak**"

#4:  "**Go Zone**"

#5:  "**Kissin' Dynamite**"

## *Blow Up Your Video - Side Two*

#1:  "**Nick Of Time**"

#2:  "**Some Sin For Nothin'**"

#3:  "**Ruff Stuff**"

#4:  "**Two's Up**"

#5:  "**This Means War**"

## AC/DC
### *The Razor's Edge* (21-23)

14th LP, released 9/90 — more than two-and-a- half years after
*Blow Up Your Video*. The *Blow Up Your Video* world tour
proved arduous. Guitarist Malcolm Young left part way
through the tour, and drummer Simon Wright departed after
the tour's end. Almost a year after the tour, 36-year-old
Malcolm rejoined his 30-year-old brother Angus, and they
wrote all of the material for this album. After demoing the new
songs to 42-year-old vocalist Brian Johnson and AC/DC's
longtime bassist, 39-year-old Cliff Williams, the group was just
about ready to rock.

Before preproduction began in late 1989 with famed
producer Bruce Fairbairn (who previously worked with
Aerosmith and Motley Crue), AC/DC needed to recruit a
drummer. Their surprising choice was 43-year-old Chris
Slade, an extremely sophisticated percussionist who worked
for several years with Manfred Mann's Earth Band and Jimmy
Page's band The Firm. (Chris had also played on Tom Jones'
"It's Not Unusual!")

The recording sessions began in April 1990. The addition
of Slade — plus the sharp production, discipline and guidance
Fairbairn supplied — helped make *The Razor's Edge* the most
artistically and commercially successful AC/DC album in the
decade since their breakthrough. *The Razor's Edge* hit #2 in
the States, and sold over three million copies. It reached #4 in
Britain, and sold another four million worldwide! The
following tour was AC/DC's most successful ever — 153

shows in 21 countries. The band worked well together and produced a killer show. Many fans felt a live album was inevitable.

## *The Razor's Edge - Side One*

#1: Not only was "**Thunderstruck**" the first song released from this album, the band also used it to start their concerts on *The Razor's Edge* tour.

#2: "**Fire Your Guns**"

#3: "**Money Talks**" reached #23 on the American singles charts in February 1991.

#4: "**The Razor's Edge**"

#5: "**Mistress For Christmas**" was inspired by Donald Trump.

#6: "**Rock Your Heart Out**"

# HARD ROCK - AC/DC

## *The Razor's Edge - Side Two*

#1:  "**Are You Ready**"

#2:  "**Got You By The Balls**"

#3:  "**Shot Of Love**"

#4:  "**Let's Make It**"

#5:  "**Good-bye & Good Riddance To Bad Luck**"

#6:  "**If You Dare**"

## AC/DC
### *LIVE* (38-35)
### *Special Collector's Edition LIVE* (36-36-31-29)

15th LP, released 11/92. The 1990-1991 *The Razor's Edge* world tour was the most successful the Australian band had ever enjoyed – they played 153 shows in 21 countries. They recorded this album near the end of the tour, and secured the services of producer during some of the final 153 shows played in 21 countries. to supervise the project. Bruce Fairbairn produced this album just before he rejoined Aerosmith for their *Get A Grip* sessions. (Bruce also produced *The Razor's Edge*, as well as Aerosmith's *Pump* and *Permanent Vacation*.)

Throughout *The Razor's Edge* tour, the performances of guitarists Malcolm and Angus Young, bassist Cliff Williams and drummer Chris Slade reflected the fun they were having – as this standout live album, covering all of AC/DC's career, demonstrated.

The band released two versions of this album. The *Special Collector's Edition LIVE* was a double compact disc package that included all 24 songs in the order they appeared in concert. The cheaper, single CD version was comprised of 14 tracks and charted at #15. The *Special Collector's Edition LIVE* reached #34. The two versions sold just under two million in the U.S. and a total of over five million copies worldwide.

# HARD ROCK - AC/DC

## *LIVE - Side One*

#1:  "**Thunderstruck**"

#2:  "**Shoot To Thrill**"

#3:  "**Back In Black**"

#4:  "**Who Made Who**"

#5:  "**Heatseeker**"

#6:  "**The Jack**"

#7:  "**Dirty Deeds Done Dirt Cheap**"

## *LIVE - Side Two*

#1:  "**Money Talks**"

#2:  "**Hells Bells**"

#3:  "**You Shook Me All Night Long**"

#4:  "**Whole Lotta Rosie**"

#5:  "**Highway To Hell**"

#6:  "**T.N.T.**"

#7:  "**For Those About To Rock (We Salute You)**"

# UNCLE JOE'S RECORD GUIDE

## *The Special Collector's Edition LIVE - Side One*

These were the songs in the order AC/DC performed them in concert.

#1: "**Thunderstruck**"

#2: "**Shoot To Thrill**"

#3: "**Back In Black**"

#4: "**Sin City**"

#5: "**Who Made Who**"

#6: "**Heatseeker**"

#7: "**Fire Your Guns**"

## *The Special Collector's Edition LIVE - Side Two*

#1: "**Jailbreak**"

#2: "**The Jack**"

#3: "**The Razor's Edge**"

#4: "**Dirty Deeds Done Dirt Cheap**"

#5: "**Money Talks**"

# HARD ROCK - AC/DC

## *The Special Collector's Edition LIVE - Side Three*

#1: "**Hells Bells**"

#2: "**Are You Ready**"

#3: "**That's The Way I Wanna Rock 'N' Roll**"

#4: "**High Voltage**"

#5: "**You Shook Me All Night Long**"

#6: "**Whole Lotta Rosie**"

## *The Special Collector's Edition LIVE - Side Four*

#1: "**Let There Be Rock**"

#2: "**Bonny**"

#3: "**Highway To Hell**"

#4: "**T.N.T.**"

#5: "**For Those About To Rock (We Salute You)**"

# UNCLE JOE'S RECORD GUIDE

## AC/DC
## *Ballbreaker* (23-27)

16th LP, released 9/26/95 — five years after their last studio effort. Following the lengthy *The Razor's Edge* tour — but before any work began on this album — AC/DC decided to return to their original, straight-ahead, hard-edged sound. In preparation, guitarists Malcolm and Angus Young spent time listening to their many old Marshall amplifiers, searching for the best sounding ones. That search led to some spirited jamming, and the seeds of several new songs emerged.

Before beginning the *Ballbreaker* preproduction in early 1994 with vocalist Brian Johnson and longtime bassist Cliff Williams, the group made a couple of important changes. First, their original drummer, Phil Rudd, was welcomed back into the group 11 years after he split for a quieter life. The second major change involved enlisting producer Rick Rubin, a long time fan who had produced the AC/DC song "**Big Guns**" for the Arnold Schwartzenegger movie *The Last Action Hero*.

As they had for *The Razor's Edge*, Malcolm and Angus co-wrote all of the music and lyrics. After a couple of months of rehearsals, the recording sessions began in New York in November 1994. Fresh from doing albums with Bob Dylan, Tom Petty and Johnny Cash, Rubin and his engineer/co-producer, Mike Fraser, proceeded to effect the return of AC/DC's vintage crunching sound — but the process wasn't easy. After months of sessions in New York didn't yield the "feel" the group wanted, they moved to Ocean Way studios in

Los Angeles. There the recording took on a life of its own. By late May 1995 everything from the New York sessions had been rerecorded. When the final mixing was completed at the Record Plant in Los Angeles on June 30, 1995, *Ballbreaker* had undergone the longest recording process ever for an AC/DC album. With that behind them, the band prepared for another extensive world tour.

## *Ballbreaker - Side One*

#1:  "**Hard As A Rock**" was the first song released from this album.

#2:  "**Cover You In Oil**"

#3:  "**The Furor**"

#4:  "**Boogie Man**"

#5:  "**The Honey Roll**"

# UNCLE JOE'S RECORD GUIDE

## *Ballbreaker - Side Two*

#1: "**Burnin' Alive**"

#2: With a different lyrical direction from anything else AC/DC had ever recorded, "**Hail Caesar**" featured one of the band's strongest arrangements to date.

#3: "**Love Bomb**"

#4: "**Caught With Your Pants Down**" featured a great riff!

#5: "**Whiskey On The Rocks**"

#6: "**Ballbreaker**" was one of the highlights of this album.

# Rush

**Rush**
1994

Geddy Lee,
Neil Peart,
Alex Lifeson

# Rush

Like many other second generation hard rock bands, the members of Rush started playing in the late Sixties, adapted the power trio format of Cream and Hendrix, and covered songs by Led Zeppelin, Deep Purple and other blues-based bands. They spent years building their reputation and core audience in the time-honored method of constant touring. Their development of instrumental virtuosity and song structure showed an increasingly progressive influence. Once they followed their natural instincts to emphasize their musical talents, and to write about real people in real situations instead of science fiction, the second phase of the band's career exploded with huge commercial success. Rush became one of the most popular bands of the early Eighties, and served as role models for thousands of musicians. The measure of their greatness arose because they did not burn out like so many others who reached the top. Instead, in the third phase of their career the three Canadians focused on perfecting their sophisticated songwriting, arrangements and performances to achieve their unique rock & roll musical vision. Along the way, Rush continued to sell millions of records and routinely play sold-out concerts.

## Rush Birth Dates

**Geddy Lee** - July 29, 1953

**Alex Lifeson** - August 25, 1953

**Neil Peart** - September 12, 1952

## Rush
### *Rush* (20-21)

1st LP, released 1/74 in Canada — 8/74 in the U.S. In Summer 1968, guitarist Alex Lifeson and his neighbor, drummer John Rutsey, jammed with another Toronto schoolmate in their basement. By September, the 14-year-old budding musicians secured their first gig, but on the evening of their debut their bass player/singer bailed out. Alex immediately called in another schoolmate, Geddy Lee. By the end of that fateful night, Rush was born. In early 1969 the band's line-up briefly included a keyboard player, but the usual egotistical/political maneuverings of 16-year-olds caused the group to split-up in Spring 1969, and then re-form in Fall. Four years and innumerable performances later, the trio recorded this ultra-low-budget album during off-hours in small local studios. The songwriting was crude and derivative of the cover songs Rush played, but the boys persevered. Several months later, when the album was nearly complete, they hired producer Terry Brown to remix the raw tapes in two days. The experience was more rewarding than any of them had anticipated. Over the next decade, Brown would produce Rush's next 10 albums.

Rush released this raw work on their own label. Within a few months, their intense gigging and self-promotion paid off with a major record deal. This became the biggest selling debut album any Canadian band ever released. In another quirk of fate, only two weeks before Rush's first extended American tour, health problems forced John Rutsey's departure from the band. A quick audition brought another

Toronto native into the group; Rush started their first tour with a new drummer — Neil Peart [pronounced PEERT].

This album eventually reached #105 on the American charts, primarily due to Rush's constant touring . Those many concert dates earned Rush a large fan base that later propelled the Canadian trio into rock & roll's major leagues.

## *Rush - Side One*

#1:  "**Finding My Way**" was a last-minute addition to the album.

#2:  "**Need Some Love**" was re-recorded after producer Terry Brown joined the project.

#3:  "**Take A Friend**"

#4:  The group re-recorded "**Here Again**" with producer Terry Brown. The band and their producer judged the first version "too lame."

## *Rush - Side Two*

#1:   **"What You're Doing"**

#2:   **"In The Mood"** was the first song the band completed. Geddy brought a rough arrangement of the song into practice one evening, and the finished tune became part of Rush's live show throughout most of their career.

#3:   **"Before And After"**

#4:   **"Working Man"** became one of the best-known and most-requested songs from Rush's early work.

## Rush
### *Fly By Night* (20-19)

2nd LP, released 2/75. Rush's first album eventually became the biggest-selling debut effort ever released by a Canadian band. However, two weeks before their first American tour, health problems forced original drummer John Rutsey to leave the band. Rush quickly recruited fellow Toronto native Neil Peart [pronounced PEERT]. The band members averaged 22 years of age during that first tour. As the tour progressed, Neil, guitarist Alex Lifeson and bassist Geddy Lee began to write songs together. Soon, Peart was Rush's designated lyricist.

Two weeks after their first American tour ended, Rush was back in the studio with co-producer Terry Brown. Ten days later, *Fly By Night* was finished. This release hit the streets just one month after the recording sessions began! Although *Fly By Night* had been written on the road and recorded quickly, the music reflected the signature sound Rush developed during Neil's first six months in the band. Many of the drummer's lyrics reflected a strong interest in fantasy and science fiction. A few of these songs also represented Rush's first attempt at more complex song structuring. In addition, the trio's performance was much tighter and more focused.

As soon as this album was released, Rush returned to the road and opened for everybody from Kiss to Aerosmith. *Fly By Night* eventually charted at #113 in the U.S.

## Fly By Night - Side One

#1:  "**Anthem**," a group composition, was inspired by Ayn [pronounced EYE-on] Rand's book of the same name. Both the book and this song would ultimately lead to the concept behind Rush's fourth album, *2112*. When drummer Neil Peart auditioned with bassist/vocalist Geddy Lee and guitarist Alex Lifeson, the first tune on which they worked was the basic riff to "**Anthem**."

#2:  Geddy took sole writing credit for "**Best I Can**."

#3:  Alex and Neil co-wrote "**Beneath, Between And Behind**."

#4:  "**By-Tor And The Snow Dog**," another complex group composition, was divided into four parts.

**Note**: The song's title was inspired by a friend's dogs — one was snow white and the other regularly bit people.

    I: "**At The Tobes Of Hades**" referred to the classical name for the underworld (Hell).

    II: "**Across The Styx**" referred to the legendary river the dead crossed to reach Hades

    III: "**Of The Battle**"

    IV: "**Epilogue**"

## *Fly By Night - Side Two*

#1: "**Fly By Night**," credited to bassist/vocalist Geddy Lee and drummer Neil Peart, marked Neil's first attempt at lyrics. After Peart wrote this, he penned lyrics for almost every Rush song that followed.

#2: The trio composed "**Making Memories**" in a car during their first American tour.

#3: The lyrics to "**Rivendell**," co-written by Geddy and Neil, relate to the House of Elrod, the Elven King, which appeared in J.R.R. Tolkien's *Hobbit*, as well as his *Lord Of The Rings* trilogy.

#4: "**In The End**" was credited to Geddy and guitarist Alex Lifeson.

## Rush
### *Caress Of Steel* (25-23)

3rd LP, released 9/75. The band finished their *Fly By Night* tour on June 25, 1975. They began to record this album with producer Terry Brown on July 1, and finished it only 12 days later. The members averaged just 22 years of age. The band wrote and arranged all this material on the road, but had been given almost no time to perfect the new songs in the studio. The result was a raw and uneven album. When Rush realized how the abbreviated sessions compromised their efforts, the young band stumbled into a severe "sophomore slump."

As usual for the early Rush albums, drummer/lyricist Neil Peart shared writing credits variously with guitarist Alex Lifeson or bassist/vocalist Geddy Lee. Although the band had already begun to tour again by the time this album was released, *Caress Of Steel* became the group's only commercial bomb (it peaked at #148 on the U.S. charts). Consequently, the following tour (only half jokingly referred to as the *Down The Tubes Tour*) did not go well and the young band became very disillusioned.

## *Caress Of Steel - Side One*

#1:   "**Bastille Day**" is still considered by many to be one of the finest hard rock songs of the Seventies. The theme and title of this track were inspired by the fall of the Bastille prison in Paris on July 14, 1789.

#2:   "**I Think I'm Going Bald**"

#3:   "**Lakeside Park**" was written about a real place near drummer Neil Peart's home in Toronto.

#4:   The mood piece entitled "**The Necromancer**" was divided into three parts. The sound suffered because the band used only three instruments.
   I:  "**Into Darkness**"
   II:  "**Under The Shadow**"
   III:  "**Return Of The Prince**," actually released as a single, never charted.

## *Caress Of Steel - Side Two*

#1:   This entire side was comprised of the epic-length "**Fountain Of Lamneth**." Rush divided the piece into six sections and several of their musical approaches on this song helped establish Rush's definitive, unique sound .
   I:  "**In The Valley**"
   II:  "**Didacts And Narpets**"
   III:  "**No One At The Bridge**"
   IV:  "**Panacea**"
   V:  "**Bacchus Plateau**"
   VI:  "**The Fountain**"

# Rush
## *2112* (21-19)

4th LP, released 4/76 – six months after *Caress Of Steel*. Most of this music was written in soundchecks and developed on stage during Rush's six-month long *Caress Of Steel* tour. Immediately after the tour finished, the band recorded this new music under the direction of producer Terry Brown. Rush learned from their last album's failures that they needed more time in the studio to develop the arrangements, melodies and lyrical themes. The result on *2112* was a conscious effort to allow Rush's music to mature — regardless of record company pressure.

The first side of this album focused on songs written around a concept inspired by Ayn [pronounced EYE-on]Rand's book *Anthem*, which had strongly influenced lyricist/drummer Neil Peart [pronounced PEERT]. The second side of *2112* was filled with individual songs the band worked up on stage. Rush's old friend, Hugh Syme, contributed some synthesizer tracks that helped expand the trio's music even more — and he also created the album cover art!

In spite of pressure from the record company to rework this album into something more commercial, in its first month of release *2112* outsold the first three Rush albums combined. The highlight of the first phase of Rush's career, *2112* charted at #61 and eventually sold over a million copies. Rush followed this release with another successful tour, which generated their first live album. The Canadian trio proved they were ready to move substantially beyond basic riff-based hard rock.

## *2112 - Side One*

This entire side (presented as *2112*) was heavily influenced by Ayn Rand's book *Anthem*.

#1: "**Overture**" featured the synthesizer work of Hugh Syme, who also designed the album cover artwork.

#2: "**The Temples Of Syrinx**"

#3: "**Discovery**"

#4: "**Presentation**"

#5: "**Oracle: The Dream**" was never performed live.

#6: "**Soliloquy**"

#7: "**Grande Finale**"

## *2112 - Side Two*

#1:  "**A Passage To Bangkok**"

#2:  "**The Twilight Zone**"

#3:  "**Lessons**" was a rare solo effort from guitarist Alex Lifeson.

#4:  "**Tears**" featured extensive keyboard work by Hugh Syme.

#5:  "**Something For Nothing**," a powerful hard-rocking song, reflected the band's statement of purpose.

# UNCLE JOE'S RECORD GUIDE

## Rush
### *All The World's A Stage* (20-22-20-20/CD-15)

5th LP, released 9/76 – six months after *2112*. Artists often use live albums to establish a career perspective and complete a career phase by showcasing new arrangements of older material.

This album proved to be the synthesis of the first phase of Rush's career – a retrospective on the group who became the biggest-drawing Canadian band in history, an accomplishment achieved with virtually no radio airplay.

At the end of the *2112* tour, vocalist/bassist Geddy Lee, guitarist Alex Lifeson and drummer/lyricist Neil Peart were all 23 years old. They recorded these songs – with minimal overdubs – on June 11, 12 and 13, 1976, at Massey Hall, in their hometown of Toronto.

*All The World's A Stage* was Rush's first album to chart in the American Top 40. This release provided an excellent showcase of the group's strongest material from the first phase of their career. It eventually sold over a million copies.

** **Special Note**: Due to time restrictions, the compact disc version of this album contained one less song than the vinyl and tape versions. However, the CD did track straight through without interruption between the songs.

# HARD ROCK - Rush

## *All The World's A Stage - Side One*

#1:  "**Bastille Day**"

#2:  "**Anthem**"

#3:  "**Fly By Night**," backed with "**In The Mood**," charted at #88 in January 1977.

#4:  "**In The Mood**"

#5:  "**Something For Nothing**"

## *All The World's A Stage - Side Two*

#1:  "**Lakeside Park**"

#2:  "**2112**"
    I:  "**Overture**"
    II:  "**The Temples Of Syrinx**"
    III:  "**Presentation**"
    IV:  "**Soliloquy**"
    V:  "**Grande Finale**"

## *All The World's A Stage - Side Three*

#1: "**By-Tor And The Snow Dog**"

#2: "**In The End**"

## *All The World's A Stage - Side Four*

#1: "**Working Man/Finding My Way**"

#2: "**What You're Doing**," omitted from the compact disc version of this album, was later included in 1990's *Chronicles* compilation.

## Rush
### *A Farewell To Kings* (18-21)

6th LP, released 9/77 – a year-and-a-half after their last studio album, *2112*. Similar to ZZ Top and Aerosmith, Rush toured non-stop throughout the mid-Seventies, allowing themselves very little time to relax and reflect before writing new material. In April and May 1977, while on the road with the *2112* tour, the group used their off-days to work hard in preproduction of this material. When the tour ended on May 21, Rush took 10 days off before traveling to Europe for the first time. After playing several sold-out European gigs (when punk music was supposedly at its peak), Rush entered Dave Edmunds' studio in the Welsh countryside. The recording sessions with producer Terry Brown took place during the last three weeks of June 1977. The result was *A Farewell To Kings*, the beginning of a new, more progressive phase in Rush's career.

Rush's first extended time away from their native Canada and their families resulted in severe homesickness, added to the exhaustion caused by their grueling tour schedule. The isolation the band felt recording this album in a foreign country compelled bassist/vocalist Geddy Lee, guitarist Alex Lifeson (both 24 years old) and 25-year-old drummer Neil Peart to concentrate their efforts and define their musical vision. They expanded their instrumental approach, by using keyboards and more intricate arrangements to better spotlight their virtuosity. Lyrically, Rush continued to use the same fantasy/science fiction literary themes of the previous four years. Instrumentally, the trio's performance advanced a quantum leap as they attempted to add more textures to their music.

When Rush returned to the U.S. they received their biggest reception to date. As the band toured through July 1978, *A Farewell To Kings* ultimately charted at #33 and was certified Gold (500,000 sold). Within a couple of years, it eventually sold over a million.

## *A Farewell To Kings - Side One*

#1: "**A Farewell To Kings**" was composed during the recording sessions in Wales.

#2: "**Xanadu**" was the first song worked up for this album. The lyrics were inspired by a Coleridge poem about mythological visions of paradise.

## *A Farewell To Kings - Side Two*

#1: "**Closer To The Heart**," one of the first numbers the trio wrote for this project, was the working title for the album through the recording sessions. "**Closer To The Heart**" charted at #76 in December 1977.

#2: "**Cinderella Man**" was developed during Rush's recording sessions in Wales. This song featured a rare lyrical contribution from bassist/vocalist Geddy Lee.

#3: "**Madrigal**"

#4: "**Cygnus X-1**" ended with the hero plunging into a black hole, a story line that would continue on their next album. Most of this song had been worked up while Rush was touring.

**Note**: Cygnus is a constellation between Lyra and Pegasus in the Milky Way.

## Rush
### *Archives*

Released 4/78. A specially packaged re-issue of Rush's first three albums, this release was timed to correspond with the band's newly found public recognition. The triple album package of *Archives* has become a collector's favorite. For details on this compilation's discography, please refer to Rush's first three albums in this *UNCLE JOE'S RECORD GUIDE*.

## Rush
### *Hemispheres* (18-18)

7th LP, released 10/29/78 — just as Van Halen finished their highly successful first world tour. Flush with the artistic and commercial success of *A Farewell To Kings* — the first album in which Rush explored a new, more progressive musical direction — the trio decided to make their next album even more progressive. But, when the success of *A Farewell To Kings* yielded more headline concert dates, the exhausted Canadians had even less time to work on new material.

The lyrical concept for this album was based on Adam Smith's *Powers Of The Mind*, a book that deals with the respective strengths of the brain's two hemispheres. Because Rush's intense tour schedule on the road did not allow for serious song development, all of this material was composed in the studio. Returning to Dave Edmunds' Welsh facilities where they made *A Farewell To Kings*, Rush recorded *Hemispheres* during their longest sessions to date (two-and-a-half months). That extended time in the studio adversely altered both the band's perspective on their music and the edge of their performances. Any artist's lyrics can become sermonizing and esoteric, and their music self-indulgent, when they lack the feedback of a live audience. By not performing any part of these songs in concert, Rush experienced exactly those problems during the lengthy recording sessions with producer Terry Brown.

*Hemispheres*, which charted at #47 and was certified Gold (500,000 sold), was Rush's last studio album that failed to make the U.S. Top 10 and sell at least a million copies. Critics and many fans viewed it as an over-extension of the trio's abilities (later the band would agree with that assessment). Ultimately, *Hemispheres* convinced Rush they had to find a different method to record their complex material.

After a successful eight-month world tour, Rush finally took their first vacation. In that time off, the trio re-evaluated their musical direction and personal goals.

## *Hemispheres - Side One*

This entire side was devoted to the further adventures of "**Cygnus X-1**," a song and character that first appeared on Rush's previous album, *A Farewell To Kings*.

#1: "**Cygnus X-1 Book II, Hemispheres**"
    I: "**Prelude**"
    II: "**Apollo *Bringer Of Wisdom***"
    III: "**Dionysus *Bringer Of Love***"
    IV: "**Armageddon *The Battle Of Heart And Mind***"
    V: "**Cygnus *Bringer Of Balance***"
    VI: "**The Sphere *A Kind Of Dream***"

## *Hemispheres - Side Two*

#1: "**Circumstances**"

#2: "**The Trees**" became a favorite with Rush's longtime fans.

#3: "**La Villa Strangiato**," an instrumental divided into 12 parts, was subtitled "**An Exercise In Self-Indulgence**" — which summed up most of this album. However, this piece developed into an impressive workout in Rush's live show. The band recorded this song in one take, but spent more time reworking it than they had spent recording the entire *Fly By Night* album.

## Rush
### *Permanent Waves* (18-18)

8th LP, released 1/1/80. This album marked the successful realization of Rush's second musical phase. Following the exhausting *Hemispheres* tour, the band took their first vacation in seven years. After each re-evaluated their individual goals, the 26-year-old musicians regrouped at a farmhouse near Ontario, Canada, to spend July and early August 1979 working up their tightest, sharpest music yet. As usual, guitarist Alex Lifeson and bassist Geddy Lee composed the music, and drummer Neil Peart [pronounced PEERT] wrote the lyrics. For the first time, Neil's lyrics focused on real subjects, such as people and technology, instead of science fiction. This change in songwriting and arranging proved to be an important new direction for the band. In the years since, each member has identified this as one of their most important transitional albums.

In late Summer 1979 Rush performed a short series of gigs to polish their new material in front of an audience. This change of procedure was calculated to prevent the problems that sapped the energy of the *Hemispheres* sessions. The band then spent September and October 1979 recording in Quebec's Le Studio with longtime co-producer Terry Brown.

*Permanent Waves* garnered Rush their first serious radio airplay, which immensely helped record sales. With the band's typical touring intensity, the five-month *Permanent Waves* world tour resulted in Rush's long-overdue international breakthrough. The Canadian trio originally planned to release a live album with material recorded near the end of this tour, but they were on a creative roll. Instead they began to use soundchecks to develop new ideas. When the tour ended, several new songs had been fully demoed. The trio was ready to record their new material in the studio. This excellent rock & roll album not only sold over a million copies, it hit #4 in America and #3 in Britain — Rush's highest charting album to date.

## *Permanent Waves - Side One*

#1: "**The Spirit Of Radio**," Rush's first bona fide hit single, was one of the first two numbers written and recorded for this album. The song was inspired by Toronto's CFNY — the first radio station that ever played Rush. "**The Spirit Of Radio**" hit #55 on the U.S. charts in March 1980.

#2: "**Free Will**" was the other of the first two songs written and recorded for this album.

#3: "**Jacob's Ladder**" used Biblical imagery to describe the search for inspiration.

## *Permanent Waves - Side Two*

#1:  "**Entre' Nous**" was inspired, in part, by Rush's concert audiences.

#2:  "**Different Strings**" featured a grand piano performance from album cover artist Hugh Syme, and lyrics by Geddy Lee.

#3:  "**Natural Science**" was put together after the rest of the album was finished. The song was comprised of several bits that had been conceived for a much longer, extended piece.

## Rush
### *Moving Pictures* (20-21)

9th LP, released 2/28/81. Rush originally planned to release a live album after the *Permanent Waves* world tour, but when several new songs took form during the soundchecks, the band returned to their remote Canadian farm to finish work on their ideas. Drummer Neil Peart [pronounced PEERT] found lyrical inspiration in the group's experiences of travel, dislocation and increasing fame. Delving into these subjects, he discovered a theme that seemed universal to all. Meanwhile, bassist/vocalist Geddy Lee and guitarist Alex Lifeson composed the band's sharpest music yet. After they recorded demos of five songs, Rush performed a two-week mini-tour during mid-September 1980 to further work out song arrangements. In early October they returned to Quebec's Le Studio with longtime co-producer Terry Brown. The sessions were Rush's smoothest to date; *Moving Pictures* was finished in just 10 weeks. The trio decided to scale back their tour to maintain their health and sanity, although when this album was released, the six-month *Moving Pictures* world tour was already on the road.

Geddy and Alex were both 27 years old, and Neil was 28 when they released *Moving Pictures*. Just as the Who failed to realize how good *Who's Next* was, and Pink Floyd didn't know *The Dark Side Of The Moon* was a rock & roll landmark, Rush weren't aware they had just recorded one of the best hard rock albums ever. The Canadian trio's biggest artistic and commercial success, *Moving Pictures* reached #3 in the States (their highest charting album to date) and sold over four million copies. With a new lyrical focus and musical sense of purpose, Rush created one of the finest hard rock albums of all time.

## *Moving Pictures - Side One*

#1:  "**Tom Sawyer**" was co-written by Pye DuBois (the lyricist for the Canadian band Max Webster). Pye gave his old friend Neil Peart a work-in-progress called "Louis The Warrior." The lyrical take on an "every man" type character was a major inspiration to Rush's drummer/lyricist, and he developed the story line even further. Before it was recorded, "**Tom Sawyer**" significantly evolved on stage. It became Rush's signature tune and one of the biggest rock & roll songs of 1981. It also charted at #44 in August of that year.

#2:  The second song completed for this album, "**Red Barchetta**" was inspired by Richard Foster's science fiction story "A Nice Morning Drive." This version was recorded in one take.
**Note**: A Maseratti Barchetta was considered to be the fastest production car of the early Seventies.

#3:  The title "**YYZ**" was taken from the code on tags marking luggage bound for Toronto International Airport (Rush's home base). The song evolved during soundcheck jams on the *Permanent Waves* tour.
**Note**: The beginning percussion in the song spelled out "**YYZ**" in Morse code!

#4:  A very insightful song about fame, "**Limelight**" was almost fully developed at soundchecks and on stage before it was recorded. Neil's lyrical inspiration was the "universal truth of finding what you wanted so bad is different once you get it." Alex has pinpointed this guitar solo as one of his two favorites in all of Rush's catalog. "**Limelight**" reached #55 on the U.S. singles charts in May 1981.

## *Moving Pictures - Side Two*

#1:  "**The Camera Eye**," the first song worked up for this album, was partially inspired by the writings of the early 20th century American novelist John Dos Passos.

#2:  Keyboardist Hugh Syme was brought in to add overdubs on "**Witch Hunt**," which was listed as the last part of a trilogy called "**Fear**." The first two sections of that trilogy appeared on the next two studio albums which were released over the next three years — talk about a long work-in-progress! A lot of work went into this piece.

**Note**: The crowd sounds at the beginning of the song were the band and crew milling about in the cold just outside Le Studio.

#3:  "**Vital Signs**," the last song completed for the album, was written as the recording sessions drew to an end. Years after the band had dropped this song from their set list in the mid-Eighties, they re-added it during the last three weeks of 1992's *Roll The Bones* tour. That experience proved so enjoyable, "**Vital Signs**" was included in the entire *Counterparts* tour in 1994.

## Rush
### *Exit... Stage Left* (20-19[15, CD]-19-21)

10th LP (second live), released 11/7/81. Recorded on their 1980 *Permanent Waves* and 1981 *Moving Pictures* tours, this album provided updates on material from the second phase of Rush's career. The music on the second side of this album came from the band's 1980 English concerts. The other three album sides contained material recorded in Canada several months later. As usual, Terry Brown shared the production credits.

Recorded live over two separate tours, *Exit... Stage Left* contained very few overdubs and many outstanding performances. Yet, rather than rest on their musical laurels, Rush started work on their next studio album while this Top 10 charting, million-selling effort was being mixed!

** **Special Note**: Just like *All The World's A Stage*, the compact disc version of this album contained one less song than the vinyl or tape versions, due to time restrictions. However, the CD tracked straight through without interruption between the songs.

## *Exit... Stage Left - Side One*

#1:   "**The Spirit Of Radio**"

#2:   "**Red Barchetta**"

#3:   "**YYZ**"

## *Exit... Stage Left - Side Two*

This side was recorded in England months before the balance of the album.

#1:   "**A Passage To Bangkok**" was omitted from the compact disc version of this album, but later included in the 1990 *Chronicles* collection.

#2:   "**Closer To The Heart**" featured spontaneous backing vocals from the Glasgow audience. This track was released as a single, with "**The Trees**" as a B-side, in December 1981. It reached #69 in the States.

#3:   "**Beneath, Between And Behind**"

#4:   "**Jacob's Ladder**"

# HARD ROCK - Rush

## Exit... Stage Left - Side Three

#1: "**Broon's Bane**" was titled with typical Rush humor — Broon was the band's pet name for producer Terry Brown. This previously unrecorded workout was an in-concert work-in-progress.

#2: "**The Trees**"

#3: "**Xanadu**"

## Exit... Stage Left - Side Four

#1: "**Free Will**"

#2: "**Tom Sawyer**" was released as single, with "**A Passage To Bangkok**" as the B-side, in October 1981.

#3: "**La Villa Strangiato**"

## Rush
*Signals* (22-21)

11th LP, released 9/25/82 – a year-and-a-half after their last studio album, *Moving Pictures*. In a radical change of procedure for the band, all three members individually worked on material for this album before officially starting to record it. The band (who averaged 29 years of age) finished one complete song in the studio and recorded some basic tracks for others, while they simultaneously mixed their live venture, *Exit... Stage Left*. Late in March 1982, when they had four songs almost complete, the band briefly toured to further develop their new, more synthesizer-driven songs on stage. In mid-April 1982 when guitarist Alex Lifeson, bassist/vocalist Geddy Lee and drummer/lyricist Neil Peart finally entered Le Studio, they faced three months of intense recording. The finished *Signals* album marked the tenth and final time Rush worked with co-producer Terry Brown.

These songs' lyrics dealt with growing up in the suburban society of the Eighties. Musically Rush developed some of their most intricate material to date, and emphasized keyboards and synthesizers more than they had in the past. Another, almost unnoticed stylistic change had also taken place. Rather than specific songs that conformed to a preconceived concept, the individual members of Rush developed several virtuoso workouts that dealt with a common theme. Pleased with the results, they would use that technique on their next several albums.

# HARD ROCK - Rush

After a holiday break, Rush's sold-out *Signals* World tour was extended into a nine-month run. This million-selling, Top 10 charting album effectively kicked off the third phase of Rush's career. It has aged very well.

## *Signals - Side One*

#1: "**Subdivisions**," the first song completed for this album, was written and recorded before the band finished their live effort, *Exit... Stage Left*.

#2: A portion of "**The Analog Kid**" was worked up before the band finished *Exit... Stage Left*. The band reprised this song during the last three weeks of their 1992 *Roll The Bones* tour. They enjoyed playing it live so much that they incorporated it into their entire *Counterparts* tour in 1994.

#3: "**Chemistry**," developed from a soundcheck jam on the 1981 *Moving Pictures* tour, marked the first time all three members of Rush collaborated on a set of lyrics.

#4: "**Digital Man**" was another song the band started working on before the release of *Exit... Stage Left*.

## *Signals - Side Two*

#1:  "**The Weapon**" was listed as the second part of an extended work entitled "**Fear**," which was spread out over three albums — part III, "**Witch Hunt**" appeared on the previous *Moving Pictures* album, and part I, "**The Enemy Within**" would be released on the forthcoming *Grace Under Pressure* album.

#2:  After the rest of the album was finished, "**New World Man**" was written and recorded in one day under the working title "Project 3:57," in reference to its length. In Fall 1982, "**New World Man**" hit #21 and became Rush's first (and only) American Top 40 hit. The B-side was a live version of "**Vital Signs**," recorded during the *Moving Pictures* tour.

#3:  Parts of "**Losing It**" were recorded before the release of *Exit... Stage Left*. Violinist Ben Mink (of the Canadian band FM) played the lead track in this final version.

#4:  "**Countdown**" was inspired when the band saw the inaugural launch of the space shuttle Columbia.
     **Note**: The bleacher section from which they watched the shuttle launch from was called Red Sector A. That name would come into play on Rush's next album.

## Rush
### *Grace Under Pressure* (20-20)

12th LP, released 4/12/84 – a year-and-a-half after *Signals* and two months after Van Halen's *1984*. The three members of Rush realized the manner in which they wrote and recorded the *Signals* album marked the beginning of a new, third phase in their career. So, after a decade of work with co-producer Terry Brown, the band decided to try a different approach in the studio. Following the *Signals* tour, the trio first spoke with producer Steve Lillywhite (who worked with U2 and Peter Gabriel) and then with Rupert Hine (who worked with the Fixx). With both Englishmen unavailable for several months, Rush regrouped in August 1983 to consider their options, and work up new songs at their farm just outside of Ontario, Canada. As the pre-production preceded, bassist/vocalist Geddy Lee and guitarist Alex Lifeson to composed more guitar-oriented, less keyboard-emphasized music, as drummer Neil Peart [pronounced PEERT] again worked mainly on lyrics. As the basic melodies and structure of four different songs came together, Neil hit upon a lyrical breakthrough: the somber nature of the daily news and feelings of introspection within the band led to the song **"Distant Early Warning**." On the surface, the song was written about a missile crossing the radar installations the United States had strung across Canada's Arctic region to warn of a Russian nuclear attack (the Distant Early Warning line, also called the DEW line). However, a twist of lyrical duality also referred to a person's fears of encounters in the real world. That duality set the tone for the rest of this album.

# UNCLE JOE'S RECORD GUIDE

In mid-September, a few weeks into the writing sessions, the band worked on arrangements of the new material during five sold-out concerts at New York's Radio City Music Hall. Immediately afterward they auditioned several more prospective producers. Their choice was Peter Henderson (who also worked with Supertramp). With all the important elements in place, Rush hit the studio between November 1983 and March 1984 — one of their longest recording sessions ever. The album's title, *Grace Under Pressure*, was as much a comment on the evolution of the album as a statement of purpose for the material.

Rush's fifth consecutive Top 10 charting, million-selling effort, *Grace Under Pressure* is considered to be one their of finest albums. But the band (who averaged 30 years of age) later said the creative pressure during the sessions tempted thoughts of a break-up!

The seven-month *Grace Under Pressure* world tour was launched in May 1984 and included the band's first trip to Japan. At the tour's end, most of the intra-group tensions had been relieved. After their holiday, Rush was again ready to test their creativity.

## *Grace Under Pressure - Side One*

#1: "**Distant Early Warning**" was inspired by the Distant Early Warning line (also called the DEW line) of radar installations the U.S. placed across northern Canada to provide an early warning of Russian attacks. This was the first song completed for the album, and set the tone for all that followed.

#2: "**Afterimage**" was inspired by the group's reflection following the death of Robbie Whelan, a close friend who was killed in an automobile accident near Le Studio where Rush was recording. The band also dedicated the album to Robbie.

#3: "**Red Sector A**," one of the first songs worked up for this album, was played live at Rush's September 1983 Radio City Music Hall concerts before the recording began. Although the lyrics mention a death camp-type prison, the song was not directly influenced by the experiences of bassist Geddy Lee's parents in a Nazi death camp.

**Note**: "Red Sector A" was the name of the bleacher section from which Rush watched the launch of the space shuttle Columbia in 1981.

#4: "**The Enemy Within**" was listed as the first part of a three song trilogy entitled "**Fear**." Each of the last two parts of the trilogy had appeared on two previous Rush albums — part II, "**The Weapon**" on *Signals*; and part III, "**Witch Hunt**" on *Moving Pictures*. Nothing like working backwards!

## *Grace Under Pressure - Side Two*

#1: "**The Body Electric**" became one of Rush's outstanding live numbers and was, in fact, performed live at New York's Radio City Music Hall in September 1983 before anything on this album was recorded. The song was somewhat inspired by Ray Bradbury's classic sci-fi novel *Sing The Body Electric*. The B-side of the non -charting May 1984 single release of "**The Body Electric**" was "**The Analog Kid**" from the *Signals* album.

#2: "**Kid Gloves**," one of the first songs written for this album, was also performed in concert before it was recorded.

#3: "**Red Lenses**" was based on Neil Peart's complex drum part.

#4: "**Between The Wheels**" was another of the first songs Rush worked up and played live before this album was recorded.

## Rush
### *Power Windows* (22-23)

13th LP, released 10/26/85. Following the *Grace Under Pressure* recording sessions and tour, Rush longed for more experimentation. The trio began preproduction in February 1985 in the same Ontario farmhouse they had been using for years. Drummer Neil Peart worked on lyrics while bassist/vocalist Geddy Lee and guitarist Alex Lifeson rearranged melodies and riffs lifted from soundcheck jams, as well as other experimentations each had worked up in their home studios. Four songs and most of a fifth were written before Rush played a few concerts in early April. Three more songs were finished before the band joined their new producer, Peter Collins, at the 1,000-year-old Manor Studios complex in England. But even with so much material written and arranged, the Canadian band took longer to finish this album than any other before it. The recording sessions stretched from April through August 1985, first in England and then in Montserrat, where *Power Windows* was finished. Andy Richards (of the Strawbs and Frankie Goes To Hollywood) joined Rush in England for synthesizer overdubs. Later, a 30-piece string section and a 25-member choir were also brought in, then more synthesizer work was done. The resulting material continued the musical and thematic experimentation begun with the *Grace Under Pressure* sessions, and included expanding the individual member's performances. However, the effect of spending so much time in recording studios (especially the British studios) convinced

Rush to approach their next recording project in a completely different manner.

Still struggling to conquer the new computer technology necessary to reproduce their most complex music to date, the 32-year-old members of Rush began their 13th American tour in December 1985. Three months later, with the bugs finally worked out, they began to record shows for a possible live album. However, when the tour ended in late May 1986, they decided to hold off that release .

Like all of the material from the third phase of Rush's career, *Power Windows* was not a run-of-the-mill, shallow hard rock album. It could be enjoyed for its musical and technical excellence, as well as the depth of its lyrics, which dealt with various mutations of power. *Power Windows* became Rush's sixth consecutive Top 10 charting, million-selling album.

# HARD ROCK - Rush

## *Power Windows - Side One*

#1: "**The Big Money**" was one of the first songs written for this album. With "**Territories**" as the B-side, it charted at #45 in December 1985.

#2: "**Grand Designs**" was completed early in preproduction, just after "**Middletown Dreams**."

#3: "**Manhattan Project**," inspired by the research that produced the first atomic bomb, was the last song the band finished.

#4: "**Marathon**" was another of the first songs written during the first week of preparation for this album. This tune became a concert highlight.

## *Power Windows - Side Two*

#1: "**Territories**" was one of the last numbers the band completed for this album.

#2: "**Middletown Dreams**," the fourth song the trio finished for this album, was completed during their second week of preproduction.

#3: Neil Peart was writing this as a ballad when Geddy Lee transformed Neil's lyrics into "**Emotion Detector**."

#4: "**Mystic Rhythms**" was another of the first songs written and recorded for this album. Because the intricacies of this song intrigued them, the group reprised this number on their 1994 *Counterparts* tour.

# UNCLE JOE'S RECORD GUIDE

## Rush
### *Hold Your Fire* (25-25)

14th LP, released 9/19/87 – two years after *Power Windows*. Rush gathered in late September 1986 to begin preproduction on this album with Peter Collins (who also produced *Power Windows*). During these afternoon sessions, guitarist Alex Lifeson and bassist/vocalist Geddy Lee developed melodies and riffs from tapes of jams done at soundchecks during the *Power Windows* tour. Drummer Neil Peart worked on lyrics written around the thematic concepts of time and instinct. In the evenings, the band worked together in the rehearsal room. Two changes in the writing process marked a departure from Rush's usual procedure. Geddy entered all of his keyboard parts and melody ideas into a computer to help him better organize the arrangements, and the band passed on any live gigs to test and develop the songs in front of an audience. By mid-December, when Rush averaged 35 years of age, they had 10 new songs to record.

Because they had found the recording procedure for the *Power Windows* album more arduous than necessary, Rush decided on yet another change of pace. They approached this album in a more leisurely manner, and, during the first four months of 1987, used different studios in Canada, England, France and Montserrat for each phase of the recording. Rush spent three weeks recording basic tracks at Oxford's Manor mansion studio complex. Before leaving England, they overdubbed with keyboardist Andy Richards at the Ridge Farm studios (Bad Company's old haunt). Traveling to Montserrat for more overdubs, they returned to Toronto to record vocals, and then to Paris for the final mixing. For the first time, another artist sang on one of Rush's songs — Aimee Mann (of 'Til Tuesday) traded lead vocals with Geddy on "**Time Stand Still**." Rush said they had more fun recording this album than any other in the previous 19 years. Their enthusiasm definitely showed in their performances.

The lyrics for this album addressed the themes of time and instincts or primal responses to life. Musically, the band pushed their arrangements and production skills further than ever. They produced each song to its fullest potential, with little forethought to live performance. The unforeseen result of this change was a far more keyboard-oriented sound than ever before. *Hold Your Fire* charted at #13 and sold over a million copies. The following tour was one of Rush's best.

## *Hold Your Fire - Side One*

#1:  "**Force Ten**," written and recorded during the last two days of sessions, was finished well after the rest of the album. Rush's old friend Pye DuBois received a co-writing credit for his lyrical contribution. The sound of a real jackhammer was used in the rhythm track. Rush used "**Force Ten**" as their opening number on their next three tours.

#2:  "**Time Stand Still**" featured Aimee Mann (of 'Til Tuesday) on backing vocals, the first time anyone outside the band made a vocal contribution to a Rush album. This was the first song written and recorded for this album. Its personal tone set the lyrical mood for everything the band subsequently recorded for this album. In October 1987 "**Time Stand Still**" was released as a single, with "**Force Ten**" as the B-side.

#3:  "**Open Secrets**" featured lyrics co-written by bassist/vocalist Geddy Lee and drummer Neil Peart.

#4:  "**Second Nature**" was the second song the band completed for this project.

#5:  "**Prime Mover**"

## *Hold Your Fire - Side Two*

#1: "**Lock And Key**"

#2: "**Mission**" featured lyrics co-written by bassist/vocalist Geddy Lee and drummer Neil Peart. Alex Lifeson has identified this guitar solo as one of his favorites on any Rush album.

#3: Geddy and Neil also co-wrote lyrics for "**Turn The Page**," one of the first songs completed for this album.

#4: "**Tai Shan**" was inspired by Neil's climb up the sacred Chinese mountain of the same name.

#5: "**High Water**" was another of the first songs the trio composed for this album.

# UNCLE JOE'S RECORD GUIDE

## Rush
### *A Show Of Hands* (19-16-20-21)

15th LP (third live effort), released 1/21/89. Artists often use live albums to wrap up a portion of their career or to satisfy contractual obligations. With all three members averaging 36 year of age and playing near peak level, Rush effectively used this release to sum up the third phase of their career. Of the 14 tracks, 12 were updated arrangements of songs from their previous four albums. Most of this self-produced effort was recorded during Rush's 1988 *Hold Your Fire* tour, primarily shows in New Orleans, San Diego and Phoenix on the final American leg of their tour, and one later show in Birmingham, England. In addition, two tracks were included from the 1986 *Power Windows* tour.

Most amazing was that bassist/keyboardist/vocalist Geddy Lee, drummer Neil Peart and guitarist Alex Lifeson produced all of this music live on stage. Unfortunately, the album's commercial impact was blunted when artwork delays postponed this release until after Christmas. *A Show Of Hands* eventually peaked at #21 on the charts.

\*\* **Special Notes**: The working title for this project was *Presto*.

This album was dedicated to the memory of Sam Charters (Screvato), one of the band's long-time crew members.

# HARD ROCK - Rush

## *A Show Of Hands - Side One*

This side was recorded in Birmingham, England in 1988.

#1: "**Intro (Stooges Music)**" was the theme music from the Three Stooges.

#2: "**The Big Money**"

#3: "**Subdivisions**"

#4: "**Marathon**"

## *A Show Of Hands - Side Two*

This side was recorded during the American leg of Rush's 1988 *Hold Your Fire* tour.

#1: "**Turn The Page**" was recorded in New Orleans.

#2: This version of "**Manhattan Project**" was taken from a Phoenix concert.

#3: "**Mission**" was recorded at Rush's San Diego appearance.

# UNCLE JOE'S RECORD GUIDE

## *A Show Of Hands - Side Three*

#1:  "**Distant Early Warning**" was recorded in Birmingham, England during the 1988 *Hold Your Fire* tour.

#2:  "**Mystic Rhythms**" had been recorded at the Meadowlands in New Jersey during the 1986 *Power Windows* tour.

#3:  "**Witch Hunt**," the second oldest song on this release, had first appeared on the *Permanent Waves* album. This track was recorded in 1986 at the Meadowlands.

#4:  "**The Rhythm Method**" included Neil Peart's drum solo and was recorded in 1988 in Birmingham, England.

## *A Show Of Hands - Side Four*

The first track on this side was recorded in Phoenix, and the rest in Birmingham, England, during the 1988 *Hold Your Fire* tour.

#1:  "**Force Ten**"

#2:  "**Time Stand Still**"

#3:  "**Red Sector A**"

#4:  "**Closer To The Heart**" was the oldest song included on this album (it had first appeared on *A Farewell To Kings*).

## Rush
### *Presto* (30-23)

16th LP, released 11/25/89 — two years after *Hold Your Fire*. Rush took a six-month vacation after they finished work on their *Show Of Hands* live album and video. During that time off, they officially changed record companies, relaxed with their families and reevaluated the band's goals.

In Winter 1988, the trio regrouped in a farm house near Toronto. As usual, guitarist Alex Lifeson and bassist/vocalist Geddy Lee, both 36 years old, developed the melodies and riffs. Meanwhile, 37-year-old drummer Neil Peart [pronounced PEERT] worked on lyrics loosely written around a theme of actively responding to life rather than passively reflecting upon it. As the trio continued to develop the basic songs, they delved deeper into the intricacies of the arrangements and began a shift towards reemphasizing power chords.

When producer Peter Collins (who worked on *Power Windows* and *Hold Your Fire*) ran into scheduling conflicts, the band recruited Rupert Hine (whose credits included the Fixx and Tina Turner). Determined to have fun while making each song's arrangement and recording the best possible, Rush recorded from June through August 1989 at Le Studio in Quebec and at McClear Place in Toronto. While *Presto* contained some of the most insightful material of their career, and the following tour saw them performing to their most diverse audience, the band felt the album didn't quite hit the mark — that the production didn't quite serve the songs the way they had envisioned. For that reason, even though *Presto* charted at #16 and sold over a million copies, the group was ready for another change.

** **Special Note**: *Presto* had been the working title for the live album *A Show Of Hands*.

## *Presto - Side One*

#1:    Drummer/lyricist Neil Peart later observed that " **Show Don't Tell**" was the direct antecedent to " **Roll The Bones**," the title track of Rush's next album.

#2:    " **Chain Lightning**"

#3:    " **The Pass**," seen by some as an update on Rush's "**Tom Sawyer**" character from the *Moving Pictures* album, became a favorite with American rock radio programmers.

#4:    " **War Paint**"

#5:    " **Scars**"

#6:    Many fans saw the lyrics for " **Presto**" as more of a personal statement than usual for Rush.

## *Presto - Side Two*

#1:  "**Superconductor**" became a strong concert piece.

#2:  "**Anagram (For Mongo)**" featured clever wordplay based on anagrams (Mongo was a reference to a favorite character in Mel Brooks' movie *Blazing Saddles*).

#3:  "**Red Tide**" effectively conveyed a sense of urgency for the welfare of the world's environment and the mental well-being of its inhabitants.

#4:  "**Hand Over Fist**"

#5:  "**Available Light**"

## Rush
### *Chronicles* (29-22-25)(27-21-21)

17th LP, released 9/15/90. This excellent compilation —
assembled by the band to satisfy contractual obligations to
their record company — included music from Rush's first
16 albums and 15 years together. To their fans dismay, no
previously unreleased material was included, although all of
Rush's older material was digitally remastered. *Chronicles*
peaked at #51 on the charts and sold over a million copies.

### *Chronicles - CD One, Side One*

#1:  "**Finding My Way**," co-written by guitarist Alex Lifeson and
bassist/vocalist Geddy Lee, was a last-minute addition to their
1974 debut album.

#2:  "**Working Man**," another Lifeson/Lee composition from their
first album, became one of the best-known and most
requested songs from Rush's early work.

#3:  "**Fly By Night**," credited to bassist/vocalist Geddy Lee and
drummer Neil Peart, marked Neil's first attempt at lyrics. After
Peart wrote this, he penned lyrics for almost every Rush song
that followed.

#4:  "**Anthem**," a group composition from 1975's *Fly By Night*
album, was inspired by Ayn [pronounced EYE-on] Rand's book
of the same name. Both the book and this song led to the
concept behind Rush's fourth album, *2112*. When drummer

Neil Peart auditioned with bassist/vocalist Geddy Lee and guitarist Alex Lifeson, the first jam they worked up was the basic riff to "**Anthem**."

#5: The group composition "**Bastille Day**," from *Caress Of Steel*, is still considered by many to be one of the finest hard rock songs of the Seventies.

#6: "**Lakeside Park**," also from 1975's *Caress Of Steel*, was written about a real place near Neil Peart's home in Toronto.

## *Chronicles - CD One, Side Two*

#1: "**Overture**," from 1976's *2112*, featured the synthesizer work of Hugh Syme (who also did that album's cover art).

#2: "**The Temples Of Syrinx**" was also taken from *2112*.

#3: This version of "**What You're Doing**" was taken from Rush's 1976 live album *All The World's A Stage*.

#4: "**A Farewell To Kings**" was composed during the recording sessions for the album of the same name.

#5: "**Closer To The Heart**" was the working title and one of the first numbers written for the *Farewell To Kings* album. This song charted at #76 in December 1977.

## *Chronicles - CD One, Side Three*

#1: "**The Trees**" was taken from 1978's *Hemispheres* album.

#2: "**La Villa Strangiato**," an instrumental divided into 12 parts, was subtitled "**An Exercise In Self-Indulgence**" — which summed up much of the *Hemispheres* album. This piece, however, developed into a very impressive workout in Rush's live show. The band recorded this in one take, but spent more time working on the piece than they had spent recording the entire *Fly By Night* album.

#3: "**The Spirit Of Radio**" (Rush's first bona fide hit single) was one of the first two songs written and recorded for *Permanent Waves*. The song was inspired by Toronto's CFNY — the first radio station to ever play Rush. "**The Spirit Of Radio**" hit #55 on the U.S. charts in March 1980.

#4: "**Free Will**" was the other of the first two songs written and recorded for *Permanent Waves*.

## *Chronicles - CD Two, Side One*

#1: "**Tom Sawyer**," from 1981's breakthrough *Moving Pictures* album, was co-written by Pye DuBois (the lyricist for the Canadian band Max Webster). Pye gave his old friend drummer Neil Peart a work-in-progress called "Louis The Warrior," and the lyrical take on an "every man" type character inspired Rush's drummer/lyricist. Before it was recorded, "**Tom Sawyer**" underwent quite an evolution on stage. It became Rush's signature tune and one of the biggest rock & roll songs of 1981 — charting at #44 in August of that year.

#2: The second song completed for *Moving Pictures*, "**Red Barchetta**" was inspired by Richard Foster's short story "A Nice Morning Drive." The band recorded this version in just one take.

#3: "**Limelight**" was almost fully developed at soundchecks and on stage before it was recorded for *Moving Pictures*. It reached #55 on the U.S. singles charts in May 1981.

#4: "**A Passage To Bangkok**" was recorded live in England and released on 1981's *Exit... Stage* Left. It had been omitted from the CD version of that album.

#5: "**Subdivisions**," the first song completed for the *Signals* album, was written and recorded before the band finished their live effort, *Exit... Stage Left*.

#6: After the rest of the *Signals* album was finished, "**New World Man**" was written and recorded in one day under the working title "Project 3:57." In Fall 1982, "**New World Man**" hit #21 and became Rush's only American Top 40 hit.

## *Chronicles - CD Two, Side Two*

#1: "**Distant Early Warning**" was inspired by the Distant Early Warning (D.E.W.) line of radar installations America placed across northern Canada to provide an early warning of Russian attacks. This was the first song completed for the *Grace Under Pressure* album.

#2: "**Red Sector A**" was one of the first songs worked up for *Grace Under Pressure*. Although it lyrically spoke of a death camp, it was not directly influenced by the experiences of bassist/vocalist Geddy Lee's parents in a Nazi death camp.

   **Note**: Red Sector A was also the name of the bleacher section from which Rush watched the launch of the space shuttle Columbia in 1981.

# UNCLE JOE'S RECORD GUIDE

#3: "**The Big Money**" was one of the first songs written for the *Power Windows* album. With "**Territories**" as the B-side, it charted at #45 in December 1985.

#4: "**Manhattan Project**," inspired by the research that produced the first atomic bomb, was the last song the band finished for *Power Windows*.

## *Chronicles - CD Two, Side Three*

#1: "**Force Ten**" was written and recorded during the last two days of the *Hold Your Fire* sessions — after the rest of the album was finished. Rush's old friend Pye DuBois received a co-writing credit for his lyrical contribution. The sound of a jackhammer was used in the rhythm track.

#2: "**Time Stand Still**" featured Aimee Mann (of 'Til Tuesday) on backing vocals — the first time anyone outside Rush had made a vocal contribution to a Rush album. This was the first song written and recorded for *Hold Your Fire*. Its personal tone lyrically set the mood for everything else. This was released as a single, with "**Force Ten**" as the B-side, in October 1987.

#3: "**Mystic Rhythms**," taken here from the *A Show Of Hands* album, had been recorded at the Meadowlands in New Jersey during the 1986 *Power Windows* tour.

#4: "**Presto**" was the excellent title track from Rush's 1989 album.

## Rush
### *Roll The Bones* (25-25)

18th LP, released 9/14/91 — two years after *Presto* and two months after Van Halen's *For Unlawful Carnal Knowledge*. Rush had worked together for 17 years when they re-grouped in late Fall 1990 to begin to work on new material for this album. They quickly discovered that their working relationship had cycled in another creative direction. The band's renewed excitement about this project and their interaction resulted in a quick transition from 10 weeks of preproduction to actual recording — Rush found themselves in the studio months sooner than planned! Recording between February and May 1991 at Le Studio in Quebec and McClear Place in Toronto, *Roll The Bones* was finished faster than any Rush album in years. Rupert Hine (who worked on *Presto*) again shared production credits with the band, and contributed some keyboard and backing vocal performances.

Lyrically, 39-year-old drummer Neil Peart [pronounced PEERT] explored the axiom "If there's a chance, you might as well take it." Musically, 38-year-old vocalist Geddy Lee decided to emphasize his bass playing, rather than keyboards and synthesizers. Thirty-eight-year-old Alex Lifeson began to play more rock-oriented guitar. The trio's new musical and lyrical direction resulted in some of Rush's most satisfying compositions. The combination worked; *Roll The Bones* charted at #3, sold over a million copies, and became Rush's most commercially successful album in years. The ensuing tour was one of their best.

## *Roll The Bones - Side One*

#1: "**Dreamline**," the first song released from this album, contained the lyrical observation "We're only at home when we're on the run." The group used "**Dreamline**" as their opening number on 1994's *Counterparts* tour.

#2: "**Bravado**" reflected drummer Neil Peart's feeling that "One needs to pursue ambitions where the odds against success are great." Alex Lifeson's guitar solo was recorded as a demo in his home studio.

#3: "**Roll The Bones**" featured several of the key lyrics to the theme of this album. A quotation from John Barth's *The Tidewater Tales*, "We will pay the price, but we will not count the cost," led Neil to lyrically conclude that "We're only immortal for a limited time." He later observed that this song was a direct descendent of "**Show Don't Tell**" from the *Presto* album. The title of this song, "**Roll The Bones**," came from the science fiction story *Gonna Roll The Bones* by Fritz Lieber. Neil kept that title in his notes for 15 years before this song was written and recorded. The main guitar solo was lifted from one of Alex Lifeson's home demos.

**Note**: The rap section in the middle of this song was done as a lark — the voice was that of bassist/vocalist Geddy subjected to some intense processing.

#4: "**Face Up**" was one of the first songs completed for this project. The lyric "Turn it up, or turn that wild card down" provided lyrical inspiration for the rest of the album.

#5: For years Rush had discussed whether they should record an instrumental track. When bassist Geddy Lee and guitarist Alex Lifeson came up with the riff to "**What's My Thing (Part IV** of the **"Gangster Of Boats" Trilogy)**," Neil Peart insisted they record this song as a true instrumental.

## *Roll The Bones - Side Two*

#1: "**The Big Wheel**"

#2: "**Heresy**" featured percussion inspired by drummers Neil Peart heard in Togo, South Africa when he toured that continent. His reaction to the native drumming was similar to that experienced by both Peter Gabriel and Paul Simon, but because Neil was himself a percussionist, his musical expression was far more primal.

#3: "**Ghost Of A Chance**" evolved from a discussion about the odds against finding a love that will last. A rare Rush song based on the personal experiences of the band, "**Ghost Of A Chance**" developed from their reflections on the uniqueness of the trio's longtime marriages. In an interesting instrumental twist, Alex's guitar solo was recorded for the second demo the band made of this song; Neil's drum part in this final version was based on Alex's solo.

**Note**: One of the members wryly commented that the group thought this song should be a massive hit, but they were resigned that it wouldn't because Rush was "just too weird for the general public's taste!"

#4: "**Neurotica**"

#5: "**You Bet Your Life**"

## Rush
### *Counterparts* (25-25)

19th LP, released 10/31/93 – about two years after *Roll The Bones*. By the end of Rush's *Roll The Bones* tour in Summer 1992, the trio concluded that the live performances of their new material sounded better than their recent albums. To correct that problem, Rush first reconnected with Peter Collins (who produced *Power Windows* and *Hold Your Fire*, and had since worked with Queensryche). Then, as they approached their 40th birthdays in Fall 1992, Rush once again gathered to begin preproduction at the Chalet Studio near their homes in Toronto.

Musically, Rush returned to their most basic power trio approach: Alex Lifeson worked on a harder-edged guitar sound; Geddy Lee de-emphasized his keyboard work and concentrated more on his bass; and lyrically, drummer Neil Peart explored the differences of perception between genders, and delved into psychologist Carl Jung's reflections on heroism and role models. In rehearsals, the band soon discovered that the unifying lyrical theme of this album had become centered around the duality of life experiences. As their songwriting progressed, the group effected a significant stylistic change. For the first time in their career, Rush concentrated on writing melodies to match or serve their lyrics. (Prior to *Counterparts*, Rush songs were usually instrumental workouts with lyrics added on.)

Rush recorded *Counterparts* between April and June 1993 at Le Studio in Quebec and McClear Place in Toronto, where they had made their two previous albums. With Peter Collins' return as producer, the trio found their trademark sound undergoing a major transformation. The very sound of Rush's instruments — and the resulting sonic impact — was greatly affected by Peter's new engineer, Kevin "Caveman" Shirley. Just as U2's engineer "Flood" helped that Irish band radically alter their sound on *Achtung Baby*, Shirley helped Rush record their music as far from their normal method as possible. At Kevin's urging, Alex sharpened his guitar sound and Geddy recorded some of his bass parts through an old, blown-up amplifier — just to change the sound. Through it all, Neil's lyrical approach became even more personal. While most of *Counterparts* lyrically dealt with relationships, it contained songs about love — but no love songs. Although Rush identified these songs as the hardest to sequence of any of their albums, the result was Rush's freshest music to date.

*Counterparts* became the biggest commercial success of Rush's third phase. It charted at #2 (their highest yet), sold over a million copies and was supported with another sold-out North American tour. The group later described the *Counterparts* tour as one of their most enjoyable. They played selections that spanned their entire career, and their performances were both playful and, perhaps, their most acute to date.

## *Counterparts - Side One*

#1:  "**Animate**"

#2:  The first song released from the album, "**Stick It Out**" featured the most radical sound Rush ever recorded. That searing sound, and the lyrical treatment of an "actions speak louder than words" theme, set the tone for the rest of *Counterparts*.

#3:  "**Cut To The Chase**"

#4:  One of the first songs completed for the album, "**Nobody's Hero**" was inspired by several friends who had strongly influenced the band. Neil Peart's initial inspiration came in part when he learned about the death of an old friend. Carl Jung's writings concerning heroism and role models also heavily influenced this song.

#5:  The lyrics for "**Between The Sun And Moon**" resulted from a collaboration between drummer Neil Peart and the group's old friend Pye DuBois.

## *Counterparts - Side Two*

#1:  "**Alien Shore**"

#2:  "**The Speed Of Love**" was one of the first songs completed for this album.

#3:  The band loved to refer to "**Double Agent**" as an exercise in self-indulgence. It was the last song they wrote and recorded for this project.

#4:  At drummer/lyricist Neil Peart's insistence, "**Leave That Thing Alone**" was arranged from two different jams the trio had worked up. Neil has said this finished version of the song — credited to guitarist Alex Lifeson and bassist/vocalist Geddy Lee — is his favorite Rush instrumental of all time.

#5:  One of Rush's most personal songs, "**Cold Fire**" transformed through several different renditions before this version came together at the end of the recording sessions. In an unusual lyrical twist, the strongest character in this song was not the narrator — nor was it the male in the relationship.

#6:  "**Everyday Glory**" was a lyrical reflection on several people whom the band knew.

# UNCLE JOE'S RECORD GUIDE

# Van Halen

**Van Halen**
1978

Alex Van Halen,
Eddie Van Halen,
David Lee Roth,
Michael Anthony

# Van Halen

Van Halen's remarkable story tracks a good-time cover band playing parties in backyards around Pasadena, California, evolving into one of the most successful and influential American hard rock bands ever. Eddie and Alex Van Halen emigrated from Holland in 1968. They first met up with David Lee Roth and Michael Anthony in the early Seventies as they competed in local bands. Getting together in 1974 as a power trio with a lead vocalist (the same format as Led Zeppelin and the Who), they began by covering songs of first generation hard rockers, especially Aerosmith and ZZ Top. At Roth's urging, they switched their name from Mammoth to Van Halen. By December 1975, they were playing complete sets of original material. They also became adept at setting up and promoting their own successful gigs at large halls like the Pasadena Civic Auditorium. Van Halen worked the Southern California bar, club, school dance and party circuit for almost three years before they were signed by a major record label in May 1977. From that point, they rarely faltered in the pursuit of their muse.

Van Halen's unique sound emerged in a way that emphasized less their virtuosity and more the image of four guys having a good time. In time, each band member would develop his musical talents to new limits. Every Van Halen album sold at least two millions copies and, after their debut, each charted in the Top 10 — an accomplishment that put them in the same rarefied league as Led Zeppelin and the Beatles. Even though they achieved that heady level of success early, the boys in Van Halen never avoided an interview or a chance to have fun.

When Van Halen changed lead vocalists — a move that killed almost every other band that tried it — the resulting music became their most artistically and commercially successful! With each successive album, their musicality and lyrical sophistication grew, but never at the expense of Van Halen and their fans having more fun than any one! With album sales in excess of 65 million and a concert show that improves with each tour, Van Halen is one of the most successful and influential American hard rock bands ever. Their story is that of every young musician's dreams.

# HARD ROCK - Van Halen

## Van Halen Birth Dates

**Michael Anthony** - June 20, 1954

**Sammy Hagar** - October 13, 1948

**David Lee Roth** - October 10, 1953

**Alex Van Halen** - May 8, 1953

**Eddie Van Halen** - January 26, 1955

# UNCLE JOE'S RECORD GUIDE

## Van Halen
### *Van Halen* (16-20)

1st LP, released 12/77. Guitarist Eddie Van Halen, drummer Alex Van Halen and vocalist David Lee Roth recruited bassist Michael Anthony from another Pasadena band to form Van Halen in Summer 1974. In late 1976, the group took a break from the Southern California bar and party circuit to record a four-song demo with Gene Simmons (of Kiss) in New York. Even though Kiss's management signed Billy Squier's band, Piper, instead of Van Halen, the Halen crew returned from their first in-studio experience with a new-found confidence in their talent.

Their big break finally came in a May 1977 Monday night showcase at the famous Starwood club in Hollywood. By chance, Warner Brothers record company president Mo Ostin and producer Ted Templeman (who worked with the Doobie Brothers and Montrose) saw Van Halen at the club. They signed the band within days.

Templeman soon took the band into Sunset Sound studios in Hollywood. In only 18 days, they recorded 27 songs from their live set and one new track, which was written during the sessions. The group recorded all their songs live in the studio, and only overdubbed instrumental tracks on three numbers. Even more extraordinary was the performance of Edward Van Halen, who was just 22 at the time (the rest of the band members averaged 23 years of age). Eddie's highly innovative guitar work won him the first of five consecutive Best Rock

# HARD ROCK - Van Halen

Guitarist of the Year awards from the readers of *Guitar Player* magazine.

Van Halen generated more energy on their debut album than any group in years. The band's standout performance was augmented by Templeman's ace production.

Although it took three months to enter the charts, this album reached #19 in the States and #34 in Britain (an amazing performance for an American band). Following the release of the album, Van Halen spent almost 11 months touring the world — first as an opening act for Journey and Black Sabbath, and then as the headline act. All of that hard work resulted in sales of more than six million copies of the Pasadena band's debut!

Van Halen's first album impacted audiences and musicians the same way Led Zeppelin's first album and Deep Purple's *Machine Head* had years earlier. Hundreds of Van Halen copy bands and imitation David Lee Roths immediately appeared. Every young guitarist was hailed as the new Eddie Van Halen. The Second Generation of Hard Rock had arrived!

## *Van Halen - Side One*

#1: "**Running With The Devil**" contained one of the few instrumental overdubs on this album. Eddie Van Halen recorded his guitar solo after the rest of the track was finished. This song charted at #84 in June 1978.

#2: "**Eruption**" was one of Eddie's warm-up exercises. This version was one of several he recorded.

#3: "**You Really Got Me**" was a Ray Davies tune, originally recorded by his band, the Kinks. Van Halen performed their raucous cover of this song throughout their club days. It became their first single and charted at #36 in February 1978. When guitarist Dave Davies (of the Kinks) heard about Van Halen's version of "**You Really Got Me**," he was amused that Van Halen was another "brothers" band. (Dave and his brother Ray never got along as well as the Van Halens.)

#4: Eddie wrote the melody of "**Ain't Talking 'Bout Love**" as a send-up of a punk rock tune. He only used two chords.

#5: "**I'm The One**"

# HARD ROCK - Van Halen

## *Van Halen - Side Two*

#1: "**Jamie's Cryin'**" was written and recorded live in the studio during the band's quick three-week session. One of Edward Van Halen's guitar parts was overdubbed.

#2: "**Atomic Punk**"

#3: "**Feel Your Love Tonight**"

#4: "**Little Dreamer**"

#5: "**Ice Cream Man**," a blues song Elmore James co-wrote with John Brim, contained the last of three overdubs Eddie recorded for this album. Vocalist David Lee Roth regularly performed an acoustic version of this song at the Ice House in the band's hometown of Pasadena, California. Legend has it that when Eddie and Alex Van Halen heard David's performance of this, they decided to ask him to join their group.

#6: "**On Fire**" was the song that Van Halen used to open their concerts during their first world tour.

# UNCLE JOE'S RECORD GUIDE

## Van Halen
### *Van Halen II* (16-17)

2nd LP, released 4/17/79 — at the same time as Bad Company's *Desolation Angels*. Van Halen started their first tour in early 1978 by opening various concerts for Journey, Montrose and Black Sabbath. By Fall 1978, they were the headline act on an expanded, worldwide tour.

In January 1979, barely 48 hours after the end of their first tour, the boys went back into Sunset Sound in Hollywood. Just 10 days later, this album was finished. Ted Templeman (who had also worked with the Doobie Brothers and Little Feat) produced the project and Donn Landee engineered the music, which was recorded live in the studio. Once again instrumental overdubs were limited to just three songs. Except for one number written in the studio, they had performed the rest of these tunes on stage — some for a number of years.

The quartet of vocalist David Lee Roth, guitarist Eddie Van Halen, drummer Alex Van Halen and bassist Michael Anthony averaged just 24 years of age when they recorded *Van Halen II*. This album sold over five million copies, charted at #6 in the U.S. and #23 in Britain. Eddie also garnered his second *Guitar Player* magazine Best Rock Guitarist Of the Year award.

** **Special Note**: David Lee Roth was wearing a plaster cast on his foot in the photo on the inside album cover. He had actually broken the foot while making the giant leap pictured on the back cover!

# HARD ROCK - Van Halen

Van Halen gave credit on this album to the first hotel they trashed — the Sheraton Inn in Madison, Wisconsin. When they stayed there again on their second tour, the hotel's management placed the group in a wing that was being remodeled. Instead of more destruction, not a piece of furniture was moved!

## *Van Halen II - Side One*

#1: "**You're No Good**" was an old standard written by Clint Ballard, Jr. and covered by many mainstream artists over the years. Since their early club days, Van Halen had played what they thought was Linda Ronstadt's version of the song, but since they only  her record on the radio (and never really listened to it!), their rendition came out radically different.

#2: "**Dance The Night Away**" became Van Halen's first Top 15 hit in July 1979. The song came together one afternoon in the studio as the boys were standing in a circle humming at each other. Eddie purposely skipped playing a guitar solo in the final version. Later, Van Halen realized Cream had recorded a song by the same title on their second album *Disraeli Gears*. (Ironically, Eric Clapton and Ginger Baker of Cream were Eddie and Alex's first musical heroes.)

#3: If you listen closely, you can hear applause at the end of Edward's guitar solo in "**Somebody Get Me A Doctor**." The band was recording live in the studio, as usual, when Eddie's performance tore everyone there apart. The song had been written about the same time as "**Running With The Devil**."

#4: "**Bottoms Up!**" was an old standard from Van Halen's bar and party sets. They used this song as their encore throughout their first world tour.

#5: "**Outta Love Again**" had been written by Eddie, Alex and David in early 1973, just before Michael Anthony was brought into the band.

## *Van Halen II - Side Two*

#1: Van Halen used "**Light Up The Sky**" to start every show on their second tour. Guitarist Eddie Van Halen wrote the basic melody right after the band finished recording their debut album. The final arrangement came together during the sessions for *Van Halen II*.

#2: "**Spanish Fly**" featured some mighty fine acoustic guitar work from Edward.

#3: "**D.O.A.**" had been written during the band's early days on the Southern California bar and party circuit.

#4: The introduction to "**Women In Love...**" contained one of the few guitar overdubs used on this album.

#5: "**Beautiful Girls**" charted at #84 in October 1979.

## Van Halen
### *Women And Children First* (19-15)

3rd LP, released 4/12/80. Often a band that fills their first two albums with songs developed over the years for their stage show runs out of material for their third album, but not Van Halen. Their creative juices were flowing! *Women And Children First* marked the first time Van Halen completely filled an album with original songs, and their performance was absolutely top notch. Vocalist David Lee Roth, bassist Michael Anthony, drummer Alex and guitarist Eddie Van Halen averaged 26 years of age when they made this album at Sunset Sound in Hollywood. The band recorded these songs live with few instrumental overdubs. Ted Templeman again supervised the production and Donn Landee engineered the quick sessions.

Although *Women And Children First* did not yield a hit single, the album charted at #6 in the States and #15 in England. It also became Van Halen's third consecutive multi-platinum release. The band's on-stage performances (and off-stage partying) were as intense as their performance in the studio. Van Halen's *Women And Children First* tour was more successful than their first two. Six years after their formation, and just three years after their first album, Van Halen was on top of the world!

**\*\*Special Note**: In late 1980, Eddie received his third consecutive Best Rock Guitarist of the Year award from the readers of *Guitar Player* magazine.

## *Women And Children First - Side One*

#1:  "**And The Cradle Will Rock...**" featured a small electric piano part blasting through guitarist Eddie Van Halen's huge stack of Marshall amplifiers — the first time a keyboard was used on a Van Halen album. "**And The Cradle Will Rock...**" charted at #55 in June 1980 as the band toured America.

#2:  "**Everybody Wants Some!!**" proved to be a great song live.

#3:  "**Fools**"

#4:  "**Romeo Delight**"

# HARD ROCK - Van Halen

## *Women And Children First - Side Two*

#1: **"Tora! Tora!"** espoused Van Halen's attitude towards touring. The song's title and lyrics were inspired by the toast and battle cry of Japanese Kamikaze pilots in World War II.

#2: **"Loss Of Control"** had been written in 1976 as a commentary on the first wave of punk rock to reach America.

#3: **"Take Your Whiskey Home"** featured a killer riff.

#4: **"Could This Be Magic?"** was an excellent acoustic guitar and vocal harmony workout. As the band prepared to record this song, producer Ted Templeman suggested a slightly different sound for the chorus. Nicolette Larson was brought in from the next studio, where she was working on a solo album, and supplied the only female backing vocal ever heard on a Van Halen record. Her harmony can be best heard on the line "Could this be magic?" right after the guitar solo — a small, but unique contribution.

#5: **"In A Simple Rhyme"**

## Van Halen
*Fair Warning* (18-15)

4th LP, released 5/23/81. *Fair Warning* marked the second time Van Halen filled an entire album with their own compositions, but this release differed from the group's first three efforts in that Eddie Van Halen actually went back into the studio after the main sessions to overdub more guitar parts. Normally, the boys practiced for a few weeks, then recorded the songs as quickly as possible. A change was also taking place within the group. Van Halen had been on tour for three years straight, with only short breaks to record. Rock & roll tours become a grind for all musicians and crews, but the pace at which Van Halen lived would strain anyone's personal strength. On the verge of exhaustion, the group's collective creativity grew thin. None-the-less, the *Fair Warning* sessions at Sunset Sound in Hollywood went well. The production was again handled by Ted Templeman (who also worked with Sammy Hagar and Eric Clapton) and the sound was again engineered by Donn Landee.

*Fair Warning* became Van Halen's fourth consecutive million-selling album and charted at #5 stateside — the highest of any Van Halen to date. Still, it did not yield a single hit, only reached #49 in Britain, and sold far fewer copies than each of their first three releases. The tour that followed was bigger and more profitable than ever, but friction was growing between vocalist David Lee Roth, bassist Michael Anthony, guitarist Eddie Van Halen and drummer Alex Van Halen. Averaging 27 years of age, the members of Van Halen had

# HARD ROCK - Van Halen

begun to show the strains of success and their intense life on the road.

## *Fair Warning - Side One*

#1: "**Mean Street**"

#2: "**Dirty Movies**"

#3: "**Sinner's Swing!**"

#4: "**Hear About It Later**"

## *Fair Warning - Side Two*

#1: "**Unchained**" was a great workout.

#2: "**Push Comes To Shove**"

#3: "**So This Is Love?**"

#4: Guitarist Eddie Van Halen wrote "**Sunday Afternoon In The Park**" for actress Valerie Bertinelli, whom he married a month before this album was released.

#5: "**One Foot Out The Door**"

## Van Halen
### *Diver Down* (16-16)

5th LP, released 5/1/82. At the conclusion of the *Fair Warning* tour in December 1981, and after five years of constant roadwork, the members of Van Halen were scheduled to begin their first real vacations. At their manager's insistence (to ensure the band's continued commercial visibility), they recorded "**(Oh) Pretty Woman**" in a single day in early January 1982. Upon its release a month later, the single began to shoot up the charts and Van Halen's record company immediately wanted an album to capitalize on the unexpected success. With their vacation plans destroyed — and little new material prepared — Van Halen was quickly booked into the first available studio. Much to Eddie's chagrin, the band worked up a number of cover songs. In just 12 days, *Diver Down* was recorded live in the studio with very few overdubs. This album marked the first time the group recorded anywhere but Sunset Sound in Hollywood — Amigo Studio in Los Angeles was the only place available on such short notice. This also marked the first time they recorded one complete song at a time, instead of recording all the music, then all the vocals. Ted Templeman (who worked with the Doobie Brothers and Eric Clapton) again produced the music and Donn Landee did the engineering. Released a month after it was completed, *Diver Down* hit #3 in America and #36 in Britain and became Van Halen's most successful album thus far. Their fifth multi-platinum release, it sold over three million copies.

# HARD ROCK - Van Halen

In spite of their success, guitarist Edward Van Halen, drummer Alex Van Halen, bassist Michael Anthony and vocalist David Lee Roth were increasingly at odds. Along with some members' increasing substance abuse problems, intra-group friction continued to build during the immensely successful *Hide Your Sheep* world tour that followed this release. The tour kicked off at the first *US Festival* in San Bernardino, California, in September 3, 1982, and ended at the second *US Festival* on May 28, 1983. By then, a change in the Pasadena-based band was inevitable.

## *Diver Down - Side One*

#1: "**Where Have All The Good Times Gone**" was written by Ray Davies and originally recorded by his band, the Kinks.

#2: "**Hang 'Em High**"

#3: "**Cathedral**" featured a brilliant volume knob switching technique by guitarist Edward Van Halen. (That was not a synthesizer!) This was also one of the prettiest songs Van Halen had recorded in this phase of their career.

#4: "**Secrets**"

#5: Eddie went back into the studio and improvised "**Intruder**" when more music was required for the beginning of the "**(Oh) Pretty Woman**" video.

#6: This cover of the 1964 Roy Orbison classic "**(Oh) Pretty Woman**" became Van Halen's biggest hit single to date when it charted at #12 in April 1982 — a full month before this album was released. The group recorded the song in early January 1982 to ensure continued commercial visibility during their first vacation. Instead, when "**(Oh) Pretty Woman**" began to shoot up the charts, Van Halen's record company demanded an album to capitalize on the unexpected success. The band's vacation was over before it began.

# HARD ROCK - Van Halen

## *Diver Down - Side Two*

#1:  "**Dancing In The Street**," co-written by Marvin Gaye, was originally a hit for Martha & The Vandellas in 1964. Guitarist Eddie Van Halen intended this riff for an original song, but when producer Ted Templeman adapted it to this R&B classic, the boys decided to try it. "**Dancing In The Street**" charted at #38 in June 1982. Eddie later identified this as his least favorite Van Halen recording.

#2:  "**Little Guitars (intro.)**"

#3:  "**Little Guitars**" was a great song based on one of Eddie's workouts.

#4:  "**Big Bad Bill (Is Sweet William Now)**" was a vaudeville classic. At singer David Lee Roth's suggestion, the Van Halen brothers' dad, Jan Van Halen, played clarinet on this version.

#5:  "**The Full Bug**"

#6:  "**Happy Trails**," written by Dale Evans, was the theme song to the *Roy Rogers and Dale Evans* cowboy TV show of the Fifties and early Sixties. Van Halen first performed this song at their legendary 1976 Pasadena Civic Auditorium show — well before they had a record deal. For several years, the band continued to play this in concert as their next-to-last song.

# UNCLE JOE'S RECORD GUIDE

## Van Halen
*1984* (16-18)

6th LP, released 1/21/84 — a year-and-a-half after *Diver Down*. In Fall 1983, following several months of touring, intra-group hassles and arguments, the boys finally regrouped for a few weeks to rehearse new songs for this album. Averaging 30 years of age, guitarist Edward Van Halen, vocalist David Lee Roth, drummer Alex Van Halen and bassist Michael Anthony were at the peak of their skills, and near the pinnacle of their animosity. For the first time, the band recorded at guitarist Eddie Van Halen's home studio, which he called 5150. When the sessions finally began, the boys recorded quickly with few instrumental overdubs. As usual for the first part of Van Halen's career, Ted Templeman (who previously worked with Sammy Hagar and the Doobie Brothers) produced the album, while Donn Landee engineered the sound. More significantly, *1984* marked the first time Van Halen's members became personally involved in producing and mixing their music.

Throughout the *1984* sessions, the boys' musical techniques evolved. Alex Van Halen's drumming was more melodious than ever, and this album marked the first time Eddie's synthesizer played such a prominent role in so many songs. *1984* proved to be Van Halen's biggest, most successful album to date. As the band's tour ripped across the States, this album spent five weeks at #2 in America, hit #15 in Britain, and sold over three million copies in the first three months of its release. A major landmark gig in their *1984* world tour was the *Monsters Of Rock Festival* at Castle Donington in England.

336

# HARD ROCK - Van Halen

But all was not well within the group. Even though more than six million copies of *1984* were eventually sold, this was Van Halen's last album with David Lee Roth, who left in an acrimonious split in mid-1985.

## *1984 - Side One*

#1:   "**1984**" was guitarist Eddie Van Halen's improvised keyboard introduction to "**Jump**."

#2:   "**Jump**" was Van Halen's first #1 charting single and one of the biggest songs of the year. Lodged at #1 for five weeks in early 1984, it sold over three million copies. "**Jump**" was the first song Eddie worked up in his new 5150 studio, and, initially, the band was reluctant to record it because the song centered on a keyboard part, instead of a guitar riff.

#3:   When a critic accused vocalist David Lee Roth of writing about nothing more than sex, partying and cars, David realized that Van Halen had never done a song about cars. Roth wrote the lyrics to "**Panama**" to cover that oversight. The third single released from *1984*, it charted at #13 in late Summer 1984.

#4:   "**Top Jimmy**" was written about the leader of a legendary L.A. bar band, Top Jimmy & The Rhythm Pigs. In the early days Van Halen played many club dates with Jimmy.

#5:   "**Drop Dead Legs**"

## *1984 - Side Two*

#1:  "**Hot For Teacher**" spawned one of the funniest, most risqué videos seen on television up to that time. The fourth single released from 1984, it peaked at #56 in November 1984.

#2:  "**I'll Wait**" was co-written by the Van Halen band and former Doobie Brother Michael McDonald. (Van Halen's producer, Ted Templeman, also handled the Doobie Brothers.) As the second single released from this album, "**I'll Wait**" charted at #13 in May 1984.

#3:  "**Girl Gone Bad**"

#4:  The melody of "**House Of Pain**," one of the last songs recorded for this album, was originally written eight years earlier, during Van Halen's club and party days around Southern California. In fact, the band recorded a different version for the four-song demo they did with Gene Simmons of Kiss in late 1976.

## Van Halen
1995

Sammy Hagar, Eddie Van Halen
Michael Anthony, Alex Van Halen

# UNCLE JOE'S RECORD GUIDE

## Van Halen
### *5150* (23-21)

7th LP, released 4/5/86. Even though their *1984* album and tour were Van Halen's most successful to date, the band went through a change of management. Intra-band friction was at an all time high when the group began preproduction for this album. Much of the music was already written and the basic tracks recorded when 32-year-old vocalist David Lee Roth left to pursue a solo career in mid-1985. When Roth's acrimonious departure was final, the three remaining members saw an opportunity for a new start. Without a moment of hesitation, the band (who all averaged 31 years of age) invited 37-year-old vocalist Sammy Hagar to guitarist Eddie Van Halen's home studio. Sammy (who previously fronted Montrose and had his own successful solo career) immediately clicked on both a musical and personal level with Edward, drummer Alex Van Halen and bassist Michael Anthony. In fact, some of Sammy's vocals from that first jam session were used on this album. At the end of that first day, the new Van Halen was officially born.

The *5150* album was recorded at Eddie's home studio, which he called 5150. The band shared the production credits with Donn Landee (their long-time engineer) and Mick Jones (of Foreigner), who was brought in near the end of the sessions to help produce the vocals. Throughout the sessions, the group's focus improved in a way they had never imagined.

A great album, *5150* became Van Halen's first #1 charting release (it stayed at #1 for three straight weeks), hit #16 in England, sold over five million copies, and was Van Halen's seventh consecutive multi-million selling, Top 20 charting effort. That accomplishment put Van Halen in the same commercial league as Led Zeppelin. The following tour developed into a raging success.

** **Special Note**: 5150 is the police code for the handling of mentally incompetent or deranged people. It was Eddie's first choice for the name of his home studio, because he said it was a reflection of the people around him. Also, in Greek mythology, 5150 was the number of millenniums Zeus condemned Atlas to carry the earth on his shoulders, and this album cover portrayed Atlas being overcome by the weight of Van Halen — heavy stuff!

## *5150 - Side One*

#1: "**Good Enough**" was one of the first songs vocalist Sammy Hagar ever sang with Van Halen. After he heard the group run through the basic arrangement once, he wrote most of these lyrics and the basis for his vocal melodies on the spot. Some of that first performance appeared in the final version of the song.

#2: "**Why Can't This Be Love**," a catchy tune that garnered the band tons of radio airplay, became one of the most requested songs of Summer 1986. It charted at #3 and became Van Halen's second single to sell over a million copies.

#3: "**Get Up**"

#4: "**Dreams**" was the last song completed for the album. When Mick Jones came in to help with the vocal mixes, he and the boys put this song together in the studio in less than a day. Working that quickly and spontaneously was a new experience for Mick, who later used the technique to revitalize his band Foreigner. "**Dreams**" charted at #22 in July 1986. It became a favorite of Space Shuttle crews orbiting earth and fighter pilots in the Persian Gulf War.

#5:   "**Summer Nights**" was the first song the group rehearsed with Sammy. He astounded the other band members when he came up with most of these lyrics and the melody line after hearing the basic arrangement only once. At that point, Eddie, Alex and Michael knew they were onto something real special. This is considered by many to be one of the greatest Van Halen songs of all time.

## *5150 - Side Two*

#1:   "**Best Of Both Worlds**" became a concert highlight.

#2:   Guitarist Eddie Van Halen had written the basic melody for "**Love Walks In**" several years prior to recording it. The third single released from this album, "**Love Walks In**" charted at #22 in October 1986.

#3:   "**5150**" was a powerful guitar workout that came together in the studio.

#4:   "**Inside**" included some in-studio tomfoolery.

# HARD ROCK - Van Halen

## Van Halen
### *OU812* (23-24)(CD, 23-28)

8th LP, released 6/11/88 — just over two years after *5150*. Following the massive *5150* tour, 38-year-old vocalist Sammy Hagar was contractually required to record a final solo album. As a favor to his friend, guitarist Eddie Van Halen (who was 32 at the time) handled the production and the bass work on Sammy's album (Sammy did all of his own guitar work). As an even tighter writing unit after finishing Sammy's album, the two then joined 34-year-old drummer Alex Van Halen and 33-year-old bassist Michael Anthony for preproduction on a new Van Halen album in Fall 1987.

The recording sessions at Eddie's 5150 studios started in December 1987 and finished in March 1988. Reverting to the technique they used so successfully on their first several albums, Van Halen recorded most of these songs live in the studio with few instrumental overdubs. This was the only Van Halen album produced completely by the band and their longtime engineer, Don Landee. It also marked Sammy's first significant recorded contribution on rhythm guitar. (Hagar was an excellent guitarist in his own right, but he was so in awe of Eddie, that he refrained from even touching a guitar in the studio until the band recorded *OU812*.)

*OU812* became Van Halen's eighth consecutive Top 20 charting, multi-million selling release and their second #1 charting album. It stayed on top of the American charts for four weeks, while it hit #16 in Britain. *OU812* sold over four million copies worldwide. The boys followed this release with one of the biggest tours of 1988. Covering 20 dates, *Van Halen's Monsters Of Rock Tour*, featured themselves, the Scorpions, Dokken, Metallica and Kingdom Come. At the conclusion of *Van Halen's Monsters Of Rock Tour*, the Southern California band continued to headline their own world tour.

** **Special Notes**: Within a month after Van Halen's *5150* tour ended, Alex and Edward's father passed away. The band dedicated this album to his memory with the inscription "This one's for you, Pa."

  The album title itself sprung from the punch line of a bad joke — "Oh, you ate one too!" Neither the joke nor the punch line appeared in any lyrics in the album. One of the titles considered for this album was *Balance*, which was later deemed more appropriate for their 1995 release.

# HARD ROCK - Van Halen

## *OU812 - Side One*

#1: "**Mine All Mine**" had first been worked up by Eddie Van Halen, Mike Anthony and Alex Van Halen on keyboards, bass and drums, respectively. Later, when the guitar tracks were dubbed, the band realized what an outstanding song they had. Sammy Hagar spent more time on these lyrics than on any others he had written in his entire career. To this day, Sammy identifies "**Mine All Mine**" as a personal favorite, and the group brought it back into their live set — with great success — during the 1995 *Balance* world tour.

#2: The first song written for this album, "**When It's Love**" also became the biggest hit single from *OU812* when it charted at #5 in August 1988.

#3: The band's desire to get back out on the concert trail inspired "**A.F.U. (Naturally Wired)**" (A.F.U. supposedly stands for "All Fired Up").

#4: Inspired by his surroundings, Sammy wrote the lyrics to "**Cabo Wabo**" while at his home in Cabo San Lucas. (The story goes that after too much tequila, one would develope a "Cabo Wobble.") Meanwhile, Eddie was independently writing tunes back at his 5150 studios. Recalling their early days on the club and party circuit around Pasadena, Edward remembered Van Halen regularly performing the Montrose song "Make It Last." With that in mind, and noting Hagar was Montrose's lead vocalist, Eddie wrote this riff with the feel of "Make It Last." When Sammy returned from Cabo, his lyrics and Eddie's riff fit together perfectly and "**Cabo Wabo**" was born.

## *OU812 - Side Two*

#1:  "**Source Of Infection**," recorded on the first take, featured a great drum workout by Alex Van Halen.

#2:  Guitarist Eddie Van Halen had developed "**Feels So Good**" on a keyboard instead of a guitar. The last single released from this album, "**Feels So Good**" hit #35 in March 1989.

#3:  While hanging out before the recording sessions began, Eddie and vocalist Sammy Hagar wrote "**Finish What Ya Started**" around 2AM one morning on the deck of Sammy's Malibu home. Later in the studio, someone in the band suggested working up a song with acoustic guitar and this country-flavored version of the tune evolved. The third single released from this album, "**Finish What Ya Started**" charted #13 in December 1988.

#4:  "**Black And Blue**" was the first song released from *OU812*. It charted at #34 and became a concert highlight.

#5:  "**Sucker In A 3 Piece**" was inspired by a business acquaintance of the group.

#6 (only on the cassette and CD): "**Apolitical Blues**" was a Lowell George song originally done by his band, Little Feat. Engineer Donn Landee had worked on the Little Feat albums and was consulted about the remix for compact disc. Sammy snatched Donn's copy of the test disc with this song on it, and took it back into the 5150 studio. The Halen boys played around with the song for a while, hung a few microphones and recorded this version live in one take. Sammy played rhythm guitar, and Edward's spontaneous guitar sound was so close to Lowell George's, it was spooky! (Eddie later overdubbed the piano part.)

## Van Halen
## *For Unlawful Carnal Knowledge* (27-27)

9th LP, released 6/30/91 – three years after *OU812*, and two months before Rush's *Roll The Bones*. Vocalist Sammy Hagar and guitarist Eddie Van Halen joined drummer Alex Van Halen and bassist Michael Anthony in Fall 1990 for preproduction on a new Van Halen album. In early 1991, the recording sessions began in earnest at Eddie's 5150 studios, with producer Andy Johns (who had worked with the Rolling Stones and Led Zeppelin, amongst other major groups).

This album contained the most complex music Van Halen had recorded. Although they still rocked hard, their new arrangements featured key and tempo changes far removed from basic three-chord rock & roll. Not only did Sammy's lyrics address real life subjects more than ever before, he also turned in some of the finest vocal performances of his career. Producer Andy Johns' methodical recording technique gave the band a chance to increase the focus on their individual performances. Most of the basic tracks were recorded live in the studio. As the recording project neared completion, Van Halen again brought in Ted Templeman (their original producer) to help record the vocals. The result was Van Halen's finest album to date.

*For Unlawful Carnal Knowledge* entered the U.S. charts at #1, and sold over three million copies. The following tour went so well that the band extended it twice, and decided to record portions of it for their first live album. To top it off, *For Unlawful Carnal Knowledge* won the 1991 Grammy Award for the *Best Hard Rock Performance With A Vocal*. Not only was Van Halen's performance on stage and in the studio better than ever, the members' personal interactions were at an all time high. They were having fun!

## *For Unlawful Carnal Knowledge - Side One*

#1: Eddie Van Halen created the opening sound on "**Poundcake**" by operating a cordless electric drill next to his guitar pick-ups. This was the first song released from the album.

#2: "**Judgement Day**"

#3: "**Spanked**"

#4: "**Runaround**" featured some great interplay between the band members, and a tremendous reprise of Alex Van Halen's drum part in the fade out.

#5: "**Pleasure Dome**"

# HARD ROCK - Van Halen

## *For Unlawful Carnal Knowledge - Side Two*

#1: "**In 'N' Out**"

#2: A great riff led to "**Man On A Mission**."

#3: The lyrics of "**The Dream Is Over**" took a lot of Van Halen fans by surprise.

#4: "**Right Now**" featured outstanding lyrics and interplay between the band members, which included guitarist Eddie Van Halen on keyboards. Eddie had first worked on the basics of this song before the band did the 1984 album. "**Right Now**" charted at #55 in March 1992, became an in-concert anthem and an award-winning video.

#5: Eddie wrote "**316**" for his son Wolfgang, who was born during the sessions for this album, on March 16, 1991. While Valerie was pregnant with Wolfie, Eddie regularly played this acoustic workout to her tummy.

#6: One of the great Van Halen songs, "**Top Of The World**" hit #27 in November 1991 and became a concert highlight.

# UNCLE JOE'S RECORD GUIDE

## Van Halen
### *Live: Right Here, Right Now* (37-38-34-36)

10th LP, released 3/6/93. The motivation for bands to release live albums is usually tied in with contractual obligations or a desire to capture definitive performances near the end of a career phase — but not for Van Halen. Their motivation to release their first live album stemmed from a strong desire to give their fans an alternative to poor quality bootleg recordings.

Guitarist Eddie Van Halen, vocalist Sammy Hagar, drummer Alex Van Halen and bassist Michael Anthony averaged 40 years of age when this was recorded near the end of their twice-extended, ultra-successful *For Unlawful Carnal Knowledge* world tour. After Eddie and Alex selected songs from various performances, they brought Andy Johns back to Eddie's 5150 studio to produce and mix the album. (Andy, who produced *For Unlawful Carnal Knowledge*, previously had worked with artists such as Led Zeppelin and the Rolling Stones.) Van Halen's 10th consecutive multi-platinum release, *Live: Right Here, Right Now* charted at #5 and sold over two million copies — an amazing feat for a double live album!

# HARD ROCK - Van Halen

## *Live: Right Here, Right Now - Side One*

#1:  "**Poundcake**"

#2:  "**Judgement Day**"

#3:  "**When It's Love**"

#4:  "**Spanked**"

#5:  "**Ain't Talking 'Bout Love**"

#6:  "**In 'N' Out**"

#7:  This version of "**Dreams**" charted at #111 in June 1993.

## *Live: Right Here, Right Now - Side Two*

#1:  "**Man On A Mission**"

#2:  "**Ultra Bass**" was bassist Michael Anthony's on stage workout.

#3:  "**Pleasure Dome/Drum Solo**" allowed drummer Alex Van Halen to stretch out his performance.

#4:  "**Panama**"

#5:  "**Love Walks In**"

#6:  "**Runaround**"

## *Live: Right Here, Right Now - Side Three*

#1:  "**Right Now**"

#2:  "**One Way To Rock**" gave the band a chance to acknowledge vocalist Sammy Hagar's solo career.

#3:  "**Why Can't This Be Love**"

#4:  Sammy preceded this acoustic workout of "**Give To Live**" with some typically glib interaction with the crowd.

#5:  "**Finish What Ya Started**"

#6:  "**Best Of Both Worlds**"

## *Live: Right Here, Right Now - Side Four*

#1:  "**316**" was guitarist Eddie Van Halen's tribute to his son Wolfgang. On the *For Unlawful Carnal Knowledge* tour, this song evolved into Edward's extended solo piece.

#2:  "**You Really Got Me/Cabo Wabo**"

#3:  This cover of the Who's "**Won't Get Fooled Again**" became a regular encore during the *For Unlawful Carnal Knowledge* tour. It also became one of the most-played songs on rock radio in early 1993.

#4:  "**Jump**"

#5:  "**Top Of The World**"

## Van Halen
*Balance* (CD, 31-22)(Cassette, 26-27)

11th LP, released 1/28/95 — three-and-a-half years after their
last studio album. Following their twice-extended *For
Unlawful Carnal Knowledge* world tour and the release of
their first live album, Van Halen's four members scheduled
some time off to relax and enjoy themselves. By the time
vocalist Sammy Hagar and bassist Michael Anthony rejoined
drummer Alex Van Halen and guitarist Eddie Van Halen in
early 1994, several events, including death and heartbreak,
had affected their personal lives. While discussing the
direction their music would take, the group chose Bruce
Fairbairn to handle the production job. Fairbairn proved
crucial to Van Halen's continued growth. Bruce, who had
worked extensively with Aerosmith since their *Permanent
Vacation* album, had also worked wonders producing
AC/DC and Motley Crue. A former musician himself, Fairbairn
brought a renewed sense of musicality and discipline to the
Van Halen sessions.

    The serious writing and recording sessions at Eddie's 5150
studios began in late May 1994. The band had demoed 20
songs in their initial rehearsals. As the recording sessions
proceeded, 14 arrangements were completed. The final
vocals were recorded at Fairbairn's Vancouver studios in late
August, and the final mixing took place at the Record Plant in
Los Angeles in September 1994. The result was Van Halen's
most guitar-oriented music in several years, some of Sammy's
finest vocal performances ever, and the band's most
rhythmically complex work to date. The songs also marked a

continuation of the more mature lyrical direction of *For Unlawful Carnal Knowledge*. The songs on *Balance* were not so much one-dimensional reflections on real life, as good, kick-ass Nineties hard rock that touched on a few, very personal themes. Lyrically, Van Halen surpassed Aerosmith and entered a territory where only Rush had tread before: an amazing transformation that the group carried into their live shows without the least bit of trouble.

The title of this album, as well the content of some of its lyrics, underwent an interesting evolution. Before beginning work on this project, their longtime friend and manager, Ed Leffler, succumbed to cancer. In his memory, Van Halen's first working title for this album was *The Club*, which is how the band referred to Ed's house (*Le Club Leffluer*). As the album approached completion, they began using the working title *The Seventh Seal*, taken from the album's opening song. During the final mixing, Van Halen decided to use a title that harkened back to the *OU812* sessions; they felt *Balance* was a better indication of their frame of mind and a more accurate reflection of their music and their lives.

*Balance* immediately charted at #1 upon its release and became Van Halen's 11th consecutive multi-million selling release. The sold out *Balance* world tour began in March 1995 and was scheduled to run for over a year.

** **Special Notes**: For the first time ever, a Van Halen song was completed during the recording sessions, but left off the album. Van Halen's first-ever, non-album B-side, was first released on the Japanese "**Don't Tell Me (What Love**

Can Do)" single, then on the worldwide release of "**Can't Stop Loving You**."

Also for the first time, the band decided to sequence their songs differently on the cassette version than on the compact disc version of the album.

## *Balance - Side One*

#1: "**The Seventh Seal**" was a working title track for this album before the final mixing was finished. The lyrics were inspired, in part, by Ingmar Bergman's film of the same name, which told of a knight playing chess with Death, and by a passage in the Book Of Revelations in the Old Testament. Vocalist Sammy Hagar described this song as a prayer to avoid Armageddon. The opening featured digitally sampled prayer chants of the Buddhist monks of Gyuto Tantric University. Eddie Van Halen created his monster guitar sound without any major effects devices — and he also refrained from playing a solo.

#2: "**Can't Stop Loving You**" was one of the last songs the group recorded for this album. In an unusual twist, Sammy wrote the lyrics from the perspective of his ex-wife. Partially because of the passion involved, this performance stands as one of Sammy's finest vocals ever.

The second song released from this album, "**Can't Stop Loving You**" was the only Van Halen single to ever feature a non-album B-side.

B-1: "**Crossing Over**" began as a demo titled "David's Tune" that Eddie wrote and recorded in 1983 for a friend who had committed suicide. Upon joining the band and hearing the demo, Sammy wanted to finish the song, but Ed declined. Years later, following the death of Ed Leffler and Sammy's father in 1993, Sammy wrote lyrics to further explore the theme of crossing over from one life into the next. Eddie finally gave his OK, and "**Crossing Over**" was finished. Still, some of the band felt the song was too personal, so it was kept off the album and appeared destined to become the only finished Van Halen outtake ever. Instead, the group was convinced to use the song as Van Halen's first-ever, non-album B-side — first on the Japanese single release of "**Don't Tell Me (What Love Can Do)**," and later as the B-side of the worldwide release of "**Can't Stop Loving You**."

#3: "**Don't Tell Me (What Love Can Do)**," the first song released from the album, was recorded live in the studio under the working title "What Love Can Do." The only overdub on this cruncher was a second guitar part in the chorus.

#4: "**Amsterdam**" referred to real places and situations in that wild Dutch city. The Van Halen brothers, who were born in The Netherlands, were at first a little surprised by Sammy's lyrical take on their "hometown."

#5: "**Big Fat Money**" opens with a bit of in-studio chatter and ends with the sound of a coin dropped on the 5150 control board.

#6: "**Strung Out**" was based on a 10-year-old tape of Eddie torturing Marvin Hamlish's grand piano with knives, spoons and forks. (Ed had rented Marvin's beach house and ended up spending a lot of money to have Marvin's prized piano refinished.)

#7 (on the CD): "**Not Enough**" was one of Van Halen's finest love songs ever. Sammy wrote the lyrics and melody for the verses. Later, he called Eddie and described what he had written. Eddie sat down and spontaneously played the piano part. As the band worked up the song, the piano was recorded inside Eddie and Valerie Bertinelli's home. For a unique tone, Eddie played his guitar through a rotating Leslie organ speaker — a technique first pioneered by the Beatles 28 years earlier. This song also featured Michael Anthony's first recorded workout on a fretless bass and some of Sammy's finest vocals.

## *Balance - Side Two*

Due to time constraints on the cassette version of this album, "**Not Enough**" was moved from the end of the first side to the second spot on this side. The balance of the tracks remained sequenced the same as on the compact disc.

#1:  "**Aftershock**," a great rocker, was written about a shaky relationship — not earthquakes.

#2 (on the cassette only):  "**Not Enough**"

#2:  "**Doin' Time**" was Alex Van Halen's workout. (When asked, he denied it was a solo, saying "It was just that no one else was playing with me.") Up until the last moment, the working title was "Drum Thing."

#3:  "**Baluchitherium**" was named after the biggest mammal ever to walk the earth — a rhinoceros-like beast from the Oligocene and Miocene epics. The name was chosen because of the "hugeness" of Edward's guitar sound. He had begun work on the riff during the *For Unlawful Carnal Knowledge* sessions. Early in the *Balance* sessions, and after working up variations of the song — including one that had vocals — the band recorded this under the working title "Heavy Groove." This song featured Michael Anthony playing a five-string bass and a rare vocal contribution from Eddie's dog Sherman.

#4: "**Take Me Back (Deja Vu)**" was recorded under the working title "Deja Vu." Lyrically, it was a follow up to "Swept Away" on Sammy's *VOA* solo album. In addition to some tasty acoustic guitar work and excellent vocals, this song featured the first extended use of a harmonica in a Van Halen song. Shortly after the *Balance* album was released, the band returned to the studio and remixed "**Take Me Back (Deja Vu)**." All subsequent versions of the album contained the remix.

#5: One of the longest songs Van Halen ever recorded, "**Feelin'**" featured some excellent lyrics, singing and musical changes. This song became a powerful, uplifting workout in concert.

# Glossary

# UNCLE JOE'S RECORD GUIDE

# Glossary

**Album** – although the term is often used in reference to vinyl phonograph recordings, an **album** is literally collection of things — be they songs or photographs. Vinyl phonograph records, cassette tapes and **compact discs** are the media on which albums are recorded. By refering to an **album** as a **CD** is the same semantic mistake as calling the **album** an **LP** — incorrect, but not the end of the world as we know it.

**Analog Recording** – until the mid-Eighties, **analog recording** was the only electronic method available for transferring voice or music onto tape or phonograph records. Skipping the technicalities, the **analog recording** process is similar to painting a line on a roadway: the line is only as smooth as the road's surface. No matter what, the line will always have the texture of that surface, just as an **analog recording** will always have the background noise and distortion inherent to the tape or phonograph record. **Digital recording** (a completely different technology) is like having that painted line suspended in the air, free of any background textures. **Digital recordings** have no tape or record noise, and no inherent distortion (you might want to see **Digital Recording** for a more objective definition).

**Artist** – a word that is used fast and loose in the music business, usually to describe performers.

**B-side** – the non-hit side of a single. Also see **flipside**.

**Basic Tracks** – the basic instrumentation of rock & roll is the rhythm section (drums and bass, and sometimes keyboards or guitar). Often those instruments will be recorded before anything else, and that initial recording is referred to as the **basic tracks** (see **Tracks** for more details). The **basic tracks** are sometimes finished on the first few takes to get a fresh, sharp feel to the music.

**Bootleg** – any recording not authorized by the **artist**. While the quality of **bootleg** recordings are usually dubious at best, the fact that the **artist** had no control over the release of their own music is odious. Because the **artist** receives no income from the project and **bootlegs** are illegal, just adds to the rip-off. Reasons enough for **UNCLE JOE'S RECORD GUIDES** not to deal with them.

# UNCLE JOE'S RECORD GUIDE

**Compact Disc** – a small acrylic disc embossed with a specially encoded **digital recording** (or digitally remastered recording). The encoded signal is deciphered with a laser beam, quite unlike the signal on a phonograph record that's deciphered by dragging a sharp diamond stylus through a plastic groove. While **compact discs** (or **CDs**) aren't indestructible, there is no degradation of sound with repeated use, nor is there any added background noise or distortion (quite unlike a phonograph record). Thus was born the phrase, "...with no record noise and virtually no distortion." With their convenience, ease of use and incredible sound fidelity, **compact discs** are the most important consumer-oriented hi-fi development since stereo was invented.

**Concept Album** – is purposely made with a theme, either lyrical or melodic, tying the songs together. The Beatles' *Sgt. Pepper* album was one of the first, Pink Floyd's *The Dark Side Of The Moon* one of the most mind-boggling, Jethro Tull's *Thick As A Brick* one of the most complete and Bruce Springsteen's *Born In The USA* one of the most popular.

**Cover Band** – a group that plays songs written and first recorded by another **artist**.

**Cover Song** – any version of a song other than the original done by the original **artist**.

**Demo** – a recording, usually very basic and rather rough, made to demonstrate a song or an **artist**.

**Digital Recording** – a relatively new process that, using computer technology, eliminates the distortion and background noise inherent to tape recording. If done properly (as on Dire Straits' *Brothers In Arms* album), the sound is incredibly clean, clear and natural. If not done properly, **digital recordings** can be harsh and unnatural, giving persnickety audiophiles something to complain about and, thus, reason to live. Most **artists** still use **analog recording** techniques in the studio (for a "warmer" sound and/or because it's cheaper), then master their work in **digital** for a cleaner final mix (see **Analog Recording** for a better analogy).

**Direct-Metal Master** – Very similar to the **half-speed mastering** process, **direct-to-metal mastering** is done directly on the record pressing-master (the metal mold used to squash the hot vinyl into a record). By skipping a couple of the middle technical steps and going directly to the metal pressing-master, the result is a very clean sound.

**EP** – an **E**xtended **P**lay record, longer than a single, shorter than an album. An **EP** might contain four songs, instead of the eight to twelve on an album.

**Engineer** – Recording **engineers** are responsible for capturing the sound on tape exactly as the **artist** and **producer** want it. However, besides making sure everything sounds right, **engineers** must also work closely and continually with the others, while not interrupting the creative process — a very difficult job. Some **producers** do their own engineering and most started as **engineers**. You can be assured that seeing the names of certain **engineers** on an album jacket, guarantees the sound will be top-notch. Check out some of your favorite albums and see for yourself!

**Flipside** – the other side of a single. Some **artists**, such as Springsteen and U2, use unreleased **outtakes** as **flipsides**.

**Gig** – a musician's term for a live show or recording date.

**Half-speed Master** – The ultimate process for making phonograph records. **Half-speed mastering** involves cutting super-quality metal record pressing-masters at half the normal speed to reduce distortion to a minimum. With those special pressing-masters actually used to squash the hot plastic into shape, the resulting album (usually made of special vinyl) plays back at normal speed, but the distortion is noticeably reduced. Adding to the quality of the **half-speed mastered** pressing is the use of the original **master tapes**, which always sound better than any other dubs (copies). Mobile Fidelity is the most reputable company responsible for the manufacture of **half-speed masters**.

**Inner Groove** – The last groove that encircles the record label on a phonograph record is called the **inner groove**. Over the years, several artists (including the Beatles, Eagles, James Gang and Def Leppard) have put material, such as applause or goofy noises, in the **inner groove**. Only a manual turntable will play the **inner groove**, which is a shame because it prevents so many people from enjoying the joke.

# UNCLE JOE'S RECORD GUIDE

**Lick** – This **lick** is a musical term, not what your mother warned you about (See **Riff** for a complete explanation).

**Master Tapes** – This refers to the actual recording tape the **artist**, **producer** and **engineer** recorded on. **Master tapes** always sound better than copies, and they sometimes prove hard to locate. If a **master tape** wasn't used for the **compact disc** mastering, then the record company did you a disservice.

**Outtake** – a recorded song, finished or not, that didn't make it onto the album, no matter what the reason.

**Overdubbing** – After recording the **basic tracks** for a song, an **artist** will often record (or dub) additional parts onto the **master tape**, parts like guitar solos or backing vocals. That process is called **overdubbing**. Some **artists** do it a lot, some not much at all.

**Pressings** – Phonograph records are made by **pressing** (or smashing) hot vinyl between two record masters. The care used in making those masters and the quality of the vinyl determines the quality of the **pressing** of the record. Although the manufacturing technique differs for compact discs, the term **pressing** still applies. See **Special Pressings** for more detail.

**Producer** – Next to the quality of the songs, the **producer** is the most important part of any recording. A good **producer** has the ability to bring out the best in both the **artist** and music, while a bad one acts as a torpedo. Some **producers** add their own touch or sound to the music, some don't. Some can turn lightweight material into hits, and some can lose everything in the mix. In the studio, the **producer** can act as the music arranger, the director of the project, an additional member of the group, the budget-master, a mediator of creative arguments, a babysitter, a cheerleader, or just hang back and keep track of where the music is going – any or all of these tasks are possible and sometimes necessary from the **producer**. Most **producers** started out as recording **engineers** and some still run their own control boards. Occasionally **artists** have enough self-control and foresight to produce themselves with the help of a good **engineer**. Generally, though, someone outside of the group is needed to keep things in perspective.

# Glossary

You'll find the names of certain **producers** consistently showing up on great records, often by very diverse groups. Following those **producers'** careers can be just as illuminating as following a musician's.

**Pseudo-Stereo** – Most pre-1966 recordings were done in mono (monaural – one channel of sound). As stereo (two channels of sound, a left and right) phonograph records first became popular, some record companies altered their mono **master tapes**, dubbing the high frequency tones onto one channel of the stereo master and the low frequencies onto the other. The result was a lousy simulated-stereo sound. Twenty years later, when many old **master tapes** were dubbed onto **compact discs**, they were left in the original mono.

**Riff** – (or **lick**) is a series of notes (sometimes a melody line) that provides an integral part of a song. If a **riff** is particularly catchy, it may be called a **hook**.

**Segue** [pronounced SEG-way] – is the mixing or blending of one song into another. Most disc jockies think they know how to do it properly (some actually do), and, occasionally, a recording **artist** will do it on an album.

**Special Pressing** – This term applies to both phonograph records than compact discs. The most common **special pressing** phonograph records are **half-speed** or **direct-to-metal masters** (see those listings for more details), and Japanese and German pressings. Both Japanese and German record companies use better vinyl and much more careful, precise mastering techniques than their American counterparts. The most common **special pressing** compact discs are **Gold CDs** and **20-Super-Bit Mastered CDs** (see those listings for more details) pressings. The quality difference is usually so great that, after hearing a **special pressing**, you may never want to listen to a normal American record again.

**Take** – Each time a song, or a portion of one, is recorded in the studio, that version is called a **take**. Most artists will do many **takes**, while some (like Springsteen and Van Halen) completely record the song on one of the first few **takes**. The latter method of recording the song, while it's still fresh to the musicians, captures a certain feeling, a special edge in the music. However, because it's so much harder to get things right on the early **takes**, almost everyone uses extensive **overdubbing**.

**Track** – refers to one of four things: a completed song; one song leading directly into another; a recording of a particular instrument (a bass **track**, vocal **track**, etc.); or a reference to the channels on a tape deck (a 4-**track** tape deck has four channels, an 8-**track** has eight, a 24-**track** has twenty-four, and so on). In regard to the latter reference, the advent of **multi-track** recorders allowed much more **overdubbing**, and thus more intense recordings and supposed **artistic** creativity.

# Recommended Reading

# UNCLE JOE'S RECORD GUIDE

# HARD ROCK - Recommended Reading

There have not been as many "in-depth studies" written about Hard Rock bands as have been done on the Beatles and the Rolling Stones. In fact, except for **UNCLE JOE'S RECORD GUIDE**, there are very few books that the bands have ever approved of. The best information resource for these six artists are the interviews they (or their associates) have done with music-oriented magazines – especially guitar magazines. Also of interest are radio features such as *Rockline*, where you can hear band members reminisce (their tone of voice can tell as much as the words they speak). With that in mind, here are a few books I've found to be helpful.

## SPECIFIC REFERENCES

### AC/DC

The best sources of information on the wildest Australian band ever are their magazine interviews. However, there is one title that *may* be of interest.

### AC/DC
Malcolm Dome.
Proteus Publishing Co., Inc.,
733 Third Avenue, New York, NY 10017. 1982.
ISBN 0-86276-011-9

This very small book was written when the band was at their peak in 1982. There is more detail on AC/DC here than you'd find in a normal rock & roll picture book, but Malcolm was stretching things as far as he could.

## Aerosmith

The best sources of information on Aerosmith are the many magazine artictles written about them over the years. Steven Tyler is *always* entertaining, and the rest of the band expounds with excellent insight on a regular basis in various guitar player magazines. However, there is one title that may be of interest.

### THE FALL AND RISE OF AEROSMITH

Mark Putterford.
Omnibus Press, a division of Book Sales Limited,
257 Park Avenue South, New York, NY 10010. 1991.
ISBN 0-7119-2303-5

This book was not written in co-operation with the band, and it is not a pretty story. Over the years, I haven't found anyone who would dispute Mark's history of Aerosmith — from the graphic details of their lowest points to a general look at their highs (career and otherwise). However, as I have emphasized in this **UNCLE JOE'S RECORD GUIDE**, Aerosmith is (more now than ever) one of the greatest rock & roll bands in the world. That they survived and rose to those heights after years of abuse only adds to their greatness and testifies to their strength of personal character. One should not dwell on how bad things were reported to have been.

# HARD ROCK - Recommended Reading

## Led Zeppelin

### HEAVEN AND HELL
Charles R. Cross and Erik Flannigan.
Photographs by Neal Preston.
Harmony Books, a division of Crown Publishers, Inc.,
201 East 50th Street, New York, NY 10022. 1991.
ISBN 0-517-583089

True Led Zeppelin fans are required to own this book. Neal Preston is one of the greatest rock & roll photographers ever, and his work illuminates this book like no other. Mr. Cross and Mr. Flannigan also did an excellent job on the research and writing.

### LED ZEPPELIN, THE DEFINITIVE BIOGRAPHY
Ritchie Yorke.
Underwood-Miller,
708 Westover Drive, Lancaster, PA 17601. 1993.
ISBN 0-88733-177-7

This is an update on the 1974 tome, *The Led Zeppelin Biography*. Ritchie York was probably the first serious writer to cover Led Zeppelin, and this is the only book that can claim it was "researched and produced with the co-operation of Led Zeppelin and close associates." It is filled with great stories and excellent insight. Another must for true Zep heads.

# UNCLE JOE'S RECORD GUIDE

### LED ZEPPELIN, A CELEBRATION

Dave Lewis.
Omnibus Press, a division of Book Sales Limited,
225 Park Avenue South, New York, NY 10003. 1991.
ISBN 0-7119-2416-3

While this book lacks the visual snap of *Heaven And Hell*, it is the easiest to read, most accurately detailed book on Led Zeppelin I have found. Another must for Zeppelin fans.

### HAMMER OF THE GODS

Stephen Davis.
William Morrow And Company, Inc.,
105 Madison Avenue, New York, NY 10016. 1985.
ISBN 0-688-04507-3

Mr. Davis used disgruntled former employees of Led Zeppelin as his main source of information for this book. Naturally, the viewpoints were a tad biased, although some of the observations were astute. You can generally discern the truth by reading between the lines. While *Hammer Of The Gods* did make the best seller lists, you are advised to consume it with a good measure of skepticism.

### LED ZEPPELIN IN THEIR OWN WORDS

Paul Kendall and Dave Lewis.
Omnibus Press, a division of Book Sales Limited,
225 Park Avenue South, New York, NY 10003. 1995.
ISBN 0-7119-4866-6

Excerpts from many interviews and lots of grainy photographs — nothing more, nothing less.

# HARD ROCK - Recommended Reading

## JIMMY PAGE, TANGENTS WITHIN A FRAMEWORK
Howard Mylett.
The Putnam Publishing Group,
200 Madison Avenue, New York, NY 10016. 1983.
ISBN 0-7119-0265-8

A very interesting look into Page's brief views on his music. Not much depth, but lots of observations and photographs crammed into a very small book.

## LED ZEPPELIN, A VISUAL DOCUMENTARY
Paul Kendall.
The Putnam Publishing Group,
200 Madison Avenue, New York, NY 10016. 1982.
ISBN 0-399-41010-4

Probably the best of the billion or so Led Zeppelin photo collections. Featuring a diary-like listing of quotes and notes about the band's activities throughout their career, the best thing about the book is that the pictures are nice.

## THE ILLUSTRATED COLLECTOR'S GUIDE TO LED ZEPPELIN
Robert Godwin.
Collector's Guide,
P.O. Box 305, 688 Brant Street,
Burlington, Ontario, Canada L7R 3Y2. 1995.

The title describes it well. Updated on a regular basis, this covers everything from legitimate releases to bootlegs, and is considered the Zep collector's bible.

# UNCLE JOE'S RECORD GUIDE

## Rush

The best sources of information on Rush are their excellent concert programs. Drummer Neil Peart always puts together a great commentary on the creation of each album. However, there are a couple of other sources that may be of interest.

### RUSH VISIONS: THE OFFICIAL BIOGRAPHY
Bill Banasiewicz.
Omnibus Press, a division of Book Sales Limited,
24 East 22nd Street, New York, NY 10010. 1988.
ISBN 0-7119-1162-2

After this was published, the band noted it was more of a fan's personal recollection than their own official biography. You should have no problem discerning the difference. In addition to some enlightening details, this book contains a number of great photographs.

### RUSH
Brian Harrigan.
The Putnam Publishing Group,
200 Madison Avenue, New York, NY 10016. 1982.
ISBN 0-86001-934-9

A very small book (less than a hundred pages), this provides a personable insight into Rush's early career. For a few years, Mr. Harrigan was the British press officer for Rush. For many years, he wasn't.

# HARD ROCK - Recommended Reading

## Van Halen

Van Halen is one of the world's greatest (and most quoted) rock & roll bands. Any interview — especially those done after Sammy Hagar joined the group — will provide you with legitimate insight to the group. However, outside of the book you are now holding (which has been hailed as definitive), I have only found one other title that may be of any interest.

### VAN HALEN: JUMPIN' FOR THE DOLLAR
John Shearlaw.
Cherry Lane Books,
Port Chester, NY 10573. 1944.
ISBN 0-946391-51-3

Judging by the title, one would think that either Mr. Shearlaw didn't like the band or he received little co-operation in writing his book. I suspect it was the latter. But unlike the many Van Halen pictorials, this book contains a lot of *real* words written about the pre-Hagar version of the band. Some of those words are actually enlightening — not many, but some.

## ZZ Top

Guitar player-oriented magazines are the best source of information on ZZ Top because guitarist Billy Gibbons tends to tell some rather outrageous stories to normal consumer-type magazines. However, there are a couple of other sources that may be of interest.

# UNCLE JOE'S RECORD GUIDE

## SHARP DRESSED MEN
David Blayney.
Hyperion,
114 Fifth Avenue, New York, NY 10011. 1994.
ISBN 0-7868-8005-8

David spent over a decade working with the Top, beginning as one of their first roadies and ending after their second round of major success. Along with his tales of rock & roll life in the Seventies, he relates many stories of life with the band. Why his birth date for Billy Gibbons is off by three months is beyond me (must have been the editor's fault!).

## ZZ TOP, BAD AND WORLDWIDE
Deborah Frost.
Rolling Stone Press
Macmillan Publishing Company,
866 Third Avenue, New York, NY 10022. 1985.
ISBN 0-02-002950-0

While this isn't as nasty as *Hammer Of The Gods*, it comes close — but several of the basic facts are there.

# HARD ROCK - Recommended Reading

## MISCELLANEOUS PUBLICATIONS

### GOLDMINE MAGAZINE
Krause Publications,
700 East State Street, Iola, WI 54990.

Billed as "a collector's marketplace," each issue of this bi-weekly magazine features a fine in-depth bio on a band or genre of rock & roll, and hundreds of ads for record dealers. Most of the advertised recordings are rare and difficult to find.

### GUITAR FOR THE PRACTICING MUSICIAN
Cherry Lane Magazines, Inc.,
10 Midland Avenue, Port Chester, NY 10573.

While the emphasis is on technique and transcriptions, *Guitar* (as it's called) always features excellent articles and interviews.

### GUITAR PLAYER
Miller Freeman, Inc.
600 Harrison Street, San Francisco, CA 94107.

In addition to transcriptions, *Guitar Player* features great interviews with the top players of every genre. Highly recommended.

### GUITAR WORLD
1115 Broadway, New York, NY 10010.

In addition to transcriptions, *Guitar World* generally has the best interviews with the top bands. Highly recommended.

# UNCLE JOE'S RECORD GUIDE

### INTERNATIONAL CD EXCHANGE
Peter Howard.
*ICE*, P.O. Box 3043, Santa Monica, CA 90408.

*ICE* is the best researched monthly newsletter in the business. Concentrating solely on compact discs, Howard and his staff dig up details on recordings, release dates and mistakes in CD mastering. My favorite feature is Pete's taking record companies to task for mastering mistakes.

### MUSICIAN MAGAZINE
BPI Communications, Inc.,
1515 Broadway, New York, NY 10036.

*Musician* is America's best overall music magazine. Very little hype, great interviews (generally done by musicians talking with other musicians) and coverage of a very broad spectrum of styles, from rock to jazz.

### NEW ROCK RECORD
Terry Hounsome.
Facts On File Publications,
460 Park Avenue South, New York, NY 10016. 1983.
ISBN 0-87196-770-7

Hounsome is a maniac for details – like who played on every rock record ever recorded. While no one could ever be 100% accurate when dealing with musicians (especially thousands of them), this is a very good reference book.

# HARD ROCK - Recommended Reading

## THE RECORD PRODUCERS
John Tobler and Stuart Grundy.
St. Martin's Press,
175 Fifth Avenue, New York, NY 10010. 1982.
ISBN 0-312-66594-6

This excellent book profiles 14 of the top producers from the mid-Fifties to early Eighties.

## THE RECORD PRODUCERS FILE
Bert Muirhead.
Sterling Publishing Company, Inc.,
2 Park Avenue, New York, NY 10016. 1984.
ISBN 0-7137-1430-1

Patterned after the *New Rock Record* book, this lists a few hundred record producers and several thousands of the albums on which they received credit.

## ROCK MOVERS & SHAKERS
Dafydd Rees and Luke Crampton.
Billboard Books, an imprint of Watson-Guptil Publications,
a division of BPI Communications, Inc.,
1515 Broadway, New York, NY 10036. 1991.
ISBN 0-8230-7609-1

An excellent time-line overview of many, many rock & roll artists.

# UNCLE JOE'S RECORD GUIDE

## ROLLING STONE MAGAZINE
Straight Arrow Publishers Company,
1290 Avenue of the Americas, New York, NY 101041.

In the late Sixties, *Rolling Stone* was the magazine that
legitimatized rock critics and brought stories of the
counterculture's lifestyle into the real world. But that was a long
time ago, and most of society has now recognized rock critics as
trendy, self-righteous bags of various hot gases. *Rolling Stone*
compensated by branching-out beyond music, into more lifestyle
and investigative reporting . When covering the music scene, they
still do an excellent job (providing someone isn't discovering a
new trend, grinding an ax or working up a treatment for a movie).

## THE ROLLING STONE ENCYCLOPEDIA OF ROCK & ROLL
Edited by Jon Pareles and Patricia Romanowski.
Rolling Stone Press/Summit Books,
Simon & Schuster Building, Rockefeller Center,
12330 Avenue of the Americas, New York, NY 10020. 1983.
ISBN 0-671-44071-3.

This is a fine general overview of a few hundred bands. Not much
enlightening detail, but lots of good, basic rundowns. If you want
to know a little about a lot (not all of it up to date or 100%
accurate), this is the one.

# HARD ROCK - Recommended Reading

## THE ROLLING STONE RECORD GUIDE
Dave Marsh with John Swenson.
The Rolling Stone Press/Random House,
Random House, Inc., New York, N Y. 1979.
ISBN 0-394-73535-8

This contains a decent section on blues artists, but the rest of the
book is filled with highly subjective reviews. If you want someone
else's opinion of a record, this is your reference point.

## SPIN MAGAZINE
Camouflage Associates,
6 West 18th Street, New York, NY 10011.

Did you ever know someone who tried so hard to be hip they
consistently looked like an idiot? In spite of a reoccurring poseur
problem, *Spin* occasionally features excellent articles on current
bands, music and lifestyles.

## JOEL WHITBURN'S TOP POP ALBUMS 1955-1992
Joel Whitburn.
Record Research, Inc.,
P.O. Box 200, Menomonee Falls, WI 53052. 1993.
ISBN 0-89820-093-8

## JOEL WHITBURN'S TOP POP SINGLES 1955-1993
Joel Whitburn.
Record Research, Inc.,
P.O. Box 200, Menomonee Falls, WI 53052. 1994.
ISBN 0-89820-104-7

Back in the early Seventies, Joel created the statistical standard for
the industry with his *Top Pop Singles* books. He has since

# UNCLE JOE'S RECORD GUIDE

expanded the line-up to cover virtually all other kinds of recordings, and there are no other books that even come close to covering statistics better than Whitburn's. Based on the *Billboard Magazine* charts, this book tells you when an album hit the charts, how long it was there and how high it got. For pure statistics, Joel's books are the absolute best. To music researchers, he is a god. Rock on Joel!

# Song Index

# UNCLE JOE'S RECORD GUIDE

# HARD ROCK - Song Index

# UNCLE JOE'S RECORD GUIDE

# HARD ROCK - Song Index

# UNCLE JOE'S RECORD GUIDE

# HARD ROCK - Song Index

## Led Zeppelin

Achilles Last Stand, 41, 43, 70
All My Love, 51, 68
Babe, I'm Gonna Leave You, 12, 59, 85
Baby Come On Home, 12, 55, 74
Black Country Woman, 30, 36, 39, 77
Black Dog, 25, 27, 46, 62, 65
Black Mountain Side, 13, 75, 85
Bonzo's Montreux, 54, 68, 79
Boogie With Stu, 24, 39, 74
Bring It On Home, 18, 79
Bron-Y-Aur-Stomp, 22, 63
Bron-Yr-Aur, 20, 38, 46, 75
Candy Store Rock, 44, 66
Carouselambra, 51, 76
Celebration Day, 21, 46, 61
Communication Breakdown, 13, 59, 86
Custard Pie, 35, 64
D'Yer Maker, 31, 35, 64, 78
Dancing Days, 30, 31, 36, 62, 66, 70
Darlene, 49, 54, 77
Dazed And Confused, 13, 46, 60, 85
Down By The Seaside, 20, 24, 38, 75
Fool In The Rain, 50, 67, 76
For Your Life, 43, 69
Four Sticks, 27, 78
Friends, 21, 61
Gallows Pole, 22, 64
Going To California, 27, 63
Good Times, Bad Times, 12, 14, 73, 85
Hats Off To (Roy) Harper, 22, 35, 64, 78
Heartbreaker, 17, 46, 59

Hey, Hey, What Can I Do, 20, 21, 52, 55, 61, 62
Hot Dog, 50, 76
Hots On For Nowhere, 44, 79
Houses Of The Holy, 30, 31, 36, 66
How Many More Times, 14, 77, 86
I Can't Quit You, 14, 53, 60, 78, 85, 86
I'm Gonna Crawl, 51, 68
Immigrant Song, 21, 52, 56, 61, 62
In My Time Of Dying, 35, 71
In The Evening, 50, 66
In The Light, 38, 68
Kashmir, 37, 69
Livin' Lovin' Maid (She's Just A Woman), 17, 79
Misty Mountain Hop, 25, 27, 62, 65
Moby Dick, 18, 47, 68, 76
Night Flight, 24, 39, 73
No Quarter, 20, 25, 31, 47, 70
Nobody's Fault But Mine, 44, 67
Out On The Tiles, 21, 75
Over The Hills And Far Away, 30, 62
Ozone Baby, 49, 54
Poor Tom, 20, 53, 67
Rain Song, 46
Ramble On, 18, 60
Rock & Roll, 24, 25, 39, 46, 65
Royal Orleans, 43, 44, 66, 79
Sick Again, 40, 76
Since I've Been Loving You, 21, 46, 63
South Bound Saurez, 50, 77
Stairway To Heaven, 26, 47, 65
Tangerine, 22
Tea For One, 44, 80
Ten Years Gone, 38, 71

# UNCLE JOE'S RECORD GUIDE

# HARD ROCK - Song Index

# UNCLE JOE'S RECORD GUIDE

# HARD ROCK - Song Index

# UNCLE JOE'S RECORD GUIDE

# HARD ROCK - Song Index

# UNCLE JOE'S RECORD GUIDE

**More Information Than Any
Human Needs To Know.**

# UNCLE JOE'S RECORD GUIDES

The **BEATLES**: ISBN 0-943031-20-6

The **ROLLING STONES**: ISBN 0-943031-02-8

**CLAPTON, HENDRIX, THE WHO**: ISBN 0-943031-03-6

**HARD ROCK, Volume One**: Led Zeppelin, Aerosmith, ZZ Top, AC/DC, Rush, Van Halen. ISBN 0-943031-14-1

**PROGRESSIVE ROCK**: Emerson, Lake & Palmer, Genesis, Jethro Tull, Pink Floyd, Yes. ISBN 0-943031-15-X

**AMERICANS, Vol. 1**: The Allman Brothers Band, Buffalo Springfield, The Byrds, CSN&Y, The Doobie Brothers, The Doors, Eagles, Lynyrd Skynyrd. ISBN 0-943031-16-8

**AMERICANS, Vol. 2**: Pat Benatar, John Cougar Mellencamp, Tom Petty, Bob Seger, Bruce Springsteen, Stevie Ray Vaughan, Joe Walsh. ISBN 0-943031-07-9

The **SEVENTIES**: Boston, The Cars, Foreigner, Heart, Journey, Kansas, Steely Dan, Styx, Supertramp. ISBN 0-943031-08-7

The **EIGHTIES**: Bon Jovi, Def Leppard, Dire Straits, INXS, The Police, The Pretenders, R.E.M., Talking Heads, U2. ISBN 0-943031-09-5

**SOLO ACTS**: Phil Collins, Don Henley, John Lennon, Paul McCartney, Robert Plant, Rod Stewart, Sting, Pete Townshend, Neil Young, and more. ISBN 0-943031-10-9

For more information, please contact:

**UNCLE JOE'S RECORD GUIDE**
P.O. Box 12464
Glendale, CA 91224